The Brontë Sisters

The Brontë Sisters

Life, Loss and Literature

Catherine Rayner

PEN & SWORD HISTORY

First published in Great Britain in 2018 and reprinted in 2021 and
2023 by by Pen & Sword History
An imprint of Pen & Sword Books Limited
47 Church Street
Barnsley
South Yorkshire
S70 2AS

ISBN 978 1 52670 312 5

Typeset in Ehrhardt
by Mac Style Ltd, Bridlington, East Yorkshire

Printed in the UK on paper from a sustainable source by CPI Group
(UK) Ltd, Croydon, CR0 4YY

Pen & Sword Books Limited incorporates the imprints of Atlas,
Archaeology, Aviation, Discovery, Family History, Fiction, History,
Maritime, Military, Military Classics, Politics, Select, Transport,
True Crime, Air World, Frontline Publishing, Leo Cooper,
Remember When, Seaforth Publishing, The Praetorian Press,
Wharncliffe Local History, Wharncliffe Transport,
Wharncliffe True Crime and White Owl.

For a complete list of Pen & Sword titles please contact
PEN & SWORD BOOKS LIMITED
47 Church Street, Barnsley, South Yorkshire, S70 2AS, England
E-mail: enquiries@pen-and-sword.co.uk
Website: www.pen-and-sword.co.uk

Contents

Acknowledgments

I would like to acknowledge and thank members of my family who have helped and encouraged me throughout the writing of this book, especially my daughter Heather, my grand-daughter Aysha, and my brothers John, who has spent many hours proofreading and editing, and David, who has supplied numerous photographs.

I have also had help from the staff at Pen and Sword Books Ltd, namely Laura Hirst and Karyn Burnham. Thanks are due to the staff of the Brontë Parsonage Museum who are always helpful, willing and knowledgeable, and a huge asset to any researcher. This book relies on the work of many previous Brontë researchers and especially to Dr Juliet Barker's extensive biography of the Brontë family.

I would like to dedicate the book to the memory of my mother, Olive Walford, who helped foster my love of literature.

Chapter One

Background and Society

To explain how and why the Brontë sisters, Charlotte, Emily and Anne developed talents and abilities that others are unable to achieve, this book will explore the background and lifestyle of the Brontë family of Haworth to try and reveal what led them to become such talented and famous writers. By researching their lives and background, their acquaintances and their environment, one can begin to understand how these women acquired and honed their skills. Their ability to write books and poetry which have survived for almost two centuries and are still widely read and studied throughout the world is testament to unique gifts, perhaps even genius.

This book describes and examines the many influences that affected the Brontë family's ideas and formed their beliefs. It is both a study of the wellspring of creativity and an exploration of how and why some writers use their own experiences and emotions in their works. It demonstrates how this contributes both to the realism of the fiction and to addressing personal and social issues. It is not compulsory to know the details of an author's life to appreciate their works but, in this case, the authors have been researched and exposed in a way that has brought an enormous amount of information to the public. Despite being born 200 years ago, a great number of their possessions still exist and many are housed at their Parsonage home at Haworth, in West Yorkshire, where they lived for most of their lives. An enormous amount of their adult writing can be seen in libraries, museums and private collections around the world along with various possessions and personal items. Hundreds of letters survive, especially those written by Patrick Brontë and his daughter Charlotte, as well as correspondence from their friends and associates. This archive gives special insight into their daily lives.

This accessible history of the family is especially relevant in the case of the Brontës because many of their own experiences appear in their novels. This representation of their lives in literature leads the reader into a deeper understanding of their psychological and emotional state and further offers the reader a more realistic appreciation of the times and background to their stories. In saying this, one should remember that these authors could also write stories, poetry and essays which were pure fantasy and contained wild flights of the imagination. This is shown especially in the remains of their juvenilia; a huge collection of childhood writings which are set in imaginary places and peopled by all manner of individuals and groups, some taken from life and some purely make-believe.

The Brontë family lived in a particularly intense environment at a time of great industrial and social changes and challenges both in Britain and other parts of the world. Many things contributed to this, not least the expanding industrialisation of the nation and the increasing discoveries in science and medicine. The mass urbanisation and growth of towns and cities affected the way people lived and worked and how the society organised itself politically and financially. The Brontës were growing up in an age where the society was rapidly changing and the old ways and organisations were under threat as more and more new ideas and inventions altered the social dynamics.

It is useful to know where the Brontë family came from and what kind of background and beliefs affected them. The family had a long history in both Ireland and Cornwall that contributed to the development of the children and to the ways in which they were educated. An unshakeable belief in God was inherent in both of their parents and their families and these principles and morals were instilled in the Brontë siblings.

Growing up in the shelter of Haworth Parsonage yet exposed to wild areas of moorland and a vast canvass of books, poetry, music and art, the Brontë children had a unique and interesting childhood which was blighted by early tragedy. The loss of their mother when the eldest of the six children was only 8, and the deaths of the two eldest girls aged only 11 and 10 years, naturally had a profound affect. These losses were never forgotten and came to be expressed and written about as a major theme of their writing and an influence on their view of the world and their religious faith.

The debate regarding the origins of our intelligence and abilities has long been attributed to Nature and Nurture. It is suggested that we are born with certain attributes and faculties which are an innate part of our genetic make-up, possibly around twenty per cent. The remaining influences on our development occur especially in childhood, from birth until our teenage years; by which time we are expected to have enough knowledge and experience to make many of our own decisions and to have established various beliefs and behaviour patterns. Our genetic make-up is, of course, the product of our parenting and all the grandparents that went before in a very long and infinitely varied queue. In the case of the Brontë children, their parents had widely different backgrounds and upbringings.

The father of the Brontës, the Reverend Patrick Brontë, was born in County Down in the north-east of Ireland on St Patrick's Day, 17 March 1777. Their mother, Maria Branwell was born in Penzance, Cornwall on 15 April 1779.

Patrick was the eldest son of a peasant farmer. His parents, Hugh and Alice Prunty or Branty, possibly had opposing religious backgrounds, one Catholic and one Protestant. This may account for their move from southern Ireland to the wild country beyond the Mountains of Mourne, in the north where they farmed a few acres of land and lived in a two-roomed cottage. The name Patrick is almost always a catholic name in Ireland and it is unusual for a protestant to name their child as such. St Patrick 's Day is a catholic celebration rather than a protestant one but his birth on that day and possible catholic sympathies within the family, may explain why their first child was given the name. Hard work and enterprise helped them to expand their farm and raise ten children, but life was often difficult for Patrick's parents. They worked very hard and their devotion and tenacity was witnessed and inherited by their son.

Maria Branwell was the daughter of a successful businessman. Her parents, Thomas and Anne Branwell, owned property in Penzance and had a busy and important social life with many friends and relatives. Their children were well educated and enjoyed a life of prosperity and affluence.

Although from widely differing origins, Patrick Brontë and Maria Branwell's paths crossed in June 1812, when Maria was visiting her uncle, John Fennell, the Headmaster of Woodhouse Grove School in West Yorkshire, a Methodist establishment for the sons of minsters. Patrick was helping to train the schoolboys in the Classics. The attraction between Patrick and Maria was instant and a friendship and then courtship followed. Six months later the couple married at Guiseley Church, near Leeds, on 29 December. Such is the way of fate, or chance, that two people meet and their offspring inherit a genetic history that goes back through the centuries.

Their Irish and Cornish inheritance brought the Brontë children a mixture of natural talents, especially in the arts. Storytelling seems to have been fundamental and one of their Irish grandparents was especially noted for this ability. The children each inherited musical and artistic abilities. Their looks were similar and Branwell, at least, had the red hair of his Irish ancestors. Their early abilities to read and to converse suggests intelligence and a love of learning. Their parents' backgrounds and influences meant that their offspring gained knowledge in a wide range of subjects including religion, politics, social and industrial change, geography, history, nature, literature and the arts.

Although the Brontë parents had a mutual devotion to knowledge and religion, Patrick and Maria Brontë had differences, not least in their accents and speech patterns. Maria would have had the cultured, softly spoken burr of the southern Cornish peninsular, whilst Patrick had the strong brogue of the northern Irish. It was this noticeable accent that probably caused his change of surname when he was registered at St John's College, Cambridge in 1802. Instead of Branty or Prunty, Patrick's name was recorded as Brontë. This was a change that he was more than willing to accept as one of his heroes, Lord Nelson, had been given the title, The Duke of Brontë.

So how did the son of an Irish labourer move to England and register at one of the worlds' most famous universities? Patrick Brontë was a man driven by ambition and an unwavering belief in God. Little is documented regarding Patrick's early life but he did not follow in his father's occupation. Instead, he attended the local school and impressed his teachers to the point that he was running and organising a small '*school*' or teaching room, for local boys when he was aged only 16. His devotion to education and his driving ambition to better himself showed an amazing self-discipline and the ability to study long and hard. He saw education as the means to improve himself and yet was fully aware that he needed the help and support of influential men in order to rise in the world.

The Rev. Thomas Tighe, the rector of Patrick's Irish birthplace, was his first guide and mentor. He was a wealthy man and a Justice of the Peace who counted the great Methodist founder, John Wesley, as a friend. It was under his tutelage and friendship that Patrick was guided to aim for England and a University education. Cambridge University opened doors for Patrick, and allied him to Members of Parliament, Clergymen and Social Reformers who would never have been part of his life had he stayed in Ireland. All his subsequent moves would be at the recommendation of someone who recognised his qualities and was willing to give this highly intelligent and presentable man a helping hand.

Following his departure from Cambridge and his ordination in to Holy Orders, Patrick's friendships and his ability to adapt and work hard saw him invited to take up a series of posts as a curate at several English churches. At each place his learning, his kindness and his ability to communicate well with people of all classes and ages, endeared him to his congregation. His recognition of the need for many social reforms and the hardships of the poorer classes led him to write many letters, throughout his long life, to notable people and newspapers demanding better conditions. Many of his letters and sermons were published. Patrick also indulged in his own literary creations, though they had a didactic purpose as well as a literary one. He could write both verse and essays and after years of writing sermons could speak spontaneously and effectively to his parishioners, both in and out of the church. In 1810, his first publication *Winter-Evening Thoughts, A Miscellaneous Poem* was published and followed by *Cottage Poems* 1811, *The Rural Minstrel,* 1813 and two books, *The Cottage in the Wood* 1815 and *The Maid of Killarney* 1818. Patrick was not unique in publishing his writings as many of his fellow clergymen had works published as a way of reaching out to their parishioners and to the population at large. In this way the word of God, which was central to their works, was spread much further afield. Patrick was, no doubt, a man who loved literature and aspired to influence and educate through the art of writing; something that his daughters would famously achieve thirty years later.

Maria Branwell was also from a large family. The eighth of eleven children, she spent her childhood in the warm and sedate surroundings of the coastal town of Penzance, Cornwall, overlooked by the beautiful island of St Michael's Mount. It was a small but busy fishing and sea port attracting trade from many parts of the world. Her father, Thomas Branwell, was a successful tea-merchant and grocer and held bonding warehouses on the quay where he traded goods. Maria and her seven surviving siblings lived in relative comfort in a style unknown to her future husband. The family had an active social life and held various important positions in the local community. Their genteel lifestyle was interrupted, by the death of their father in 1808 and their mother the following year, but not discontinued. There was money and plenty of well-to-do relatives and property for the Branwell girls to continue living in comfort, without the need to go out and earn a living.

This does not mean that the children were lazy or indulged. The boys were trained in business and the girls were educated in the arts and literature, music, singing, dancing and female occupations such as needlework and embroidery. Maria was bright and willing to learn. She had been brought up in the Church of England but the family leaned towards the teachings of John Wesley and supported the building of a chapel near their home. Religion was central to Maria's beliefs and behaviour, and she had trust in God in all things.

In her first letter to Patrick written during their courtship Maria wrote,

> *If I know anything of myself, I am incapable of making an ungenerous return to the smallest degree of kindness, much less to you whose attention and conduct have been so particularly obliging. I will frankly confess that your behaviour and what I have seen and heard of your character has excited my warmest esteem and regard, and be assured that you will never have cause to repent of any confidence you may think proper to place in me, and that it will always be my endeavour to deserve the good opinion which you have formed.... In giving you these assurances I do not depend upon my own strength, but I look to Him who has been my unerring guide through life and in whose continued protection and assistance I confidently trust. (26 August 1812).*

> (J R.V. Barker, 2010) p. 59.

In these ways, there were recognisable links between Patrick and Maria. Their love of nature and literature was a common bond, their knowledge and understanding of various branches of religion and their acknowledgement of the work of John Wesley and his brother, Charles, was another and this linked them to the Rev. Thomas Tighe, Patrick's original mentor. People whom Patrick had known at Cambridge were uncannily linked to Maria who held a book of verses and sermons written by Patrick's friend and roommate, Henry Kirke White. Maria's aunt, Jane, married John Fennell, an acquaintance of Patrick's, when he was a curate at Wellington, and who introduced Patrick to Maria. This interweaving of people and places brought about the union of this diverse but harmonious couple.

Patrick and Maria Brontë had grown up in a world that was rapidly changing. In the hundred years between 1770 and 1870, the whole of Britain saw a revolution in all aspects of its social and political existence. The development of industrialisation and its advance into the lives of the population was absolute. The invention of many materials and machinery, the discovery of new lands and minerals and the changes in transportation altered the way of life of the British people forever. Expensive and exotic goods came in from the newly conquered lands; cotton, gold, tea, sugar and spices were just a few. The invention of steam power and the sophistication of weapons meant that the deployment of men and arms could be shipped all over the world. The growth of huge factories and mills drew rural societies into towns and made them cities, where overcrowding and poverty increased as more and more people poured in to them looking for work.

In the early nineteenth century, the factories were converted to steam-powered machinery that could spin the yarn and work the looms, faster and more efficiently and their instalment eventually overtook a trade that had been a cottage industry for centuries. Everything began to get bigger, faster and more competitive. Huge buildings grew in cities like London, Manchester and Liverpool, overshadowing the poor housing of the workers and dominating and defining the metropolises. Bridges, tunnels, mines, roads and eventually railways, altered the landscape and destroyed many areas of the countryside. Despite this, it allowed for movement of goods and people on an unprecedented scale. This huge growth had to be managed and the political leaders, magnates and business corporations fought to constantly increase growth and maximise profits. For some it was a time of wealth and prosperity, for those who had the misfortune to be born into poverty or the labouring classes it was a time of extreme hardship and a limited life span.

Some progress was good and beneficial to all members of the society. The growth in education and research into diseases were two of the benefits, as were the provision of housing, sanitation and the improved methods of transport and the availability of different foods and clothing. Much of the industrial revolution relied on the fast and new developments in the coal mining industry. It was coal which fed the furnaces that empowered the steam-driven machinery, the boats and the railway engines. The whole was a mass of interlinked inventions and discoveries which built up and allowed the British Empire to grow and thrive.

Along the way there were many casualties, much distress and an exodus of some to foreign lands, many driven by poverty rather than an urge to explore.

This was the tumultuous world of Patrick and Maria Brontë. It is important to recall that in the late years of the eighteenth century and the beginnings of the nineteenth, England was often at war and many important events were taking place in other parts of the world. These conflicts formed the backdrop to the lives of this couple who, through education and exposure, especially in Patrick's case, were affected by them. Patrick had an interest in military history throughout his life and whilst at Cambridge, when there was threat of invasion by the French, he joined the university volunteer corps and, like his fellow St John's College undergraduates, trained under the officer in charge, Lord Palmerston. Patrick would have been fully aware of the French Revolution, begun in 1789 by the storming of the Bastille. It was the biggest revolt by the underclasses ever seen in Europe and during ten years of unrest it unnerved the English crown, its government and its people. By the end of the 1700s England finally saw the loss of its colonies after the long American wars of Independence ended. There were also successes and Patrick will have read the newspaper accounts of Nelson's triumphs and eventual death at Trafalgar, fighting against the French and the Spanish. He would have followed the rise of Napoleon and the peninsular wars, and celebrated the victory of his hero, the Duke of Wellington, who eventually defeated the French at the Battle of Waterloo in 1815. Living on the south coast of England, Maria would also have knowledge of the wars and naval battles, the leading officers of the day and their losses and gains.

Patrick and Maria witnessed political change at a time when the king had a direct effect on Parliament. The Act of Union of 1800 was designed to unite England and Ireland but was upset by George III's decision to deny the Irish full emancipation. The Act of Union of 1801 united Scotland and Wales without this proviso and 1807 saw the Act to abolish slavery, led by another of Patrick's heroes, William Wilberforce. Wilberforce had been one of Patrick's benefactors when he went to Cambridge, as a sizer, dependent on the charity and good will of several high-ranking individuals who gave money to support poorer undergraduates. In 1811, Patrick was not only aware of the Luddite riots but was actively affected by them in his curatorship in the parish of Hartshead, near Dewsbury in South Yorkshire. A local mill was attacked and people killed when the owner attempted to introduce machinery that would take the jobs away from the workers. Patrick was challenged one night on his way home; he never forgot this encounter and owned a pistol for the rest of his life. The Luddite riots were often talked about to his children and were recorded in detail by Charlotte in her novel, *Shirley*.

As can be seen in both Patrick's and his children's writing, this interest and involvement in the political and social upheavals of the times were a major part of their lives. In childhood, the Brontë siblings read newspaper reports of battles and conflict and political and social unrest both at home and abroad. Stories told to them by their father and local gossip by way of the family servants, led them to write copiously about all aspects of human life in their juvenilia; the amalgamation of stories, poems and articles they wrote as children, containing many thousands, possibly millions, of words. This was a household and a family where there was a constant interchange of information and ideas which the children were openly encouraged to discuss.

Chapter Two

The Birth of Genius

Knowing that Patrick and Maria Brontë were intelligent and educated people who had similar interests and grew up in a time of massive change does not explain how, or why, their children developed exceptional literary talents. Many families could follow a similar pedigree with no remarkable offspring, so other influences must have been involved. Throughout history there have been people of exceptional talent and there will always be degrees of ability that differ from person to person and race to race, it is a part of the human condition and it is influenced by many factors. One line of my own family were wood carvers and cabinetmakers for centuries. Was that due to family influence, early teaching, an inherited ability, or none or all of those things? I do know that even in early childhood I liked the feel, smell and shape of trees and wood beyond that of my friends and acquaintances and it is an abiding sensation that has never left me.

Does being highly talented or gifted in a subject or ability, equate to genius? What of people who are unable to express their capabilities for lack of opportunity, lack of language or social skills? Is genius a modern invention used to describe those who have better memory and recall, or ability to think in the abstract or to invent and produce new and exciting innovations? Can you be a genius in areas that do not involve obvious human achievements such as empathy, endurance and humour? Are there genius criminals, terrorists or bullies? Can you be a genius and a killer? Who decides which traits are positive and beneficial to the society and which are not? Over time, different attributes are recognised and rewarded whereas others are ignored or reviled. To be an exceptional warrior with the strength and cunning to kill and maim the enemy may be the highest ability and honour in one era and can be abhorred in another time and place.

We label people and in so doing, categorise them in a way that they may find hard to escape from; the poor, the labourer, the addict, the mentally ill, the disabled and in some cultures, the female. To speak of female genius in the Middle Ages in Britain was a misnomer. Genius, in some cultures, is still a distinctly male prerogative. Historically men have usually been the gender who made the decisions and demonstrated their skills whilst the females worked as homemakers and child-bearers. It can be argued, that there is absolutely nothing wrong with that arrangement if both male and female are happy and equally respected in their roles. It is only when there is disharmony and inequality of recognition and value placed on a person that they may feel their talents are unrecognised or undervalued.

The melting pot of human genetics has produced every variation of the human form and enhanced its ability to function and to think. Many see progress in terms of the development of the human mind and its ability to evolve and to rationalise. Not every person appears to have, or to use, their faculties for any purpose other than survival, but throughout history many artists and thinkers have devised ways and means of influencing their society and enriching and promoting its progress.

What happened in Britain towards the end of the eighteenth century was a sudden and dramatic rise in scientific knowledge that started a chain reaction of events that introduced a new and 'modern' lifestyle which revolutionised the way people worked, and played, and thought. Patrick and Maria Brontë were born at this time and witnessed the changes which gradually infiltrated every part of the country and its people. Their different backgrounds did not divide them but, instead, united them as a couple, with a variety of experiences and knowledge with which to inform and educate their children.

This is one of the many keys to intellect: an early and profound family involvement from parents or guardians who are educated and able to impart knowledge, provide stimulation, and encourage questioning. It is not a prerequisite for intelligence, but it is an aid that can assist the child to develop and use their abilities. Some of this can be seen nowadays in the upsurge in home schooling and in the philosophy of the Montessori teaching, where the child can dictate its own pace of learning and concentrate for as long as necessary on anything which takes its interest, without the interruption of set meals, sleep times or other restrictions. It is controversial but it produces interesting results which show that some children thrive and progress far better than those in the state school system.

Obviously, childrearing has been performed in a myriad of different ways throughout history and debate continues to this day as to the 'correct' method. It would be nonsense to rear a child in a tribal rainforest in the same way as one in England or in the Arctic about the knowledge and skills that they may need, but do they all require a similar nurturing by a devoted guardian or parent? Is it necessary, or desirable, for children to have a single person or parents overseeing their development? In some societies children are more a part of a general, extended network, in a Kibbutz, for instance. Do they not thrive and develop just as well? Studies show that some children born in some of the most extreme, violent and harsh conditions may flourish and develop a rich and productive 'intelligence' as much as any other child.

This suggests that it is the child themselves, their genetic make-up, their personality and reasoning, that is fostering their abilities. Although we may believe that a 'good' upbringing, comprehensive education and the opportunity to try and do all things, engenders intelligence, it may be that it only helps to fuel what is already innate. As no two children have ever had the same upbringing due to their unique genes and subjective experience of childhood, it is almost impossible to find out what, and where, their intelligence or aptitude comes from. Years of research have not produced a convincing answer that fully explains child development or why some children, even in the same family, or even as twins, develop at different rates and in different ways.

Some key twentieth century studies promote parental love as the key to the flowering of intelligence (See John Balby, *Child Care and the growth of Love*). Some show that utter devotion and stimulation by the parents in isolation from an influential and possibly corruptive society can produce genius (See Michael Deakin, *The Children on the Hill*). Books and essays on the growing discipline of Child Psychology argue a variety of reasons for intelligence and its ability to flourish, but theory changes constantly. It is easy to generalise, which is not productive, but there are repeated patterns that appear to show that children who are allowed the freedom to develop their talents without interruption achieve higher levels of skill. If this is also done with the full love and support of their adult carers they seem more able to develop higher levels of emotional understanding and the ability to integrate into society with better knowledge of the world and the people around them. This is not universal and not an exact science and ironically, as education becomes more widespread and available to many children, the home environment itself has changed. We now have a situation where many children in Britain have access to global education and information, but may lack the very basic nurturing of parental and extended families that once offered them the necessary security and love in which to develop. It may well be that to be a fully developed and happy person, able to reach full potential and exercise and develop intelligence and ability, childhood should be safe, secure, stimulated and surrounded with love. Nevertheless, it can be seen, and notably in the Brontës' childhood, that adversity and tragedy can produce insight and knowledge that may also stimulate the creative mind.

In the Brontë household were six young children who were helped and encouraged to learn and develop, within the safety and protection of their home, and with the support of two intelligent and diverse parents. The children were given access to read and to study almost whatever subject and reading material was available. They were taught by parents who had total belief in education as the key to success. Added to this, the children had to conform to the social norms and mores of the age and from their clergyman father, they had a deep grounding in Christianity and the belief in a benevolent God. They were well fed and dressed and did not suffer abuse or unkindness at home. They had love and laughter and toys and books, the company of their siblings and an almost unrestricted freedom to roam on the moors which lay to the west of their home.

Unfortunately, tragedy struck when the six siblings were all under 8 years old and their mother died from cancer. Within a few years, the two eldest girls succumbed to tuberculosis and also died. These events caused the remaining family members deep suffering and a grief that stayed with them throughout their lives and was incorporated into themes of loss and death in their play and their writings. It is part of the attraction of their works and the longevity of their books and poetry, that there is a universal appeal to profound human feelings of grief and an empathy with suffering. Had they not had these painful experiences they may have been unable to express such strong and lasting emotions.

It is important to note at this point, that the Brontë family were growing up at a time when women were still unable to take active roles in many parts of society. Very gradually, this was beginning to change so that ideas and long-held beliefs about their roles and responsibilities began to be challenged. The industrial advances of the nineteenth century upset many of the male and female roles and the class system that had survived for centuries. Britain mostly led this revolution; largely through the ability of its inventors, its natural resources, the vision and investment of men of wealth and influence and the opening of free trade across the world. Being at the forefront means coping with all the mistakes as well as the opportunities and financial gains. Emerging nations today start off on a footing not even dreamt of in the nineteenth century.

Industrialisation has many facets and one is that it brings together people and cultures that have for centuries been separated. As the agricultural land and people were called upon to give up their skills and property for roads, railways, towns and cities, not only the land map altered, but the inhabitants themselves. People had to adapt and mix in a melting pot of new ways and new ideas. Gradually old systems and beliefs changed and many people became urbanised. Lives, once dominated by the seasons, by labour and by their environment and local knowledge, were being eroded and replaced, sometimes for better and sometimes for worse.

The changes in Britain slowly affected and altered the rest of the world and there was a scramble for the wealth and resources now available to anyone with the might and manpower to invade and exploit. Weaponry and navigational skills brought British soldiers and sailors to all parts of the globe where their superior arms and knowledge helped them to subdue many nations and to plunder their wealth. At the time, this was viewed as a national triumph: the overcoming of the ignorant and uneducated by the intelligent and the superior. This was also often seen as the religious order of the day, that God favoured the conquerors and that those with skill and ability should rightly succeed over those deemed as 'lacking'. It is only in hindsight that men realise what they may have destroyed along the way.

It can be understood why the industrialists believed that what they were doing to the land, its people and the world in general, was good and right. It was progress. It was changing the old for the new and making a bigger and better place for mankind. In part, this was true. There were many advantages to better and safer travel, to exploiting resources, minerals and foods, to increasing the nation's wealth and therefore providing better services for its people. The middle and upper classes thrived and their education and health improved. Investment in the infrastructure was now possible and a huge network of canals, roads and eventually railways, revolutionised the transportation of goods and people. The time to travel from York to London by horse or carriage was measured in days in the eighteenth century. The fact that it can be done today by train in less than two hours is the direct result of industrial progress based on scientific research, massive investment and intensive labour.

It took many years, but progress did eventually cascade down to include the poorer classes. Education, often in the form of religious instruction, and better conditions for the working classes and the very poor, gradually improved in the nineteenth century, helped along by various Acts of Parliament, which finally recognised that conditions for children and adults in many industrialised towns and cities were totally unacceptable and the cause of much misery and disease.

It is of course very clear that almost all inventions, political power, social regulation and even the reforms, when they came both in the new industrialised nation and previously, were in the hands of the upper- and middle-class male section of the population. Women had little or no academic education, no voting rights, and were mostly prevented from ownership of property or inheriting wealth. Women were the property of their husbands, their fathers or a male relative, as were their children, and there were little or no divorce laws or rights for women. Nurturing was a woman's place, she was the carer and homemaker; her role was to nurse her children and obey and serve her husband. The home was bereft of any modern appliances that we now take for granted. With no electricity, no modern fabrics, no hot water and no heating other than coal fires, women of all classes and income struggled to run their households and rear their children. For many there was little or no time to concentrate on activities beyond their home sphere or their allotted work.

Again, it can be argued that for some this was an accepted, and possibly enjoyed, state of affairs at the time. If the men were doing so well and were busy conquering the world, there was little need for women to interfere. Was there any point in educating women or considering their views? What would be gained by altering the balance of the male and female roles that had evolved over millennia? It is understandable how and why male dominance had occurred and why even women themselves were not necessarily keen to change it.

Although they were very few, some females from the eighteenth and nineteenth centuries do enter our history books for their unusual and exceptional abilities. They include the mathematician, Maria Agresi born 1718, the historian, Catherine Macauley, born 1731, the astronomer Caroline Herschel, born 1750, the prison reformer Elizabeth Fry, born 1780 and the nursing reformer,

Florence Nightingale, born 1820. Female writers were also emerging. Jane Austen, born 1775, satirised the behaviour of middle-class women perpetually in search of a good marriage. In 1792, Mary Wollstonecraft wrote her seminal work, *A Vindication of the Rights of Women*, one of the first feminist works, whilst in 1818, her daughter, Mary Shelley, produced her novel *Frankenstein*, a treatise on the human condition. By the mid 1800s Harriet Martineau was leading women forward with her views on such major topics as the abolition of slavery and the concept of feminism. She is also regarded as the founder of modern sociology. Mrs Gaskell was laying bare the plight of women and the working classes in the industrial north of England.

When the Brontë sisters came to write their novels, they were keenly aware of many of the dilemmas facing women of the time and most of their books demonstrate issues around the role of the middle-class gentlewoman with no fortune or fulfilling future. There were other female poets and writers who had something to say and used their considerable talents to voice their concerns, but they were in a very small minority.

Interestingly, the male dominated world did not all agree that women should be kept in the home or subjugated to their male counterparts. In the nineteenth century the social conscience of some leading men had caused them to fight not just for the causes of women, but for anyone, anywhere in the world, who was the subject of abuse or domination. This included slavery, for which cause William Wilberforce led the reforms through Parliament which eventually brought about its abolition, in theory if not in total practice. John Stuart Mill was another writer, philosopher, social economist and reformer who recognised and fought against women's inequality and in 1869 wrote his famous essay, *The Subjection of Women*. There were others who gradually helped to persuade and educate leading politicians that equality was worth the investment and that education of everyone, despite gender or class, was the key to a better workforce and a happier population but it was not until the twentieth century that this view became universal.

Chapter Three

Yorkshire Beginnings

The Brontës first active links with Yorkshire began in December 1809 when Patrick Brontë was appointed curate at All Saint's Church, Dewsbury. It was his belief in the Evangelical movement, which promoted the enthusiastic spreading of the word of God through preaching, and Yorkshire's associations with the Wesley brothers that may have prompted him to come to the county. Patrick was a popular curate and a great help to the vicar, the Rev. John Buckworth and his wife. Handsome, dedicated and devoted to the parishioners, Patrick's empathy with the poor and his determination to fight good causes and defend anyone falsely accused or unlawfully treated, endeared him to his flock. To reach out to as many people as he could and offer them instruction and comfort, he began to write the first of various poems and essays of simple religious thoughts that were printed locally and shared amongst a variety of people.

By March 1811, Patrick accepted a post as perpetual curate at Hartshead-cum-Clifton, a few miles from Dewsbury. The population of the two towns were mainly woollen workers in the local mills and many lacked education or religious direction. Patrick was soon accepted into their community as a fair and compassionate man. It was here that Patrick met again his friend, John Fennell, who had married Jane Branwell, an aunt of Patrick's future wife. In April 1812, Patrick's friend the Rev. William Morgan, whom he had also known from his days in Shropshire, came to Yorkshire to work in Bradford and the two men remained good friends for many years. William met, and later married, John Fennell's daughter Jane. By December, in a double wedding at Guiseley Parish Church, Patrick officiated at the wedding of his friend, William Morgan to Jane Fennell, and William returned the compliment by marrying Patrick to Maria Branwell.

1812 is a year well remembered both at home and abroad for many reasons. It saw the defeat and retreat of Napoleon's troops in Russia and the appalling loss of life that ensued. America continued to fight both the British and their own indigenous people, as they strove for independence. The British navy was becoming the largest and most effective in the world for both war and trade. These events would have fascinated Patrick and his contemporaries and the newspapers would have been full of reports on the fighting and the challenges taking place, socially and politically, around the world.

In Yorkshire, another battle was taking place as the Luddite riots, which had begun in Nottinghamshire with the introduction of machinery into manufacturing, had spread northwards and rioting was taking place in many of the mills. Patrick could sympathise with the plight of the local mill workers who were seeing their livings taken over by machines, but he believed in the upholding of the law and could not condone their actions when they broke up machinery and threatened and attacked the mill owners. He became personally threatened when he came face to face with some of the rioters one dark night, but they eventually let him pass. Years later Charlotte was to write vividly about the Luddites with a fictional but accurate account of their attack on Rawfold's Mill near Cleckheaton, no doubt based on first-hand accounts related to her by her father.

By January 1813 Patrick needed a house for his new bride and left his lodgings at Thorn Bush Farm and rented a house in Clough Lane at Hightown, near Liversedge, not far from Hartshead Church. Whilst living there he continued to write poetry and published *The Rural Minstrel*. Patrick was steadily gaining a reputation for his writing which continued as an extension of his preaching and was intended to educate people by spreading knowledge of Christianity and the teachings of the Bible.

It was in the house on Clough Lane in January 1814, that the Brontës' first child, Maria, was born. Maria was baptised at Harsthead Church by the Rev. William Morgan and the Morgans and Fennells were godparents. Later in the year Patrick became acquainted with Thomas Atkinson, the vicar of Thornton, a village around four miles east of Bradford, and it was suggested that they exchange livings. This move would bring Maria nearer to her relatives, the Fennells, and double Patrick's stipend. Before the move could be finalised, Maria gave birth, on 8 February 1815, to her second child, a daughter named Elizabeth. She was named after her aunt, Mrs Brontë's sister, who came to visit and help look after her during her confinement. Aunt Branwell, as she was known, was 38 and a spinster. She was deeply religious, a strict Methodist but with some Calvinistic leanings.

In May of 1815, the Brontë family and their new help, a servant girl named Nancy Garrs, made the exchange to Market Street in Thornton. The house was smaller than that at Liversedge, with only two levels and six rooms but convenient for the church and for visiting friends and parishioners. The house was comfortable and had a tiny front garden facing the road and another larger yard at the back against the rising hillside. This house, altered and restored, still stands and can be visited in its present capacity as an Italian coffee shop. One can sit with friends in the very rooms where Maria Branwell nursed her babies and Patrick tended to his parish work.

Patrick's church at Thornton was the Old Bell Chapel, now a ruin, and even in those days, dark, dismal and damp, but it overlooked fields, woods, and a valley, and beyond lay hills and moorland. In 1815 this was a picturesque rural village, but with a growing population of around 7,000 people, so its narrow streets, courtyards and cottages were overcrowded. The Brontë family were soon acquainted with their neighbours but as in all of their homes, and with all of their friends, they always kept a little apart from people who were not of the same class. Patrick and his wife saw and mixed with people of all classes as befitted the role of the vicar, but personal friends were often of a higher and more gentrified nature. This included the Firths who lived at Kipping House in Thornton. John Firth was a doctor whose wife had been killed when her gig overturned. Their only child, Elizabeth, then 18, became friends with Maria Brontë and later Maria's sister, when she returned for the christening of her namesake, Elizabeth Brontë.

Acquaintance with the Morgans, Fennells, and Firth families and other clergy and prominent neighbours helped to elevate Patrick away from his roots and allowed his wife to live a life similar in some ways to that which she had enjoyed in Cornwall. The round of tea parties, visits and general socialising was enjoyable, and with her sister often there to share in the household responsibilities and with a larger amount of income, including the £50 per annum allowance left for Maria by her parents, the family were doing rather well.

Napoleon was finally defeated by the Duke of Wellington in 1815 at the battle of Waterloo and there was great rejoicing throughout Britain. Patrick would have been especially affected due to his interest in wars and his military leanings.

Patrick revered the Duke, and his children later inherited his admiration for the soldier and statesman. One of Patrick's first duties at Thornton was to hold a service of thanksgiving for the defeat of Napoleon. It is against the background of such world-shattering events that the Brontë children were raised.

Inevitably, Maria soon became pregnant again and over the next four years gave birth to four more children, Charlotte in 1816, Patrick Branwell (known as Branwell) in 1817, Emily in 1818 and Ann in 1820. What had once been a comfortable house for the family of four and a servant was now overcrowded and uncomfortable, especially as an extra nursemaid, Nancy's sister, Sarah, was also living there. Two adults, six children, two servants and extended visits from aunt Branwell, could not have been tolerated without a degree of organisation and administration. Patrick needed peace and quiet whilst at home to write his sermons, study and conduct church business. The children would need constant attention to guide them through the hazards of deadly childhood diseases and natural accidents. They also needed fresh air and exercise and the beginnings of a sound education.

What were the Brontë children experiencing in these early years at Thornton? One can imagine a fairly crowded but ordered house to begin with, where the mother was constantly pregnant or nursing, with a growing brood of noisy and active children. Yet this was a household where the parents had strong faith and a belief in education that they no doubt instilled in their children from birth. The house had to be organised and the children kept occupied for their father to function in his duties and there must have been a lot of time spent on instilling good manners and controlled behaviour. These children would not be running around in the streets, but rather they would be spending time in learning to speak, to learn their letters, to read, the girls to sew a little and the only boy to take a primary place in the hierarchy of the children and be taught strictly boyhood occupations and pastimes.

This was an age where children had no rights and many were given little attention or education; their thoughts and feelings often ignored or seen as of no value. I suggest that it was different in the Brontë household. Patrick and Maria welcomed and loved their children and wanted the best for them so it is likely that their early years included love and attention in a settled and safe environment. This provides the necessary circumstances for children to thrive. If you also had children who were already intelligent, enquiring and observant, you would expect them to learn easily and quickly and so appear rather forward for their ages.

There were three and often four adults in the house to supervise and teach the children and adults who visited and to whom the children were taken to see. The children were well fed compared to many in the village, both physically and spiritually, and this would help to keep them healthy and, despite various childhood illnesses, all six children reached the age of 10 years. This was rather unusual for the times when death at or around birth, or in the first five years, claimed the lives of approximately one in three children.

The growth of the family in such a short time would necessarily make the children close both physically, emotionally and intellectually. They would share everything; eating, sleeping, playing and learning together. Whilst Branwell would be especially indulged, all the children developed a close bond that lasted throughout their lives, despite separation and, at times, quite differing ideas and lifestyles. This affection and respect for each other may have been due to their closeness in age and environment, or it could have been part of the taught and copied behaviour between their parents or friends who showed affection between themselves and towards the children. Godparents often played an important part in the lives of the children whom they were bound by God to support; a promise made during the christening service. The Brontë children all had godparents who played important roles, especially in their childhood.

Whether the Brontë siblings met and played with other children whilst living in Thornton is unknown but it is unlikely that no other children visited the house or were a part of their lives. We do know that the parents were keen for the children to only mix within or above their class and in Thornton this would mean only the children of the local professional people, relatives or close friends. The six children had probably no real need to socialise with other children and as time went on they certainly appeared quite self-contained.

As a Protestant with both Evangelical and Wesleyan leanings, Patrick could preach his views and beliefs from a wide palette. There is no doubt that the Brontë children were brought up by both of their parents to have a deep and lasting faith in God and the teachings of the Bible. This belief would have affected every part of their upbringing. They were expected to behave, to be polite and to love and respect their parents. They would attend church from a very young age and have prayers and bible lessons at home.

Despite their position in Thornton and their circle of friends and the respect of their parishioners, it was obvious to Patrick that he needed a bigger house and a wider parish in which to spread his Christian message. Yorkshire was in a turmoil of unrest with some people losing their faith or failing to attend church altogether and Patrick felt it his duty to do everything he could to help to address this issue. In this and other matters, he was quite a philanthropist. Although of high Tory leanings, Patrick Brontë was a man raised from poverty and he did not forget that fact even when he was moving in much higher society. He fought throughout his life to improve the lot of the poor and the disadvantaged and it is to his credit that he tried so hard to help others, acting with true Christian principles.

In June 1819, following the death of the perpetual curate of St Michael and All Angels Church in Haworth, ten miles from Thornton, Henry Heap, the Vicar of Bradford, put Patrick's name forward as the next incumbent. Unfortunately, this angered the local church trustees, who had not been consulted and for a while there was deadlock with no vicar in place. The Archbishop sent Patrick to preach there and he won the approval of the local people. Controversy still ensued as Henry Heap then tried to install the Rev. Samuel Redhead, whom the now angry parishioners drove out of the town. Under the orders of the Archbishop, Patrick, reluctantly at first, began to take services at Haworth, and by January 1820, the month in which his last child Anne was born, arrangements were made for his move to the town. His stipend was set at £180, plus some small benefits, like his surplices, and he would have, rent free, the Parsonage at Haworth for his lifetime.

Before moving to Haworth in April of 1820, the six children were aged between 3 months and 6 years. Six children in six years had no doubt taken its toll on their mother and was probably a contributor to, if not the cause of, her failing health. The family had been popular in Thornton and had various close friends and acquaintances both within and outside of Patrick's congregation. Maria had many friends and relatives on whom she could rely and Patrick kept some of his friends from Cambridge and his various ministries. He was socially and politically active and had already shown signs of wanting to bring about reforms. Whether Maria relished the move to Haworth is not recorded and she had, in any case, little choice in the matter as it was her duty to follow her husband wherever he went. The move meant that she had to leave much of the support of friends like the Firths and the Fennells and in an age where travel was difficult and arduous, she would have been largely unable to keep up acquaintances, except by letter.

Patrick was probably looking forward to the challenge of his new and often unruly parish which spread over a large area and included several villages and much moorland and outlying farmsteads. It is unlikely that he would not also consider his children's education and position in his new parish but he was a largely self-educated man who, it would appear, had always expected to home school his children in their childhood and possibly adolescence. He and his wife were both capable of teaching their children and, Patrick especially, had a higher education and a University degree which was beyond the qualifications of most teachers of the time. There were no formal schools in Haworth but schooling their children would not have been an issue for the Brontë parents. Another bonus for Patrick, who also had a great love of nature and the outdoors, would have been the moorland which reached the back door of the Parsonage and spread for many miles to the west; a veritable playground for his growing children.

The amount of unrest and threat in the West Riding of Yorkshire in the early nineteenth century and the levels of poverty and industrialisation cannot be underestimated. The times were dangerous and hard for most people. Overcrowding in the towns caused poor living conditions, which led to disease, hardship, misery and sometimes violence. In the West Riding, the mills were one of the main employers but the introduction of machinery was taking jobs away and no matter how hard the working conditions for the mill workers, they did not want to lose their jobs and incomes. Bradford and Keighley, the two nearest towns to Haworth, had grown into large, ugly conglomerations of buildings, mills and streets with very little space or fresh air. The smell and dust from the furnaces, the machinery and the domestic fires would have filled the air and damaged health. Life in these towns was noisy, dirty and full of the smells and detritus of people crowded together. Acts of Parliament to resolve social issues were slow to be introduced and lagged way behind the problems being faced by the population. It is not, therefore, unreasonable to assume that Patrick saw the move to Haworth as an escape from some of the worst ravages of the times and the surrounding hills as a haven for his children.

The eldest of his children, Maria, was now 6 years old. What had she seen, experienced and learnt in those years? It is known that, as the eldest, she felt a responsibility and affinity with her siblings. Charlotte described her to her friend Ellen Nussey, years later, as a wonderful child who was a 'little mother' to the others. Her father regarded her as very clever, able to read and understand newspapers and discuss topical issues from a very young age. She was bright, pious and a model of kindness and femininity. She was revered by her younger brother and sisters and portrayed by Charlotte in Jane Eyre, as the model for the character, Helen Burns. Elizabeth Brontë, at 5 years old, was also bright but untidy, funny and altogether different in temperament.

It has long been debated that the position of a child in a family can dictate how that child is valued and treated. Elizabeth was the second girl. Was she less noticed and less indulged in that position? When three more girls arrived did her status reduce or grow? Did she, like many children, behave in ways that, consciously or unconsciously, helped her to attract attention? If she could not emulate her 'perfect' sister, did she use other ways to be different and memorable?

Modern child psychology now recognises and places emphasis on position and changing dynamics within a family and how it affects both the parents and the children. The youngest and the oldest are not treated the same as the siblings in between, nor are the first boy or the first girl. Who was the least attractive, valued, recognised or loved child in the Brontë household? If you disregard the eldest and the youngest and the first boy and girl, there are three sisters all vying for special status: Elizabeth, the second daughter; Charlotte, the third daughter; and Emily, the fourth daughter, all have a niche to make and all need as much attention as the others. It is hard for any parent to juggle the needs of their children and give as much, if not equal, attention to them all. The culture of the time would treat the male, and especially the only male child, as special and deserving of preferential treatment and this puts him in a difficult position and can lead to all types of resentment and sibling rivalry. Were Patrick and Maria aware of the need to encourage sharing and respect amongst all of their children? Did they see this as an important part of a good Christian upbringing and did this lead to a more harmonious group than may have happened under different circumstances?

It is hard to know the facts but the well-documented lives of the Brontë children, especially the four youngest, and their letters and those of their father and friends, suggest a closeness and affection between the siblings. Whether this behaviour was taught or natural to them is hard to define but that it existed is indisputable. Although they naturally paired up at times, they remained a unit and worked and lived together to the extent that they could think and speak for one another. This is not unusual in siblings, but in the case of the Brontës it appears to have been life long and, at times, all consuming. As they grew up they seemed to feed off each other's ideas and imaginations so that the whole was greater than its component parts. Only as adults did they go in any different direction from each other and often only because work and the necessity of earning an income, dictated the circumstances.

There are many examples of children growing up together, apart from outside interference or the dictates of formal education, who develop extraordinary skills and academic and artistic ability. In 1970 a journalist for the BBC, Michael Deakin, made a documentary for Yorkshire Television called, *Shows Promise – Should Go Far*, which was later turned into a book entitled, *The Children on the Hill*. This family of four siblings, whose anonymity has always been preserved, were raised in a cottage on a remote hill in south Wales where their parents exercised complete control of their environment. The children followed a Montessori type system that allowed them freedom to learn what they wanted, when they wanted to, and for as long as they wished. Their parents protected them from all outside influences: most other children, television and formal schooling, and let them develop in an atmosphere free of aggression, violence or chastisement. There has never been a follow up to this book, and so it is not known how these children developed in adulthood, but at the time of the documentary two of the children were described as geniuses; one excelling in mathematics and one in music, way beyond their tender years. By watching their activities and helping to develop their skills, the children's parents, especially their mother, had seen and encouraged various interests and traits and allowed the children free rein to indulge and progress in their chosen and natural talents.

There are some parallels between these children and the Brontës, not least the vivid imaginations and the sharing of time and effort between them. For several years, the four youngest Brontë children lived in a similar isolation; a house on a hill surrounded by fields and moors in which they had time and opportunity to learn about and appreciate nature. They, too, had a wide, though more controlled and restricted, education. Manners and good behaviour would have been of greater importance and religion played a major part, but the Brontë children were able to indulge in a purely childhood environment of play and learning that was often self-directed and self-imposed. They too became artistically predisposed and academically proficient and it is interesting to wonder if this was one of the factors in determining their abilities and literary skills. Is it better that children are left to grow and develop this way, or do they need a formal and restricted education that 'socialises' them amongst dozens of other children of similar age and background? This argument has raged throughout modern education and remains unresolved.

Perhaps it is the case that there should be choice, and children should not be forced to attend school unless there is a demonstrable benefit to that child at that time. Perhaps modern living and the move of women into all areas of the workplace and to the opportunities it affords, prevents or restricts them from keeping their children at home. Do parents want, or are they even able, to spend many years with their children acting as parent, teacher and coach? As stated, we can only ever have one childhood and none of us knows if we would have fared better, or been happier, had we moved to a different house or school, mixed with different people or been raised by different adults. We can argue that compared with many parts of the world, we in Britain have a better education system than most, and years of reform and hard work have created advantages and opportunities to children beyond anything ever offered in the past. Modern technology and scientific advances are constantly adding to knowledge and changing the face of education. Are we now producing children of higher ability, happier and more fulfilled than before or are we, as a society, over indulging them to the point where there is little or no incentive for them to work and to strive?

Education is not an exclusive or defined subject. Education includes emotional and psychological development, socialisation and self-discovery as well as knowledge of the world in which we have arrived. Should adults separate the 'education' part of our development from the rest of our progress as children? Should formal and informal education be defined or isolated so that it must take part in specially designated places, i.e. schools? Did our schooling make us the adults that we have become or did our families, friends, or environment?

Would we have become what we are anyway because it is how we are genetically programmed? Most current theory suggests that all experiences and all learning, plus our genetic make-up, contributes to the development of the human being but it is interesting to note that in some circumstances, some people achieve a far higher standard than others, especially in the arts and sciences. It is also notable that these circumstances are not always those that would seem advantageous to child development. Many repressed and disadvantaged people have developed unique abilities and some people thrive on adversity.

Whatever Patrick's thoughts and beliefs about the move and the transposing of his family from the friendly yet overcrowded life in Thornton to the busy but more isolated township of Haworth, the move was approved and arranged. On 20 April 1820, two carts transported the Brontë family, their two servants and all their belongings, over the moors from Thornton to a place that would remain their home for the rest of their lives.

Chapter Four

Haworth and the Parsonage

The Haworth to which the Brontë family arrived in 1820 was a busy and industrious place consisting of four main villages, Haworth, Far and Near Oxenhope, and Stanbury, and several surrounding hamlets. Four thousand people lived in this area and were experiencing some of the effects of industrialisation. For centuries, Haworth had stood on the main route between Bradford and the Lancashire mill towns of Colne and Nelson, offering rest and sustenance to the drovers and packhorses carrying cotton and wool between the two counties.

Haworth itself was, and still is, situated on a hillside overlooking the River Worth valley. It has a main, steep cobbled street winding up from the valley bottom, with many shops, houses and businesses on either side. This street finally levels out at the top of the hill for a few yards, into a small square surrounded by public houses, shops and the church of St Michael and All Angels. A small lane running up the side of the church leads to Haworth Parsonage, whilst the main road divides from the square and carries on to the villages of Oakworth and Stanbury.

In 1820, the working population of Haworth and its local communities consisted mainly of home spinners and weavers, millworkers, quarrymen, dairy farmers and shopkeepers. There were a few gentlemen landowners and mill owners who lived in their large manor houses but the main population lived in small, often overcrowded, cottages in the town and surrounding villages or out on the large number of smallholdings spread across the open hills and fields between and above the four townships. Much of the moorland could not be farmed due to the heather and poor soil, but sheep and cattle were kept in even the most outlying areas. The people held many different religious beliefs, possibly owing to the sprawled out and divided parish. Methodists, Baptists, Wesleyans, Protestants, Catholics and various Non-conformists have had their chapels and churches in the neighbourhood throughout the centuries. The church that Patrick Brontë came to was on ground used for worship probably since the Norman conquest. Rebuilt in the 1880s, only part of the tower of the old church can still be seen.

The Church of St Michael and All Angels dominated the village of Haworth from its superior position on top of the hillside. Looking at the church and Parsonage today it is a little difficult to envisage the scene as the Brontës first encountered it. The church was smaller and very old and damp. It had a graveyard on two sides that was already overflowing with burials and an unhealthy overcrowding which meant that the earth was regularly dug up and more and more bodies added. The church lane was devoid of other buildings beyond the church except a barn on the opposite side of the lane facing the Parsonage. The Parsonage, which did not have its current extensions, was the last and highest house in the village and whilst overlooking the church and graveyard from its east and south side, faced miles of open moorland from its back, west facing, walls. A small garden surrounded the house on three sides but there were no trees in either garden or graveyard.

The Parsonage at Haworth was, and remains, a most important and dominant building in the story of the Brontë family. This house, built in 1778, was constructed almost entirely from materials found on the moors. It is a foursquare Georgian building laid out on a grid of two levels with a small cellar, and no attics. It had four downstairs rooms surrounding a hallway and five bedrooms leading from a small landing. Each room had at least one window and all but two had a fireplace. The house was built from local stone probably quarried on Penistone Hill just above and beyond Haworth. It was well built and still retains much of its former stonework, lintels, window and doorframes. It has been altered over many years to include a whole new wing in the 1880s and a back extension in the 1960s. The house has been reroofed at least twice but retains some of the original stone tiles. Similarly chimneys and chimneystacks have been replaced, and the wall that once surrounded the house has almost all gone, so externally there have been many changes.

Internally the house had a major overhaul in the 1850s initiated and paid for by Charlotte Brontë from some of the money she made as a famous author. These alterations included a new roof and the enlarging of the parlour and upstairs bedroom by moving the dividing walls. This narrowed the hallway which was offset by a new archway. When the new incumbent, The Rev. Wade arrived, following Patrick's death in 1861, he had no qualms about altering the house for his requirements and discouraged any visitors who had hoped to keep it a shrine to the memory of its famous family. His new extension to the north side of the house destroyed the former kitchen and added a separate dining room, bathroom, library and bedrooms.

When the Brontë family came to Haworth the Parsonage was rather detached from the rest of the village and would have been a cold and austere building unprotected from the weather, especially the prevailing westerly winds. It had small gardens on three sides surrounded by a garden wall, beyond which lay two graveyards, the church and the moors. The positioning of the Brontës' home and its relationship to the village and the elements cannot be over emphasised in the story of the Brontës. This house, the only one that the four surviving siblings ever knew, was their home, their schoolroom, their safety and their enclosure, for almost all of their lives, and it had a major effect on them.

Anyone who stays in the same house throughout their lives will inevitably form a deep attachment to it. It is imbued in the developing mind and in memory and is a central part of ones growing up and view of the world. It may have a positive or a negative effect at different times, or some of both. Most childhood memories will be set within its walls and most of one's experiences will take place there. Home becomes the familiar, the normal and the protective shield to most people unless things happen within its safe harbour which upset and disturb its inhabitants. As no-one can have totally good experiences throughout their lives it is inevitable that, at times, home is not the safe haven of security but more a place of bad memories and experiences; a prison even, from which one may try to escape. The longer one stays in the same dwelling the more and varied experiences will occur there.

The Brontës' home was central to their early development. The Parsonage was not just a domestic space but the place where interaction took place between Patrick and his wide circle of churchmen, friends and parishioners. This house saw a lot of visitors because it was a house built and supported by the church and therefore used for its business and purposes. Patrick was expected to host and sometimes accommodate church officials from bishops to curates. Some reports still exist of different visitors' experience of the Parsonage in the time of Patrick's incumbency, describing the house variously as, 'comfortable, cold, large, rather small, very clean, spotless, welcoming and neat'. It was a house that was ordered yet sometimes chaotic with many people living in close proximity. It was a house where the inhabitants were often on show to visitors and had to demonstrate a high standard of good behaviour.

Whilst this house saw many happy and social interactions, it was also a place of illness and death. Maria, one of the children of the previous vicar, the Rev. Charnock, died in the house when a baby and her father died there in 1819. This was perfectly normal in so far as nearly all people were born and died at home, as they had done for centuries; it is only with the advent of hospitals and nursing homes that this has been reversed. In the Brontë family, the death of their mother and two elder sisters also occurred in the house, after weeks of illness and suffering. The effects of these events are examined in detail in later chapters as to their effect on the remaining family, but it is important here to recognise how a home includes and encloses all the drama that takes place within it. We use expressions like 'walls have ears' or 'if only these walls could speak', as we wonder what events have taken place within a certain room or place. It is why so many are drawn to old houses, battlefields, castles and historic sites. It is to feel the history and to wonder at the lives of all the people who lived and died there.

It is difficult to prove whether a house or a room can hold something of the essence of the past and the lives of the people who inhabited it. Many people are drawn to 'haunted' places and believe in the existence of 'ghosts'. This may include a wish to connect with someone now dead, or a hope to feel something from the past. Belief in something can make it real for that person and it can be a religion, a philosophy, a person or an object. If someone believes that they have seen, or felt, or encountered something or somebody from the past, it is very difficult, and perhaps unnecessary, to disbelieve them. Although current scientific thought and theory may try to disprove such phenomena this issue has never been totally resolved.

When the Brontës were living in Haworth the new and changing face of science and medicine was discovering and challenging all manner of previous beliefs. There was a surge in psychological sciences that began to examine the emotions and the psyche and tried to explain how and why people behaved and experienced life in the way they did. New ideas about the links between one's mind and one's body were being explored and expounded. Phrenology, psychology and psychiatry were new sciences which were investigating phenomena that religion or nature had failed to explain. As industrialisation forged ahead, the personal health of the labourer became an issue. Men like the didactic authors, Samuel Smiles, J.S. Mill and Jeremy Bentham expounded the belief in the work ethic and the application of Utilitarian principles in working towards the greater good for the greatest number of people. This included the belief that people with healthy minds in healthy bodies could work to create a vigorous and growing economy. One's health was also linked to the importance of religion as a doctrine that kept the worker always with his eyes on the afterlife; despite whatever ills he suffered in this one.

If you believed in an afterlife in religious terms in Britain during the nineteenth century, then you believed that life continued after death either in a 'heaven' where you were not only in communion with God, but also restored to your dead relatives, or a perpetual 'hell' where you suffered for all eternity. It would be almost unreasonable not to believe in ghosts and the return of the dead to help or haunt the living. This belief in an afterlife has endured in every culture throughout the history of mankind and still endures and is still impossible to prove or disprove as we still do not have indisputable evidence of a person raised from the dead, who can confirm an afterlife. However, there are many people who have had strange near-death experiences, who claim to have seen and spoken to ghosts, or have seen or felt inexplicable sensations. Death may always fascinate and disturb the living and in the nineteenth century, as in all those before, people searched for ways and means of explaining death and what happened to their bodies and 'souls' afterwards.

One can interpret Haworth Parsonage as a typically 'haunted' house in so far as it was a house, like many others, that survived long enough to incorporate the history of various families and enveloped the multiple good and bad experiences encountered within its walls. The house becomes a kind of crossroads; a passing to and fro of people and events and, in the case of the Parsonage, a crossroads in a multiple sense of the word.

Haworth Parsonage stands with its walls facing the four points of the compass. It is at the centre of the four directions with each wall facing a different aspect. By the 1830s, and with the building of the Sunday school, the north side of the Parsonage faced both a civilised and educational establishment. To the east it overlooked the church; its religious links, and further down towards the town; its social and secular, populated area. To the south it stood adjacent to a graveyard;

its connection to death and the afterlife and to the west it overlooked miles of open moorland; its affinity to nature and the elements. This was an unusual and special building where at any time, day or night, the inhabitants could look out of any window and see a wide range of human and natural elements.

Haworth Parsonage is 250 metres above sea level and, with almost no shelter, was very much exposed to the weather at a time of lower temperatures than today. The seasons were more pronounced and notable for their weather and temperature patterns than in current times. The Brontë's letters, poetry and books speak constantly of the weather conditions because it dictated a lot of their behaviour; their ability to leave the house, play or work in the garden, light fires, open the windows or go into the neighbouring towns and villages. The moors would be dangerous and unsuitable for children, or adults, at certain times of the year unless they had the footwear and clothing that could protect them from ice, rain and snow. The weather would affect who left the Parsonage and who visited, when they came and for how long they stayed. To this day, ice and snow can make both Main Street and Church Street a steep and dangerous climb and descent.

In the 1800s, horse-drawn carriages could not negotiate the steep main street in bad weather, which meant that the delivery of people, goods and food would be affected. With only open fires for warmth and cooking, the Parsonage would not be a warm place in the winter and spring unless there was a good supply of peat or wood to burn and this had to be sourced, delivered and paid for. So, the weather dictated a great deal of how life functioned in the house and what occupations took place within its walls. The seasons meant that whilst one could write without a candle into the late evening in the summer months, the cost of a candle and the ever-present danger of causing a fire may inhibit study and activity at other times of the year.

Another feature of a family home is the way in which the dynamics and movement of the family affects the placing of the inhabitants in different rooms and social spaces. The Brontë family consisted of eight people and two servants when they arrived, and they all had to be accommodated according to their gender, status and needs. Whilst this was a large house in comparison with many in the town, it would still mean a constant shifting of rooms, of furniture, beds and household items. The children would share beds for warmth as much as necessity, they would wash and bathe together, study and play together using different spaces in and around the house according to the climate and their needs. How does one accommodate six small children at any one time when there are such variables as sickness, visitors, quarrelling, education and sleep? Patrick Brontë needed a peaceful and ordered household in which to work and a standard of behaviour amongst his family that was expected of, and dictated by, their social position. The house had to be run well and smoothly at all times.

Unfortunately, nothing is predictable and the decline and death of Mrs Brontë within eighteen months of their move to Haworth will have literally turned the house upside down. A cosy bedroom could as easily become a place of pain and death, and live on as such in the children's memory. A bright and welcoming parlour could, on a different day, be a cold and morbid space. Only the solid walls of the house itself remained a constant as even the sturdy, locally built furniture, was often, of necessity, rearranged. This type of change and movement can both upset and stimulate children. Some like their own space and possessions and others are happy to share. The Brontë children probably shared all of their toys and books, beds, clothing and meals in an interchange that was normal and natural to them. There was a constant movement within the Parsonage, an ebb and flow of human occupation and experience.

This house was also a place where one could live amongst the very rituals and accompaniments of the rites of passage. Patrick performed many christenings, weddings and funerals. The ringing of the church bell heralding a happy event, or the tolling to mark a death, was a background noise that would echo throughout the house and gardens. The constant digging and the sound of the stonemasons' hammers and the sight and smells of the graveyard, were an ever-present backcloth to the Brontës' lives, where the living inhabitants of the Parsonage were in such proximity to their neighbouring dead.

These are some of the influences that made Haworth Parsonage such a unique and unsettling place to live. One can view it as a building at the centre of surrounding natural and social conflict, a boundary between the free and largely uncultivated moorland and the restrictions of the ordered town. Neither may have been less cruel or comforting than the other but they met and crossed in this extraordinary house. If one walked through the house from front to back, east to west, in the first half of the nineteenth century, which one could easily do at that time, one would move through an invisible barrier that exchanged a social and ordered, manmade environment for a natural and disordered one. Standing at the back door of the Parsonage or, better still, at one of the back bedroom windows, one had a 180-degree view of moorland. The view from the front windows and doorway was of the church, the rooftops of the town and the graveyard. The contrast is extraordinary.

It is important to emphasise how much the moor was part of the house and how the elements entered and supported it. The materials which formed the house came from straight-cut ashlar stone from the moorland quarries and were jointed with the local millstone grit. The quarries also supplied the flagstone floors and the stone tiled roof. One can describe the Brontës as living within the bedrock of the moor itself. The Parsonage can be viewed as linked to the four elements: Air, Fire, Water and Earth, in the following specific ways. The house was built on reclaimed moorland earth, peat was cut from the moors to burn in the hearths and water was provided from moorland springs that fed the well in the back garden. Wind blowing directly into the house from the moors filled it with fresh, but often chilling air. The Parsonage is therefore a house built on, and out of, the moor itself, which has become part of its existence.

And yet, as explained, this was a house that 'belonged' to the church as one of its appendages and was paid for and constructed for religious purposes. It had a steady stream of intelligent and learned visitors, and contained many books and newspapers alive with current affairs and political argument. Education and knowledge were as much a part of the house as its moorland construction. This was a home where civil and uncivil met, and where conscious and unconscious, familiar and unfamiliar interchanged and followed through and beyond. It was a place where a child could observe and assimilate the clash between opposites and form opinions and make choices.

Even now one can imagine that the Parsonage and its surroundings would be an exciting and stimulating playground for six small children. Apart from the nine rooms, it had a hallway, a cellar, a back kitchen, gardens and a surrounding wall. It had the lure and repulsion of graves and gravestones, a church to explore and, whenever the conditions permitted, miles and miles of moorland, dotted with smallholdings, animals, water and hills. Interesting people visited their home, bringing lively conversation and exciting books and journals. The children were given almost free rein to study a wide range of subjects including art, music and science. They were not inhibited physically or mentally, especially compared with other children of the time. Their only restrictions appear to be those of normal, early Victorian manners and class. It is not surprising that they all expressed a deep love of their home, Emily wrote the following lines:

> *The house is old, the trees are bare*
> *And moonless bends the misty dome*
> *But what on earth is half so dear,*
> *So longed for as the hearth of home?*
>
> (E. Brontë, *The Complete Poems*
> *of Emily Jane Brontë*, 1941)

No matter how often they had to leave it, they always returned whenever they could and even when they felt oppressed by it. Charlotte, as an adult, often felt trapped and overwhelmed by her home and longed to travel and 'escape', especially after the deaths of all her siblings. Branwell, appears to have wanted to leave the confines of the house in his later years, and his family at times, but always came back and eventually died there. Emily may have been almost agoraphobic when absent from home and, after her aunt's death, never again left it. Anne endured being away from home for the longest time, out of duty, earning money as a governess, but she too suffered and felt the awful pull of homesickness whenever she could not return.

One is reminded of Mr Tulliver's eviction in George Eliot's *The Mill on the Floss*, who 'Couldn't bear to think of himself living in any other spot – where he knew the sound of every gate and door…because his growing senses had fed on them.' (Eliot, *The Mill on The Floss* 1977)

The Brontës' 'growing senses' were permeated with their home and its surroundings; I suggest, that this strange dwelling juxtaposed between, and yet so much part of, conflicting opposites may have helped to create a special atmosphere in which the sensitive and discerning child could develop an extraordinary intensity of imagination that critics would later hail as genius. Whatever reasons or theories are put forward as to the Brontës' literary gifts, their home cannot be underestimated as a source of their creative talents.

Chapter Five

Parents and Children

The Brontë children, as already described, had parents who had a standing in the local community and had been well educated in their respective schooling, Patrick especially so. Both had studied and read widely, and both had social refinement and social skills. They would be considered middle class or lower middle class and this would affect with whom they made friends and which social circles they and their children would inhabit.

There was, and still is to a degree, a separation between class, colour, culture and financial status and gender in many parts of the world. These divisions were rigidly defined and in early nineteenth-century Britain would limit, or increase, the behaviours of the various social groups. Maria Brontë had been brought up with a certain level of wealth and social status, whereas Patrick had educated himself into a higher social position, but one that had always relied on benefactors. Patrick's position in the church put him in a position above most of his parishioners, and allowed him access to the landed gentry. Despite being a rather impoverished clergyman with no personal fortune, he could correspond with and meet many people to whom he and his family would not usually have had access.

Patrick can be viewed as a man craving status and attention, or as a philanthropist wanting the best for the people he cared for, both personally and professionally. When their children were born, Patrick and Maria would have wanted them to excel and held hopes that they would succeed above and beyond the talents and class of their parents. This meant in realistic terms that Branwell would be the focus of the family's fortunes and would exceed his father in both education and a career, and that the Brontë girls would be highly educated gentlewomen who would make excellent marriages which would keep them financially secure for life. The process of realising these dreams and expectations would have begun from birth.

Whatever Patrick and Maria's hopes or expectations for the gender of each child is unknown, but there appears to have been almost as much drive and encouragement shown to the five girls as to the only boy, in a way that was unusual for the time. Many families saw their daughters as needing only enough education and accomplishment to make a decent marriage. Their experiences were limited to household duties, needlework, sewing, housekeeping and the ability to amuse and care for their husbands. The Brontë parents do not appear to have followed this pattern and the girls were at least as well schooled as their brother. This may well have been due to Patrick's belief in and experience of education as the route to success.

So, from the beginning, the Brontë siblings would have received love, kindness, discipline, a sense of sharing and encouragement to study. They would be expected to behave well as representatives of their parents and to demonstrate their position as the son and daughters of a clergyman. Their mother had received a refined upbringing which made her sensitive and kind, according to those who knew her, as well as instilling an abiding faith in God. These traits would have been passed on to her children and they would have also observed her obedience to her husband's needs and wishes.

Patrick was most likely the archetypal patriarch. He was following his God; a figurehead who was both benevolent and forceful and whom dictated the secular behaviour as well as the divine. I suggest that Patrick's faith was immovable and he followed the Bible and its teachings rigorously. This would not necessarily make him a tyrannical or unjust father, but it would certainly mean that his word was final and his beliefs absolute. He would, therefore, naturally rear his children very closely in the beliefs he held: that they must be answerable to God, that they must prepare in this life the seeds of an everlasting one, and that they should follow unquestioningly the 'path to righteousness'.

One can already see the mixture of influences that emanated from their parents and how they affected their offspring. They had a father and mother and servants, aunts, uncles and godparents, who had similar ideas or who, in the case of the nursemaids, would be expected to follow the wishes and instructions of their employers. We know very little of the children's lives at Hartshead and Thornton apart from information in letters that concentrate on visits to relatives and small outings. We can only imagine their daily routines as based on the knowledge we have of their parents, extended family and their environment. Their mother and nursemaids would concentrate their waking hours on feeding, washing, dressing, teaching and entertaining the children. There were no nurseries or schools to send them to so all events took place within the home or its close environments. Patrick had an overcrowded parish to oversee, would have been very busy throughout the day and probably saw little of his children at times. Nevertheless, this was a father who had set and determined ideas. Prayers and Bible readings were said every day in the home with both the children and servants in attendance.

At Hartshead, Thornton and during the first year at Haworth, Mrs Brontë devoted herself to her children and their welfare. She had the help of first one and later two nursemaids, but the education and control of the children probably fell to her whilst they were all so young. Having six children in six years would have taken its toll on Maria's health and strength, and one can see that she had little time between pregnancies to fully recover. The local attention of the children's godparents will have helped and visits from her sister, Elizabeth, may also have been welcome, but Maria does not appear to have had much time for rest or for following her own interests. Like all other wives and mothers, her husband, children and home were her focus and her priority.

We know from letters that Charlotte described her eldest sister, Maria, as always helping and playing with her younger siblings. Patrick described his eldest child as being remarkable in her intelligence and abilities. It is so sad that neither Maria nor her sister, Elizabeth, survived beyond childhood to demonstrate their talents, but we are already aware that these children were individual and clever in comparison with others of their age and time. Was this accidental? Was it a quirk of genetics that made all six children develop talents and imaginations above and beyond those of most other children? Was it the influence of their parents with their love of learning and deep faith that helped to produce quick and intelligent children or was it the environment in which they were raised? One suspects that each played a part but why then do not all children have exceptional abilities?

Modern child psychology has examined thousands of children, their IQs, their families and their environments to try and answer this question because it does not automatically follow that if you provide the 'perfect setting' for a child to develop, that child will grow into an intelligent and fruitful member of the society and will have insight, empathy or kindness towards other human beings.

Nor can those who are more talented or more able be relied upon to use their gifts wisely.

We cannot stand outside of our own upbringing so we may not know which events occurred, or when that made us decide to do one thing or another, especially before we formed recognisable memory patterns and recognition of people and objects. Our lives are out of our own control for the first and most formative years, so it is mainly copying and conditioning that dictates our behaviour and feeds our senses in a never-to-be-repeated or altered way. The young Brontë children had what could be described as a good moral upbringing. They were taught right from wrong, shown how to behave and allowed to engage with the wider world through books and conversation and people who were almost always, adult. They were guided and guarded by loving parents in a settled environment where there was enough sustenance and shelter to keep them as safe and healthy as possible. They were not encouraged to be loud or boisterous or to quarrel, but allowed to question in a polite and interested manner. Being so close in age would cause both harmony and discord at various times, but it would always be overseen by adults who had the children's best interests at heart and wanted them to grow into sensible and intelligent adults. One can see that there is a propensity here to raise healthy and bright children, but the Brontë children's upbringing was not all cheerful or harmonious. A year after the family moved to Haworth disaster entered their lives and caused irrevocable changes.

Chapter Six

Childhood and Loss

By January of 1821 Maria was 7 years old and Ann 1 year. The house would have been full of the noise and the commotion of six small children and four adults and yet order and harmony would have to be maintained. At the hub of this family was Mrs Brontë dealing with her children, attending to her husband and organising the servants and all the household matters. Her role was the lynchpin that held the family together. The Brontë family had nine months of settling in and getting used to their new home when, after the strain of six pregnancies, possibly also miscarriages, and the amount of work involved in raising her family and maintaining her role as the Parson's wife, Mrs Brontë became ill with what the doctor finally diagnosed as cancer of the stomach, though possibly of ovarian cause.

Whilst many illnesses and diseases could be diagnosed at this time there was very little that could be done to cure them or even treat many of the symptoms, including pain. Cancer, especially in the later stages, can be appallingly painful and even with modern drugs like morphine it is still hard to treat and control. From January until September 1821, Patrick watched his wife slowly die as the disease took hold and spread. He stated afterwards that he had never seen anyone suffer so much as his wife and that at times she was in agony both physically and mentally.

One can only imagine the effect that this illness had on the children. Their mother was separated from them and lay upstairs in bed for weeks in a perpetual state of pain and worry. Patrick tells of this time when even his strong faith wavered and he despaired for his wife and children. He spent many nights nursing his wife and days trying to fulfil his parish duties. He recalls that even the childish prattling of his children upset and disturbed him as he realised the enormity of what was happening. His wife needed peace and quiet to try and rest, and six small children could not provide that.

The effects of their parents' situation must have caused the children worry and upset their daily routines. The elder children would be especially aware of their mother's illness whilst the younger ones would want and need all the care and affection that a growing child usually gains from its parents. One imagines the children huddled together for comfort and reassurance as their father strove to stay calm and continue his ministerial duties. The eldest child, Maria, became the `little mother' to whom the younger ones turned. Her father probably asked, or expected, her to take on this role and possibly confided some of his problems and worries to her. Maria was put into a position where she had to behave in a way that belied her age and made her into a mini adult. Although there would be practical help from the family servants, they were not substitute mothers; it was not their role to give the affection and instruction that Mrs Brontë had given her children.

During the final weeks of her illness a nurse was hired to attend Maria and to allow Patrick some rest, but this was not a satisfactory arrangement and she was dismissed. Patrick asked his wife's sister, Elizabeth Branwell, to come again from Cornwall to tend to her sister and the children. Aunt Branwell, as she was always known, was different from her sister in many ways. She was older and set in her ways with stricter religious and social views. She had led a pleasant and happy life in Cornwall and disliked the colder climate of the north and possibly the people and their ways; she had never married or had children of her own. It was a hard thing to ask of her to travel the long way to Haworth and to take on the role of nurse and child minder but she did, and her presence in the household was a great comfort to both Patrick and his wife. Whether the children responded well to their aunt is not recorded. At times during their mother's illness the children stayed with their various godparents but they wanted and needed to be at home.

On the day of their mother's death, the children each visited her in her sickbed as was custom and practice at the time. To lose one's mother at any age is traumatic, but to lose her when one is very young and unable to comprehend her loss may be even more disturbing. Modern day studies of the effect of parental loss on children are comprehensive and much more is known and understood about the long-term effects. Although death was a far more regular, even common, occurrence within the home in the nineteenth century, the emotional effects would not be lessened.

One can see that their mother's death would affect each child in a different way. Anne was only 18 months old and she, Emily and Branwell could not recall her to memory when they were older. Maria and Elizabeth knew her well, and Charlotte was also acutely aware of this mother who was once there and now gone. It is impossible to calculate how deeply each was affected at the time but their writing demonstrates that they each would grieve throughout their lives. Years later Charlotte stated that her only memory of her mother was one of her playing with Branwell in the front parlour. One day her father showed her the parcel of neatly bound letters that her mother had written to him during their courtship. Charlotte described her feelings in a letter to her friend, Ellen, saying that, 'I wish she had lived, and that I had known her'.

It is a brutal but obvious fact that Patrick Brontë needed a wife and a mother for his children and within a few months of Maria's death he began to contact likely females. This is no statement of Patrick's love for his wife, it was more of a necessity than a reflection on his marriage. The family friend, Elizabeth Firth, had recently lost her father and Patrick wrote to her suggesting that they become more than friends. His proposal was instantly refused and caused a rift between the two families for several years. Remarriage was not unusual for a man in Patrick's position. With the loss of so many wives in childbirth, men would often remarry, sometimes repeatedly. The strict male and female roles did not allow for men to be homemakers and child-minders. Sadly, Patrick's gauche attempts to obtain a wife fell on very stony ground.

Possibly with the realisation that he was, at 45, not the handsome and entertaining curate of his younger days and whilst also being very aware that he had six motherless children, Patrick did the only thing he could and approached his sister-in-law, Elizabeth Branwell, to stay at the Parsonage and look after him and his children. This arrangement was initially to be a temporary one until he eventually found a wife or until the children were older. It is unlikely that this decision was made after consultation with all the children, though possible that Patrick spoke to the elder ones as he included his children in his affairs more than most parents of the time. The outcome was that aunt Branwell stayed on at the Parsonage after her sister's death and the children had a temporary new 'mother'.

Whether this arrangement worked well at the time is not known but by 1823, Patrick again tried to resolve his widowhood and he wrote to a former lady friend, in an attempt to rekindle their relationship. His insensitive letters show how wrong he was to assume that this woman, Mary Burder, had any feelings for him except contempt, having been rebuffed by Patrick some fifteen years earlier and having had no contact from him in all that time. Despite her obvious scorn at his offer of marriage, Patrick tactlessly wrote to her again in 1824, but this time the lady did not even reply. At the age of 47, Patrick had to accept that a remarriage was not imminent or even likely and that his sister-in-law, would need to remain a permanent resident for the foreseeable future.

One wonders how well this arrangement suited Elizabeth Branwell and whether she would have preferred to return to Cornwall. Had she made a deathbed promise to her sister to care for her children? Did she feel it her duty to stay and support the family? Did she resent the fact that she had, by default, five nieces and a nephew to care for with little or no prospect of living the life that she had so enjoyed in Cornwall? At this time, the law prevented a man from marrying the sister of his deceased wife, so Patrick and Elizabeth could not have lived together as man and wife, even if either had wanted to. Both would have been dependent on each other in so many ways, but were prevented from showing affection or intimacy towards each other. If Elizabeth was unhappy with her situation in what way did this affect her relationship with each child and what was each child's relationship with their aunt?

There is no doubt that aunt Branwell cared well for the children. She provided stability and knowledge of household management and female occupations and manners necessary for their upbringing. Branwell was very much his father's responsibility and he taught him and encouraged him in his studies. Whether aunt Branwell was demonstrative in her affections for the children or whether she had favourites is not known, but Branwell was especially close to her and she probably singled him out because he was the only boy. Anne too knew no other mother figure and her aunt appears to have favoured her as the youngest and possibly the quietest and most obedient of the children.

Therefore, in the months and years following the loss of their mother, the six children lived in an environment that was both homely and familiar but turned strange and different as the adult dynamics altered. It is known that these motherless children sought comfort amongst themselves as much as from any external affection that may, or may not, have been shown towards them by the adults in the house. With his busy role, it is likely that Patrick left most of the childrearing to their aunt, but he appears to have had the main say in how they were educated and what they had access to in the way of books and information. The children certainly loved and respected their father but whether they were demonstrative in their affections with him is difficult to tell. This was not an age when people showed a lot of overt affection towards each other or their offspring. The emphasis was on good manners and obedience and, in the Parsonage, a strict belief in God and the teachings of the Bible. The soul rather than the body was valued as the most important part to nurture and this was based on bending to the will of God before any personal needs or preferences.

There were no excesses at the Parsonage. The children had physically enough to survive but emotionally they may well have felt deprived. Academically they were very well catered for and encouraged in all manner of the arts and sciences as well as the political and social affairs of the day. Most of their formal learning took place in the house around the dining table in the parlour or, for the girls, in aunt's bedroom, where they would learn to sew, or in the kitchen where they learnt the rudiments of baking and housekeeping. Branwell was taught by his father, probably in Patrick's study, receiving the same classical education that Patrick had known and in the same male orientated manner that would see him educated in history and politics, both ancient and modern, and studying Greek and Latin as he grew older.

There was however a vast play area on the doorstep of the Parsonage and it was in amongst these moorlands that the children discovered, and fostered, their love of nature. Weather permitting, the children were allowed to roam on these moors more or less unrestricted. As young children, they would be accompanied by a servant, or possibly their father, but as they grew older they ventured out as a group or in pairs, depending on the circumstances and dynamics. As youngsters, there was always a tendency for play to be in either the gardens or on the moors rather than venturing into the town. It is an odd child who would not see those moors as a huge adventure playground and to want to revel in the freedom it offered against the restrictions of their home. On the moors they could run, shout and behave with the wildness and exuberance that is a part of childhood.

They would see this wide area in all its beauty and at its most dark and dangerous. The hills and valleys were populated by farms and animals but up on the moorland the environment was still very natural and full of birds and wildlife, flowers and heather and pure spring water. It was here that the children learnt to know and appreciate the flora and fauna of the moors and to closely inspect the behaviour of domestic and wild animals and observe the natural cycles of the seasons. This was a time a hundred years before the building of the reservoirs, necessary to carry water to the growing cities of Leeds and Bradford, which later flooded and spoilt the natural lie of the land. The children had various favourite spots on the moors, some of which are no longer visible as they lie under water.

From the back bedrooms of the Parsonage the children could view the landscape of the moors and watch the skies. At night, they would view the stars and the phases of the moon. This was a time before any artificial lighting and on clear nights they would have seen a vast spectacle of stars and constellations. Time spent on the moors nurtured these children as much as that spent in the Parsonage and they grew to love all that it had to offer. Again, the position of their home was unique in the way that it could provide shelter and contain all the social affairs of the day but also offer a vista of the natural world not known or seen by people living in towns and cities.

We simply do not know precisely how the children behaved and developed over the first five years at the Parsonage, but we do know that it was the centre of their world and between it and the moors they had everything a child could need, except the love and care of their natural mother. It would seem that Maria, as the eldest child, took a great interest in helping and teaching her younger siblings and they all adored her. She was lively and intelligent and it was she who would read to the younger ones and make up stories for them. Storytelling is an art when performed and delivered in a certain way which captures and illuminates the emotions and thoughts of the listener. Patrick's Irish ancestry claimed some fame in this area of literary skill and Patrick had inherited the ability to tell or write a good story. As his children grew, they would hear the tales of their families in both Ireland and Cornwall, and listen to the stories of all manner of real and imaginary deeds. Living in such proximity and so close in age, the children would sleep in shared beds and it was the elder girls' habit to entertain their siblings at night with tales or plays that would be acted out and discussed. When Charlotte was at school in her mid-teens, she had to be stopped from telling stories to the other girls because they became so frightened. This history of storytelling and the ability of the children to make up their own stories and imagine all manner of people and events was probably nurtured in their bedtime tales and developed into their world of fantasy and imagination.

An event took place in 1824 that would affect the Brontë family forever. On 30 January, a school opened at Cowan Bridge near Kirby Lonsdale in Lancashire that offered an inexpensive education to the daughters of poor or impoverished clergymen. The school's founder, the Reverend William Carus Wilson was a strict Calvinist who had little interest in the physical welfare of the pupils and believed that only hard work and the removal of all pleasure and personality would fit these unfortunate girls for work as teachers and governesses. He wrote tracts for children about the fires of hell, to which each would undoubtedly go if they did not conform to the school's strict regime.

Under the guidance of this man, the Clergy Daughters' School at Cowan Bridge opened its doors to girls as young as 5, but offered a damp and dank atmosphere in a low valley where there was little heating in the winter and a lack of fresh and clean air even in the summer. The girls were crowded into dormitories, were ill fed, not given enough opportunity to wash properly, and followed an exhaustive routine of lessons and Bible studies. It was a harsh and sometimes cruel environment which caused many of the pupils great suffering and sickness.

Unfortunately, Patrick Brontë saw this school, with its annual fees of only £14, as an answer to a prayer. He could afford to send his daughters away to be educated. He believed that they would be in a strict but caring environment where they would learn all the female attributes necessary to fit them for work in the limited professions open to them. Patrick would continue to school Branwell at home and aunt Branwell could return to Cornwall. The Garr sisters were already talking of leaving and Patrick would only need one housekeeper to see to himself and Branwell. This was a financial solution to his hard-pressed funds and would allow him the opportunity to have some peace and leisure time to himself.

Before Patrick could avail himself of the Clergy Daughters' School, all six children succumbed to measles and then whooping cough. They were ill for weeks and it was a very trying time for everyone. At a time when the death rate amongst children in Haworth was so high, mainly due to childhood diseases, Patrick must have been extremely worried. It took a long time for the children to fully recover and it is possible that Maria and Elizabeth were still frail when Patrick took them on the long journey by coach in July of that year to their new school, twenty miles away. A month later Charlotte was taken to join her sisters and in November the 6-year-old Emily followed.

One can understand why Patrick thought that the school would benefit his daughters' education and prepare them for adult life and why he may not have investigated it too thoroughly with regard to the children's physical welfare. He too believed that children needed to fear God and to behave in a way that prepared them for both adulthood and the afterlife. This school had a major, if rigid, religious doctrine and promised many skills and accomplishments. Taking his eldest three daughters in July and August he probably saw the school bathed in light and sunshine and did not notice its low-lying prospect and isolation. In November, he and Emily would have travelled there and arrived mainly in darkness and Patrick was perhaps eager to return to Haworth, especially if the weather was poor. There is a record that he may have stayed overnight, but whether he saw his daughters on each visit is unknown. No school is going to advertise its faults and failings and Patrick no doubt received a warm and affable welcome on each occasion he visited and left his daughters in a situation he believed to be greatly beneficial to them.

By January 1825, with four of the Brontë children away at school, the Garr sisters left the Parsonage to be replaced by a 53-year-old widow named Tabitha Aykroyd. Aunt Branwell had probably agreed to remain until Anne was old enough to join her sisters at school. Tabby, as she was known, was in many ways a far more motherly substitute than aunt Branwell. She was a warm-hearted lady with experience of children and came with a wealth of knowledge about Haworth town and many of the people in it. She too was a storyteller and the children learnt a great deal about their hometown and its history over the years from Tabby. She was also a gossip and knew much of the social and intimate details of her neighbours. Tabby was a Methodist and this was a faith that was in some ways more welcoming and tolerant than the Church of England but had equally strong views about behaviour and social class. Tabby was hired as a servant but over the thirty years that she lived with the Brontë family she became more of a companion and foster mother to her charges and the children grew to love her. She was also highly superstitious. Tabby could recall seeing 'fairies' in the valley bottom before the building of the mills and her influence on the children's imaginations would have been considerable.

Patrick and aunt Branwell were oblivious to the conditions at the Clergy Daughters' School until a letter arrived in February 1825 stating that Maria was seriously ill. Patrick hastened to Cowan Bridge to bring her home and saw that she was rapidly succumbing to consumption. Over the next frantic weeks Patrick, aunt Branwell and Tabby nursed the sick child but on 6 May she died and was buried alongside her mother in the crypt of her father's church. Two weeks later a servant from the school arrived with Elizabeth, also fatally ill. This time Patrick was galvanised into rushing to the school but, because of an outbreak of typhus fever, the pupils who were well had been sent to the Reverend Wilson's home near Morecombe where Patrick found Charlotte and Emily and brought them home to Haworth.

The next few weeks saw Elizabeth's death in a repeat of the last days of her sister. Branwell and Anne had lived through the trauma of their eldest sister's illness and death and were now going through the same rituals with Elizabeth. This time Charlotte and Emily were at home and also suffered the ordeal as the adults tried in vain to nurse Elizabeth back to health. The effects of the two deaths on the remaining children and the adults changed their lives and relationships forever. As was the practice at the time, all the children would see, and were probably present, when death occurred and were expected to kiss the corpse and view it lying in the bedroom until the funeral day and then in its coffin. We forget that corpses stayed at home until burial and were on view for family and visitors, to pay their respects. Branwell was deeply disturbed by these images and recreated them in several of his writings.

There is also another worrying aspect of these repeated deaths. When children lose a parent or a sibling, they are often upset more by the fact that they do not understand why and how that person has died and, more importantly, where they have gone to. When Maria and Elizabeth died in quick succession no-one knew who would be next or how soon another death may occur. This would make everyone very anxious and the children, fearing that there may be another death as part of this awful cycle, would be especially loath to be parted from their surviving parent or each other.

Patrick was, no doubt, utterly devastated by his daughters' demise and one wonders whether he blamed himself for a certain lack of care. His worry and possible guilt made him especially vigilant over the health of both himself and his remaining family. Aunt Branwell must have realised at that point, if not before, that the likelihood of her returning to Cornwall was gone. The traumatised children needed her guidance and stability now more than ever. Tabby would have done all in her power to comfort everyone and to protect the remaining children at the saddest time of their young lives.

Charlotte was now the eldest child and this had a profound effect on her and on her behaviour towards her siblings. She took the role of elder sister very seriously, looking out for her brother and sisters in an affectionate but possibly a rather official and domineering way. The elder sisters whom she had adored had now gone and she had to take their place in a complete role reversal. She too was loving and caring but Charlotte could be sharp and demanding as well; always expecting others to maintain her own high standards. In adulthood, when Branwell succumbed to women, drink and drugs, she appears to have berated or ignored him rather than offer support. Charlotte despised what she saw as weakness or affectation and had little time or sympathy for it.

We do not know when, or even if, Charlotte ever told her father of the true horrors of her childhood schooldays but they obviously had a most profound and lasting effect. When she wrote *Jane Eyre* she used the experiences of the Clergy Daughters' School to describe Lowood and the trials of the school girls including Helen Burns, the fictional version of her sister, Maria. Despite opposition to her novel and even a threat to sue, Charlotte always maintained the description to be true to life and the staff and conditions responsible for the deaths of her sisters.

Chapter Seven

Education and Exploration

It is easy to imagine that the four remaining children turned even more to each other as they suffered the enormity of their losses. The house must have been a sad and morbid place for these previously active and enthusiastic siblings and it is likely that they spent more and more time out of doors away from all the reminders of those harrowing weeks.

Notwithstanding, some important and lasting circumstances occurred following these deaths. It would be many years before Patrick sent any of his children away from home again and this created a unique bond between the children and between them and their surviving parent. Patrick was now far more protective of his children and especially concerned with their health. He had the experience and the materials to carry on their home schooling and, economically, he had a smaller household to sustain. Patrick had a medical book which still exists and it is full of his annotations regarding numerous illnesses and how to deal with them. It would seem that Patrick spent some time researching medical matters and had some medical knowledge and insight. He certainly believed that clear water, pure air and good plain food contributed to health. He had few qualms therefore about his children spending time out of doors at any available opportunity. It is also likely that both for their health and social position, his children did not mix with the local children for play or lessons but would only see them at church or on errands through the village.

By the summer of 1825, and for the next five years, the four children lived for most of their formative years in and around Haworth Parsonage. They depended on each other absolutely and when their papa and aunt were occupied with their own work and interests the children had free reign of the locality and their own play. Charlotte once likened this period in their lives to 'mushrooms growing in a cellar'. This was not a derogatory observation. It does in fact demonstrate how children forced into a situation can flourish. They had everything they needed to grow. Even though, to outsiders, their situation may have seemed dark and undercover, these were the very circumstances necessary for their development.

This childhood microcosm of the Brontë children contained books, conversations with informed and educated adults, close and loving relationships, lots of exercise and communing with nature throughout the seasons and in all weathers, a safe and sheltered home, a healthy diet and plenty of sleep and, perhaps most importantly, a knowledge of the church and the Bible which offered them a way of understanding and coping with the loss of their mother and sisters. These children were, in fact, very privileged to have all this on which to learn and grow.

Confined in some ways but so free in others, the children rapidly progressed in all aspects of their education and development. The unique position of their home and the moors gave enormous opportunities to feed the imagination. Life and death surrounded them, the huge expanse of the moors fed their minds as much as the confines of the Parsonage. They learnt about the human condition and how nature attacks and overwhelms whatever man tries to accomplish. Emily wrote years later about the insanity of nature and its unrelenting fight for survival which involves growth, destruction and rebirth.

It was in these five important years that the Brontë children used each of their senses to know and understand the world around them and this acute observation and appreciation of the environment and the people who populated it, helped them to become highly perceptive writers.

Charlotte wrote of these extraordinary, often happy days,

> *We wove a web in childhood,*
> *A web of sunny air;*
> *We dug a spring in infancy*
> *Of water pure and fair*
> (C. Brontë, *The Brontës: Selected Poems*, 2003)

These halcyon years formed their personalities and established their beliefs. They fostered their growing interests in art and literature which allowed them to develop and write colourful stories. One catalyst to their early writings may have been the arrival of a box of toy soldiers brought home by Patrick, with other gifts, for his young family. The children's knowledge of politics, war and battles was already advanced, both through their reading of local newspapers and magazines and Patrick's own tales and interest. The toy soldiers were adopted by the children and given names and identities based on leading men of the day. Gradually, the soldiers and their activities were developed and transposed into a race of people living on an island off the coast of Africa which the children named The Great Glasstown Confederacy.

It did not take long for the children to write up the saga of these people in little books that copied, in miniature, the magazines which they read. Producing their own secret magazines, the children described all the social structures, class, war and peace of their made-up characters. They played out the lives of the kings and queens, the politicians, the explorers, the armies and the life and loves of their characters, with increasing enthusiasm and complicated interaction.

This was a full-time occupation which only stopped for formal lessons. The children became their characters and when conversing in the persona of each, would talk and behave like them. They would discuss and act scenes in bed at night or when walking on the moors. They could see, and be, the people they had created. On cold wet days, or as a punishment, they may be confined to the small cellar at the Parsonage where, in the semi-darkness, they could add further frightening and mysterious aspects to their tales. They would listen to the gossip that Tabby was always pleased to share and her tales of misdoings in the town and it would all add to the melting pot of their dreams and be reworked into their stories. This constant source of information may have heightened their need to know more about human events and behaviour.

Some of their early miniature books still exist and both their innocence and maturity is evident. As the children grew older their writing became more prolific and they produced various tales in magazine form, essays and poetry. Initially, Branwell was the lead author but gradually all the children joined in. By 1829 Branwell was producing *Branwell's Blackwood's Magazine* which was later adopted and adapted by Charlotte into the *Young Men's Magazine*. Branwell and Charlotte's writing was a hive of activity into which they only gradually let Emily and Anne contribute. As often happens amongst siblings, they form partnerships, fall out, regroup and continue, and this pattern may be repeated throughout their lives. For most of their childhood and teenage years, Branwell and Charlotte were natural partners, both in age and outlook: eldest boy, eldest girl and with similar ideas and interests. Emily and Anne were also close in age and temperament. Whilst Emily is often viewed as introverted and self-contained, she had a very close and sustained relationship with her youngest sister and Anne reciprocated. Later their partnerships became firmly established. Charlotte and Branwell concentrated on their nation of Angria and the Angrians, and Emily and Anne created their own kingdom of Gondal and the Gondals. Each make-believe realm was peopled by beings who could transmute into different versions of themselves and could even die and be resurrected. This gave the four Brontë 'Genie' absolute powers to control each person and event in their stories in a way that was denied to them in the real world.

As they developed, the children could add more characters and involve more complicated relationships and plots. Their observation and knowledge of actual politics and social relationships and events helped them to create complicated societies in their make-believe worlds. By their teenage years, exploration of love and sexual behaviour had entered their work and a more mature and controlled writing developed which included caricature, satire, symbolism and metaphor. People were analysed and all their strengths and faults exposed and worked through. The battles and play of childhood become the plot and intrigue of youth and adulthood.

It is hard to explain the extent and force of the children's fantasy worlds. They were as real to them as their own lives and sometimes intertwined, and interfered, with reality. In a diary paper written by Emily in June 1837 when she is nearly 19 years old, she records that, (the punctuation is my own),

> *Tabby is in the kitchin – the Emperors and Empresses of Gondal and Gaaldine [are] preparing to depart from Gaalding to Gondal to prepare for the coronation which will be on the 12th of July. Queen Victoria ascended the throne this month. Northangerland in Monceys Isle – Zamorna at Eversham. All tight and right in which condition it is to be hoped we shall be on this day 4 years, at which time Charlotte will be 25 and 2 months – Branwell just 24 it being his birthday – myself 22 and 10 months and a piece, Anne 21 and nearly a half.*
>
> (J.R.V. Barker, 2010.p. 315)

This extract says so much about Emily's state of mind. She is an adult and she is writing about real people and events in the same vein as those of her make-believe world and they appear to have equal status. Whereas many children grow out of the need to create and indulge in daydreams and make-believe, the Brontë children clung on to their creations into adulthood and possibly throughout their lives.

What one sees in these children is a childhood interest and occupation that grows until it becomes obsessive. Whilst one can argue that their stories, with their constant characterisation and plot organisation, gave ample practice for their mature poetry and novels, there were occasions when it appears to the modern eye, that the obsession with make-believe was unnatural or unhealthy. Charlotte described a time when teaching a group of young girls when she became lost in reverie and oblivious to the noise and activity around her. It is indicative of obsession and possible mental confusion that allows the mind to wander and play when the person is in a situation which they dislike or where they are unable to cope.

When life becomes too difficult, too alien or too sad, one can only escape into the imagination. The Brontë children had learnt to do this from a very young age and it remained a comfort, especially in times of stress such as Charlotte was experiencing as a teacher at Roe Head school, or when they felt under threat from real and adverse events.

When Emily and Anne visited York in their twenties they played out some of the characters from their *Gondal Saga*. This may seem harmless fun, but could also be a sign of something strange and slightly odd behaviour for two women on an outing to a new city. It could indicate an inability to face reality and a need to dwell in the safety and security of childhood with a necessity to control events, real or imaginary. It could be that their natural shyness and lack of sophistication in such an environment caused them to hide behind personas with which they were familiar and under which they could metaphorically disappear. Why would two women in their mid-twenties, who would normally be married with children, be playing games in the manner of children twenty years younger? Here were two women who were well educated, had travelled, gone out to work, experienced many social situations and met a variety of people, indulging in childish make-believe. Their behaviour highlights the importance they attached to their stories and dreams. It shows that, despite their situation and their ages, fantasy dominated their thoughts and was still a huge pleasure to them. We cannot know but we can wonder at the extent of their fantasy world and to what degree it interfered with, or crossed over, into reality.

Harmless or otherwise, their desire to read and write copiously and their access to a wide range of information fed their growing understanding of the world and fostered their ability to create huge metropolises inhabited by vast populations of people of all ages and lifestyles. Part of the inspiration for their fantasies came from *Blackwood's Magazine*, a monthly journal published in Edinburgh and borrowed from Mr Driver, one of their neighbours. This magazine, first published in 1817, was a continuing source of information focusing especially on political and literary debate. It was a Tory paper which fitted their father's political leanings and it glorified and honoured the great statesmen and writers of the day. It is probably from this magazine that the Brontës learnt much of their knowledge of home and foreign affairs and the machinations of the royal courts. The children thrived on its reports on a wide variety of subjects including travel, the arts, adventure and discovery, history and the biographies of prominent writers and politicians.

This magazine was the template for the 'little books' that the Brontë's wrote in childhood and they copied its style and used its words and phrases so that their writing was not only imaginative but also informed and adult in content and language. This gave much of their early works a maturity that would not otherwise have developed until much later. *Blackwood's* was not their only inspiration, but it was the most influential. Their literary intake came also from books and articles, pamphlets and leaflets in the Parsonage and a deep knowledge of religious texts. The Parsonage books were a collection of fiction and non-fiction but all were instructive and interesting. These included works such as *Aesop's Fables*, Bewick's *History of British Birds*, *The Arabian Night's Entertainment* and poetry by Coleridge, Dryden, Butler, Southey, Wordsworth, Keats, Burns and Byron. Sir Walter Scott became a favoured author. Branwell studied the classics in the works of Homer and Virgil but the girls were also introduced to these and knew a great deal of ancient history, even if they did not study the Greek and Latin languages until they were older. In their teens, the girls all studied German and French.

The family also had access to the Keighley Mechanics Institute which was founded in 1825. This organisation offered lectures on a wide variety of subjects in a fortnightly programme open to all. These included scientific demonstrations and talks by visiting academics and prominent figures in many walks of life. There was also the Keighley Circulating Library from which the children could borrow books and, for a while, they were able to access a lending library in Keighley High Street. There is some speculation that the children also had access to the private library of the Heaton family who lived at Ponden Hall about two miles west of Haworth. The Heaton's were local mill owners and also trustees of Haworth church and lands. They would be well known to Patrick and his family and visits and exchanges may have taken place.

Not only did the Brontë children have a wide range of books and magazines, and a vast area of nature to explore on their doorstep, their father, despite his limited income, paid for them to have both music and art lessons. These probably began around 1829. Charlotte suffered from extreme short-sightedness causing her to peer closely at objects and writing. This caused her drawings and paintings to be painstakingly copied out, often miniaturised and highly detailed. All four children had good artistic abilities, with Branwell encouraged to paint with oils and eventually testing his skills as a portrait painter. Musically, Emily was possibly a gifted pianist but they all sang and played various instruments including the piano and the flute and, in Branwell's case, the church organ. These skills developed over time but it is important to note the wide range of instruction and experience that the children were exposed to and why they developed such abilities in so many areas of the arts.

During these precious years when they had access and encouragement to study, and when exercise took the form of long and informative walks on the moors, the children learnt and practiced their storytelling skills. These were firstly discussed between themselves, often at bedtime and then acted out in the form of plays and finally, by round 1828, they began to write them down. A shortage of paper, a desire to keep their stories secret from the adults, and the influence of *Blackwood's Magazine* meant that they produced tiny books which followed the style and layout of *Blackwood's* but in miniature, and printed in writing so tiny as to need a magnifying glass to be read. Miraculously some of these early booklets still survive and can be seen at the Haworth Parsonage Museum. They are less than 7cm in length and width and are hand-sewn together from scraps of various types of paper. The drawings and writing are tiny but are reproduced in a printed form to resemble an adult magazine.

Hundreds of fragments of stories and poems from the Glasstown and Angrian Sagas still exist and a limited number of poems written to accompany the Gondal stories. These manuscripts contain thousands of words and many sketches. Time and again the dominant characters such as The Duke of Wellington, The Marquis of Duro, Napoleon Bonaparte, Arthur and Charles Wellesley, grow prominent, die and are reinvented as another character or as one of their own family members. The stories are full of reference to foreign places, especially Africa, which was currently being explored and discussed in the newspapers. Charlotte, especially, liked to describe exotic lands and fertile valleys, vast deserts and majestic mountains and they show the influence of the children's reading of the *Arabian Nights* and an advanced knowledge of history and geography.

Sometimes the stories are serious and brutal, at others they are gentle and the characters are kind and thoughtful. Often the children use their stories to make playful references to each other and to target or mock a characteristic. Charlotte often sees part of Branwell's personality in his characters and uses her own characters in a way that will show his defects without actual confrontation. Therefore, one sees the brother and sisters arguing with each other through their characters, a clever device that allows indirect criticism and mockery without giving first-hand offence.

It is in this development of wit and sarcasm that the Brontës' writing begins to alter from a childhood occupation to a more mature and sophisticated arrangement of language and styles. The more they became immersed in their studies and the more information they received, the more they could articulate and debate. The children were now developing different and separate characters and, whilst still very close, were evolving their own personal tastes and opinions. Charlotte and Branwell often bantered words between each other but Emily and Anne did not escape sibling rivalry and were also, at times, the butt of the elder children's barbed commentary.

The role that the house and the moors played in the education and experience of the children must be appreciated to understand how they developed their talents. As previously noted, Haworth Parsonage is an extraordinary house which stands at a crossroads between the church and state, and nature and the landscape. The familiarity with it that the children felt, and the time spent within its walls, made the Parsonage both a refuge and a prison at various times in their lives.

The fact that the house was Patrick's until his death meant that as he grew older and more frail, the likelihood of his demise was a constant fear to him and his children. Without him they would be bereft of both a dwelling and an income. As the four children could remember no home other than the Parsonage, it was a very special place. They must have known every nook and cranny, every sound and every smell. It must have imbibed their senses and been an ever-present edifice and backdrop for most of their experiences. During their lifetime, the Parsonage had one small cellar leading from a door in the hallway down a narrow, curved staircase into a short oblong room with a vaulted ceiling. It still exists but has been extended. It was a dark and possibly dank place, cold all year round and used for storage and for aunt Branwell's beer making. It may also have been used as an extra playroom for the children or as a place of punishment. It would certainly have helped to fire the imagination and would be an extra room where they could sit and plot their stories using the atmosphere to frighten each other by creating ghostly events. The *Gondal Saga* contains stories of the Palace of Instruction, where children are sent to live underground as punishment and all manner of awful things happen to them.

Living in a house surrounded on two sides by a graveyard, where the sounds and sights of death and mystery were so close, must have informed their play. It is hard to imagine nowadays the absolute darkness of night in previous centuries. The only artificial light came from firelight, candles, gaslights or oil lamps. In the winter, and in any house where there were financial constraints, the lighting of candles and lamps would be either restricted or they would not be used at all. In the Brontë household, candles were an extravagance and were also a fire hazard dreaded by Patrick, who had buried many children and adults burnt to death in house fires.

This appreciation of the long dark hours in the winter months explains why the children spent a lot of time on their bed plays and in acting out adventures. There was not the light to see to read or write but there were many hours of darkness when they could invent fabulous stories and exotic characters. Out on the moors, usually in daylight or evening gloom, they had the space, the light and the stimuli to lend free rein to their night time fantasies. The convoluted landscape of the hills and moorland and the centuries of farming and water have shaped the hills and valleys around Haworth into a beautiful landscape. It was an empty canvas that gave the Brontë children carte blanche to paint on to it their own ideas and events. Each time they returned, the moor was there again and they could fill it with new and exciting people and adventures that, at night, could be transferred into plays or, by day, written about as part of their stories.

These moorlands contained large empty spaces, but also the homes of a number of people who worked this attractive yet harsh environment and tried to make a living from it. Nothing can live on heather moorland except wild birds and small animals. Those who tried to farm the lower slopes were tough Yorkshire folk and often different from the people in the towns and villages in their manners and customs and in their accents and their beliefs. The Brontë children will have met and known them as they wandered the moors. In fact, they may have been more familiar with some of these families than with many of the Haworth villagers. Travel was so limited that many people did not stray far from where they were born, so traditions carried on from one generation to the next with little or no interruption. It was a way of life that was unchanged for centuries until the encroachment of mechanisation in farming in the twentieth century and the building of the reservoirs.

One can appreciate how these children could be considered as isolated but they were, in fact, better informed, better cared for, and better supplied with stimuli than most other children in the area. They had both freedom and close supervision. They had family love, but also suffered family loss and tragedy, and they had a living expanse of moorland filled with birds and animals in which to wander at their ease and pleasure. They were, in many ways, very blessed.

Chapter Eight

Ambition and Restraints

These happy days of learning and exploring had to come to an end at some point, and this was prompted after Patrick became seriously ill in 1830 with inflammation of the lungs which made him very weak and confined him to bed for three weeks. The question of how his family would survive if he died was again brought to the fore. Charlotte and her sisters were only ever going to be able to work as teachers or governesses because of their social position. Despite their high levels of knowledge, their limited time at school and their lack of refinement meant they required extra, and necessary, skills that would qualify them for these particular roles. They needed extra schooling, formal qualifications and teaching skills, and they needed the support and references of people already in these professions.

Patrick realised that he must begin to equip his children to earn their own livings and to support themselves in the event of his death. Although probably reluctant to approach the subject and with Charlotte naturally fearful at the prospect, Patrick had to find a suitable school for his daughter which would prepare her in all the accomplishments necessary for her to find work. Charlotte was now 14 years old and childhood had to come to an end.

A school was found, at Mirfield, called Roe Head. It was about twenty miles south-east of Haworth, and it proved to be a turning point in Charlotte's development. Despite Charlotte's initial misgivings and her memories of the Clergy Daughters' School at Cowan Bridge, this new establishment, set up by the Wooler sisters, could not have been more different. The school was a large, clean and airy house. The food and accommodation were good and the small number of girls were kind and friendly. Miss Margaret Wooler, the principle, was an astute and intelligent woman who could see the potential in her pupils and used praise and encouragement to stimulate learning. There was a strict but fair timetable which included French, Drawing, Music, Literature and Sciences.

The girls had beautiful grounds in which to exercise and they all thrived in this calm and pleasant establishment.

Within days Charlotte had made the acquaintance of Ellen Nussey who would remain her closest friend, outside of her family, for the rest of her life. She also met the Taylor sisters, Mary and Martha, whose intelligence and outspoken views helped to draw Charlotte out from her shyness and indulge in discussion and argument over a wide range of topics including religion and politics. Despite homesickness Charlotte flourished and worked diligently to rise to the top of the class. Pupils who knew Charlotte at Roe Head spoke of her reluctance to play games or take part in physical exercise, but they greatly admired her knowledge and self-discipline and they especially noted her ability to tell thrilling stories; some of which were so frightening that Miss Wooler had to ban them being told at night in the dormitory.

Charlotte's success at Roe Head and the excellent reports from her teachers show how the regime suited her love of learning, and for the first time she could overcome her inhibitions and make lasting friendships with people of different ages and with different views to her own. Roe Head opened a whole new world to Charlotte, very different from the years spent at home learning with her siblings. Although school did take up most of Charlotte's time and energy, her enthusiasm for her world of Glasstown did not diminish and neither did Branwell's. With Charlotte away at school, Branwell wrote more and more and this included series of stories in volumes, poetry, letters and essays. Without his co-author, he gave way to total indulgence in his own fantasy. He did not join in with Emily and Anne who, by now, were in their own world of Gondal and were also writing prolifically. Branwell had total control until Charlotte came home for the holidays and they took up their writing together once more. It would be interesting to know how Branwell felt when Charlotte returned home full of stories of school and her new friends and of all the real and invented tales she had been storing up to share with her brother.

Charlotte stayed for three terms at Roe Head and came home with a silver medal to mark her achievements. She was changed in many ways and had more confidence. She corresponded regularly with her new friends and exchanged visits so that her siblings also gained acquaintance with other young people of similar ages. Mary Taylor, who lived with her family at The Red House, Gomersall, was intelligent, opinionated, boisterous and very able to hold an argument. Her outspoken opinions and lively manner would have pleased all the Brontë children and must have led to many a heated debate. Ellen was quiet, gentle and very ladylike. Both girls' families had wealth and social standing and when Branwell accompanied Charlotte one day to Ellen's home at the The Rydings near Birstall, he told her that he was leaving her 'in Paradise'.

The contrast between Charlotte's two closest friends, with their different opinions and personalities, all helped Charlotte to observe and accept difference, and to see arguments from opposing sides. The Taylor family were political Radicals and their beliefs were the very opposite of Charlotte's staunchly held Tory views. Mary Taylor described in a letter how she and Charlotte argued furiously over their politics; an area where Charlotte lost her reserve and could hold her own against the full force of the Taylor family on her visits to The Red House. The Taylor's are delightfully captured in Charlotte's book *Shirley* as the Yorke family.

The Nussey's were also a large family but lived a more genteel lifestyle and held political and religious views like, but less forceful than, the Brontë family. Whereas Mary Taylor could brutally tell Charlotte that she was ugly and old fashioned, Ellen spoke only kindly and in her quiet and thoughtful way supported and admired her friend throughout her life. Some of the many hundreds of letters written between Ellen and Charlotte still exist and they show a mutual affection in a relationship usually led by Charlotte. The juxtaposition of Charlotte between these two women, who both had a tremendous effect on her thoughts and feelings, helps to explain some of Charlotte's schizophrenic need to behave like them both. She could be quiet, shy and home loving, and yet also be ferociously sarcastic, fiery and determined, with a will to travel and explore. She was both the dutiful daughter and loving sister whilst living in a fantasy where she could be anything or anyone, and be as bold and brazen as she wished. Her novel *Jane Eyre* is sub-titled 'an autobiography', and in it Charlotte shows how the small, plain and ugly girl can, and will, stand up for herself and what she believes in, and this is something which Charlotte tried to do.

Mary Taylor grew up to live life to the full. She travelled on her own all over the world at a time when women barely crossed the street alone. She taught in a boys' school in Germany, she ran a shop in New Zealand for many years, she wrote a novel and was a busy and staunch political activist for all of her long life. Ellen stayed in England, moving around only to stay or live with various members of her family. She led the life of a gentlewoman of small but private means and never had to go out to work. One can see flashes of Mary's ambition and Ellen's reticence in Charlotte's personality and lifestyle.

Having left Roe Head, Charlotte returned home and was able to pass on her learning to her sisters and to further indulge in and expand the Glasstown saga with Branwell. Patrick was fully recovered and as hale and hearty as ever and the fear of his imminent death seems to have been dispelled. The growing children spent the next three years at home following the same round of study, exercise and fantasy that they had done previously. By now their knowledge was vastly increased and their ability to copy other writers and styles was growing. In many ways, they were reporters; they knew the layout and content of *Blackwood's Magazine* and also *Fraser's Magazine*, to which aunt Branwell had begun to subscribe in 1831. This ability to report events, describe people and to observe the interchange of social behaviour would prove enormously useful when they turned their attention to novel writing. Charlotte especially, and possibly due to her poor and failing eyesight, was a miniaturist; all her drawings and all her early writings show the detail of minutia and the need to concentrate on every detail and every line. Her three siblings did the same to a lesser degree but they were all concerned with the intimate detail of drawings and of music and of writing. They all had the ability to memorise detail and to faithfully record it in various mediums.

These skills were practised during their teenage years to the extent that they could write reasonably skilful poetry; an art based on the use of language, symbols and metaphors to create a mood or scene. The use of metaphor was also expertly applied throughout their novels. Emily especially could invoke emotion by applying metaphoric symbols in her work. After Charlotte went away to Roe Head, Emily and Anne did not want to share their writing with Branwell and branched away from Glasstown with their own Island, Gondal, set in the North Pacific Ocean. They wrote poetry to accompany the many stories of the lives of their heroes and heroines but not in any linear or progressive account, rather as expressions of feelings and the dramas felt by their protagonists. Unfortunately, none of the *Gondal Saga* remains, only some of the poetry which accompanied it, written after 1836.

The vastness of these imaginary islands and the amount of work and time the children put into them is astonishing. The fact that they carried on writing and inventing well into adulthood is a measure of their compulsion to fantasise and their collective interdependence. Their stories continued to occupy and inspire them, bringing comfort, adventure, and excitement into their lives. To call this obsession childish is to denigrate and malign what it meant and what it achieved. The Glasstown Saga developed over time into a new land where Charlotte and Branwell were the only authors. They named this new land Angria and it became their passion from 1834 onwards. The new Angria, and the continuing Gondal, further developed the children's skills and this prolonged apprenticeship later produced adults with perfected writing skills who could plot, describe, and conjure up all manner of people and events. When these abilities were further added to their own lived experience, they could produce novels of exceptional skill and realism.

Branwell and Charlotte appear to have been the most ambitious of the four children. After her eighteen months at Roe Head School, Charlotte had acquired some friends and some social graces. She had gained respect from those around her and enjoyed their company. She had also achieved high academic success. This probably increased her self-esteem and whetted her appetite for further adventures away from home. She could now visit her new friends in their homes and meet and socialise with people from other social classes who had a more varied and experienced background.

Branwell's position was that of the dominant male amongst his siblings and it was never, at this time, in any doubt that he would make an important and recognised mark for himself in one of the professions, or as an artist. Branwell, like his sisters, had artistic as well as literary talents and was tutored by the Leeds portrait painter, William Robinson. Branwell chose oils as his medium and achieved moderate success but was not exceptional. It is believed that he may have tried, and failed, to enter the Royal Academy of Arts, in London. Whether he did or not, his artistic career lasted only a brief time at a studio in Bradford in mid-1838 before it became obvious that he was unable to make a living from it.

We do not know what ambitions Branwell had for himself but he wrote to many of the major poets of the day for their opinions on his poetry and to *Blackwood's Magazine* on several occasions suggesting that he become a contributor and offering various examples of his writing. Most of this was met with a profound silence. Only Hartley Coleridge (son of Samuel Taylor Coleridge) replied and Branwell spent a wonderful day with him at his home at Nab Ridge on Rydal Water in the Lake District. He did receive some encouragement, but it was with his translations of Greek that he appears to have had real talent. Unfortunately, his dismissal from a succession of various jobs over the years diminished his hopes and his confidence, and his subsequent addictions robbed him of all ambition and talent. There is no doubt that Branwell had a high level of ability in the arts, but it was never constant or stable enough. He flitted from writing to painting to translating to working as a clerk and a tutor, but was a man undecided in his ambitions and lacking in areas of self-control. He came to see alcohol as the panacea for his perceived misfortunes and this, possibly along with the pressure on him due to the high expectations of his family, helped to bring about his eventual downfall. One feels that Branwell had none of the fortitude and dogged determination of his sisters. His continuing use of alcohol and laudanum, and the elation and depression that these substances fuelled, led to his final breakdown in health and spirits and his eventual death.

Whilst Branwell is not the focus of this work, it is most important to regard the effect that this once revered and beloved brother had on his siblings and how his decline affected their lives and their works. They lived in adulthood with a brother who was unstable. Branwell could be aggressive and contrite, bombastic and unreliable; traits that would have been intolerable to his family and cause them all deep distress and embarrassment. The effect on Patrick was especially hard as he watched his only son spiral out of control, and it must have further added to his worries about the family finances and their social position. A vicar with an alcoholic for a son would not be acceptable to the church or to his parishioners. It would, however unfairly, have demonstrated a lack of parental guidance and of a sound Christian upbringing and taken away some of Patrick's credibility in the neighbourhood. If he could not control his own son how could he save and care for other people?

One wonders at what point the alienation of Branwell began. The Brontë girls had a strict moral code instilled by their aunt both as females, and as daughters of a clergyman. Politics, religion and culture kept them in a female place that was set and rigidly applied by law and within the society. Branwell, like many men of the time, had little overt control over his behaviour by any social or cultural influences. Patrick tried to keep him at home, to nurture and teach him but Branwell appears to have resented his father's overprotection and sought to indulge in behaviour that deliberately upset his father's strong beliefs and challenged his authority. Whether Branwell's behaviour was also due to underlying mental health issues is unclear, but it must have grieved them all and they each reacted to him in their separate ways. Patrick constantly forgave his son's behaviour and tried to support him with money, often paying his debts. Charlotte despised his weaknesses and eventually absolved herself of all responsibility for him. After his final dismissal from Thorpe Green, where he had worked with Anne but had begun an affair with his employer's wife, Anne's distress and embarrassment turned even this tolerant young sister against him. It was probably only Emily who could handle Branwell and it was her strength and her ability to stand up to him that meant she was often the only member of the household willing and able to deal with him.

The first break with Branwell as a writing partner had occurred when Charlotte attended Roe Head and began to make new friends. They had moved from the Glasstown world to the Island of Angria, but separation broke them again when Charlotte accepted an invitation from Miss Wooler, in 1835, to return to the school as a teacher and to take Emily with her as a pupil. Whilst this arrangement was good for the girls' further education, it deprived Branwell again of Charlotte as co-author. The fact that Branwell hung on to Angria but also wrote various works of his own, shows that at this time he still had writing ambitions.

Charlotte's return to Roe Head was not a happy one for her or Emily. Emily suffered from appalling homesickness and Charlotte begged Miss Wooler to send her home. This eventually happened and Anne took her sister's place; her first venture into formal education and her first experience of living away from Haworth.

As a pupil, Charlotte had thrived on hard work and the society of her contemporaries. This time she had to change sides and she found that, as a teacher, she lacked the skills, the patience and the inclination to deal with young children. She found her pupils idle and unintelligent, a drain on her time and her nerves. It was drudgery to her and kept her mind and thoughts away from her fantasies and this was anathema to her. In 1836 she wrote,

The thought came over me am I to spend all the best part of my life in this
wretched bondage, forcibly supressing my rage at the idleness the apathy and the

hyperbolical and most asinine stupidity of these fathead oafs and on compulsion
assuming an air of kindness, patience and assiduity?

She continued:

I longed to write. The spirit of all Verdopolis – of all the mountainous North
of all the woodland West of all the river-watered East came crowding into my
mind. If I had time to indulge it I felt that the vague sensations of that moment
would have settled down in to some narrative better at least than anything I
ever produced before. But just then a Dolt came up with a lesson. I thought I
should have vomited.

(J.R.V. Barker, 2010.p. 296)

These are the words of an angry and frustrated writer, and a woman who is living in the terrible claustrophobia of a place where she feels confined and duty-bound for a limitless time. When Charlotte eventually took a short break to visit Ellen in May 1836, her friends worried at her mental state and inability to relax and rest. By the end of the year Charlotte was in a state of nervous exhaustion and her mental and physical health would remain precarious for many months. In December, she wrote to the Poet Laureate, Robert Southey, with some of her verses. He eventually replied the following March 1837 with his famous advice that,

The day-dreams in which you habitually indulge are likely to induce a
distempered state of mind, and in proportion as all the ordinary 'uses of the
world' seem to you 'flat and unprofitable', you will be unfitted for these, without
becoming fitted for anything else. Literature cannot be the business of a woman's
life, and it ought not to be. The more she is engaged in her proper duties, the less
leisure she will have for it, even as an accomplishment and a recreation.

(J.R.V. Barker, 2010) p. 304.

These famous lines clearly echo the dominant attitude of the times. Women have too many domestic obligations and chores to which they should, and must, apply themselves; there is no room for indulgence in areas traditionally accepted as part of the male domain. Men have the knowledge and they have got things to say that women cannot possibly know or understand and should not meddle with.

We are lucky that Charlotte did not take the advice of the great man but she did take notice of his letter and wrote on it the words: 'Southey's advice to be kept forever. My 21st birthday, Roe Head, April 21st, 1837'.

It was a great trial to her to both acknowledge the wisdom of Southey's words, which were not unkindly meant, whilst recognising that writing was her calling. Charlotte struggled for years between doing her duty and conforming to social norms, and indulging herself in literature and fantasy. The longer she stayed teaching at Roe Head, the more she sank into depression. By December 1837, when Anne was very ill with gastric flu, Charlotte's worry over her sister caused a major fallout between her and Miss Wooler, leading to Charlotte taking Anne home to Haworth. It is easy to see how the spectre of the Clergy Daughters' School at Cowan Bridge may well have prompted Charlotte's reaction, but it left her friend and mentor deeply upset.

Charlotte had fire and resolve when necessary and the experience of loss to prompt her, but she was often ready to forgive her friends and to acknowledge their help and advice. She did not stay angry with Miss Wooler for too long and even agreed to return as a teacher to the new premises at Heald's Hall, Dewsbury Moor, to which the school had removed over the Christmas Holidays. Unfortunately, once again, Charlotte's mental and physical health suffered from the long hours, the strain of doing a job she hated and the inability to settle her mind. With her health of grave concern to her friends and family, Charlotte left the school in May to recuperate back at the Parsonage.

Charlotte's inability to cope with teaching meant that no-one was adding to the family income. There was still only Patrick's stipend and a little money from their aunt. Branwell was struggling to make a living at his studio in Bradford and none of his sisters were bringing in a wage. The girls had all had a good education and were now in their late teens. It is not unreasonable, therefore, that by September 1838, Charlotte was back with Miss Wooler and that Emily had got a teaching post at Law Hill School, Southowram, near Halifax.

Emily's life at Law Hill was a round of utter drudgery. Like Charlotte she had no affiliation with children and no wish to teach them. Unlike Charlotte, her environment and fellow teachers were not kind or sympathetic and her hours of work were from six in the morning until eleven at night with only a half hour rest. Emily managed to stay at this job for over six months and despite the hardships wrote some of her most beautiful and expressive Gondal and personal poetry.

Over the next three years, Charlotte and Anne tried, and mainly failed, to obtain work for any length of time. Working as governesses they each had a series of unsuccessful posts with families who often treated them worse than the servants, and whose children were unruly and disobedient. Anne had the patience that Charlotte lacked but was often overwhelmed by her charges and the demands on her time and person. Each time the sisters returned home their anxiety lifted and they could write and enjoy each other's company but it did not help the family income. Finally, in 1841, Anne found a position as a governess to the Robinson family of Thorpe Green near Little Ouseburn between York and Boroughbridge, in the North Riding of Yorkshire at which she stayed for the next four years.

During these unsettled years, each of the Brontës encountered challenges and experienced wider social contacts. None of them knew what they wanted, or how to obtain emotional and financial success. Branwell was already drinking heavily and was dismissed from various posts; Charlotte realised that as a teacher or governess she was neither suitable nor inclined; Anne wanted to do her duty and was more willing to sacrifice self for the good of the family. Emily appears to have settled into a routine at home in which her father relied on her company and support. Emily was probably the happiest as she had a life in the home she loved. She had open access to the moors and she had her family and pets around her. She could write more and more of the *Gondal Saga* and indulge all her fantasies.

The appearance of love, or the notion of marriage, is unusually absent for a family containing adults in the prime of life. It does not seem to be a primary ambition. The girls, especially Charlotte, appear rather dismissive of it and Emily shows no inclination whatsoever. Despite this, inevitably, there were still occasions when men flirted and toyed with their affections. One of these was their father's new curate, William Weightman, who sent them all Valentine cards. Charlotte also received a proposal of marriage around this time from Ellen Nussey's brother, Henry. She rejected him as they both knew that it was not a love match. Charlotte respected him and the marriage would have related her to her beloved Ellen. Yet, at this time in her life, like Jane Eyre, Charlotte wanted to marry only for love with all the fervour and romanticism of characters in her juvenilia.

Ambition was still in their minds and in 1841, despairing of finding a post that suited her and aware that Mary and Martha Taylor had recently gone to a finishing school in Brussels, Charlotte discussed the idea of setting up a school of their own. She envisaged situating the potential school at Burlington (Bridlington) where she had spent a happy holiday with Ellen. For this idea to become a reality they would need more training in languages, especially French, and more qualifications and certificates to attract the right sort of pupils. Charlotte appealed to her aunt to fund a trip to a school in Belgium for her and Emily to receive the knowledge and experience necessary. Charlotte was not averse to cajoling and the use of emotional blackmail to get her father and aunt's consent. She wrote to her aunt, who had already agreed to help fund a school, saying,

Papa will perhaps think it a wild and ambitious scheme; but whoever rose in the world without ambition? When he left Ireland to go to Cambridge University, he was as ambitious as I am now. I want us all to go on. I know we have talents, and I want them to be turned to account. I look to you, aunt, to help us. I think you will not refuse.

(J.R.V. Barker, 2010) p. 425.

Charlotte's enthusiasm was fired and fed by letters from Martha Taylor, still at school in Brussels, and Mary Taylor, now on a four-month tour of the Continent. They each described the sights and sounds of their foreign experiences. Charlotte finally won over her aunt and father and preparations were made for the next stage in the lives of Charlotte and Emily, a stage that would bring more heartache and experience than Charlotte could imagine.

Chapter Nine

Work, Travel and Unrequited Love

When Charlotte and Emily left Haworth in February 1842 on their long journey to Brussels, Branwell was working as a clerk-in-charge for the railway based at Luddenden Foot Station near Hebden Bridge. He drank regularly in the local hostelries and often arranged for others to cover his duties for him. Anne was still working as a governess for the Robinson family in a position which she only gradually began to tolerate. She travelled on holidays with the family to Scarborough in the summer, a location which Anne found hugely enjoyable, and she took great pleasure in being by the sea. She also eventually became fond of her charges and they grew to respect her. Despite missing her home and family, Anne did well at her work and continued with the *Gondal Saga* whenever she could. Without the support of Charlotte, Branwell appears to have turned away from Angria and concentrated more on his own sketches and poetry, when he did write, which was happening less and less.

It is difficult for us to imagine today the type of journey the Brontë girls and Patrick undertook to get to Brussels, or the enormity of the whole Brussels venture. They were not a wealthy family, like the Taylors, and yet Patrick and aunt Branwell had faith in the girls' abilities and were prepared to sacrifice a great deal to give them the opportunity to further their ambitions. Their venture was enterprising and, as Charlotte had stated, as ambitious as their father's journey to England, thirty years before. Neither sister had left the north of England and whilst they were cultured and informed within their local circle, they had no experience of foreign travel or foreigners. We do not have Emily's description of the journey or her thoughts on this event which took her so far from her comfort zone. We can only assume that she went willingly, but it was possibly with tremendous effort for a woman notably shy with strangers and rather insular in her habits.

The travelling party, which included Mary and Joe Taylor who were also en route to Brussels, set off on Tuesday 8 February, and after many hours on trains, reached London where they all spent three days of sightseeing, which included the British Museum, The Royal Academy and The National Gallery. The packet boat trip from London Bridge to Ostend was long and the sea was rough. Charlotte was very sick causing them all to stay in Ostend for twenty-four hours to recover. They then travelled to the Porte de Flandre and stayed overnight. It was on Tuesday 15 February, a week after setting off, that Patrick took his girls to the Pensionnat Heger on the Rue d'Isabelle in Brussels, where they would spend the next nine months.

Patrick took advantage of his time in Belgium to visit the battlefields of Waterloo, the victory ground of his hero, the Duke of Wellington, before returning home via Calais; another long and tiring journey for a man now in his sixty-fifth year. He must have wondered about his life, and the lives of his offspring, during this long journey. His children were all now away from home and working or studying, and he was returning to a house where only his ageing sister-in-law and the servants were in residence. Had his children fulfilled any of the early promise they had shown? Was Branwell destined for bigger and better things? Were his daughters going to have their own successful school? Would they marry? Would he live to see them settled and happy? These and many other thoughts must have accompanied him on his way home.

Charlotte and Emily appear to have settled in well at the Pensionnat and Charlotte, especially, thrived once again in the role of pupil to a strong and experienced teacher. Monsieur Heger and his wife owned and ran two schools, The Pensionnat for young ladies, and the adjoining Athene Royale for young men. Monsieur Heger was the master at the boys' school but taught in both. Charlotte was immediately attracted to his intelligence and his masterful ways. Here was a man that Charlotte could admire, a man who could stretch her talents and capabilities and who was as hard on her as she was on herself and she rose to the challenge.

Monsieur Heger recognised in the Brontë sisters a very powerful ability to study, but also the power to reason and, especially in Emily, the power to philosophise; to see life and events from a different perspective which incorporated an understanding of how and why people behaved as they did. Emily was a great observer without herself taking part. She stood aside and watched others and drew her own conclusions. Often, she did not find it necessary to speak, but she absorbed everything around her and was able to translate and transform that knowledge into the written word. At times that ability even transcended language. Emily was different to almost any other woman of her time or background. She behaved differently, talked little but experienced many things. She loved her home and family, but could be strict and severe with both herself and others. She was not a woman to whom most people warmed and she seems to have had no aspirations to be other than she was. When taunted by the girls at school her reply was, 'I am as God made me'.

The little we know of Emily, in comparison to Charlotte, suggests a self-contained and private person who embraced the natural world in favour of the human one and who had no interest in making friendships, or even acquaintances, outside of her family. She had her writing, her music, her art, and nature, and appears to have valued, or needed, little else.

Emily certainly did not embrace Monsieur Heger in the way that her sister fell for his charm and his temperament. Emily remained aloof and isolated at the Pensionnat and had neither the time nor the inclination to mix with her fellow school pupils. Despite Monsieur Heger's growing admiration and respect for Emily she did nothing to attract his praise or approval other than to work hard. Emily learnt a great deal at the school, advancing especially in both German and French. Her love of music and her proficiency as a pianist led the Hegers to invite her to teach some of the other students, for which she was paid a small sum. Regrettably, her inability to socialise, or to tolerate their poor talents, created an atmosphere of loathing in Emily and fear and dislike from her pupils.

Charlotte, alternatively, blossomed at the Pensionnat during these months. She was doing something she loved in a new and stimulating environment where she had the attention of a man she really admired. Such was her enthusiasm that she either offered, or was invited, to stay on as a teacher following their intended period of study. Unfortunately, fate intervened and news that aunt Branwell was gravely ill caused Charlotte and Emily to return home to Haworth in November 1842. By the time they arrived back their aunt was already dead and they were too late to even attend her funeral.

Emily had absolutely no desire to return to Brussels but Charlotte, now fully overwhelmed by Monsieur Heger and possibly enamoured towards him in a way that she had never felt about a man before, returned alone in the role of teacher. She was also invited to give English lessons to Monsieur Heger and his brother-in-law, so that she saw and interacted far more with the man whom she was now possibly secretly in love with. It was a recipe for disaster and by April 1843, the lessons were suddenly terminated. Whether this was at the instigation of Madame Heger or her husband is not known but one, or both, of them recognised that Charlotte had come to view Monsieur Heger as much more than her teacher and mentor.

In August, the Hegers went away on holiday and Charlotte was left almost alone at the Pensionnat. Bereft of company and miles away from home, Charlotte experienced a collapse. It is possible that she had some degree of mental and physical breakdown and certainly a crisis of faith. Her experiences and feelings over these weeks are accurately recorded in her novel, *Villette*. Charlotte struggled on for another few months in Brussels, largely friendless and longing for a man whom she obviously revered but who was in no position to return her admiration and affection.

On 1 January 1844, Charlotte left Brussels and never returned. Her unrequited love for Monsieur Heger was to affect her emotionally, possibly for the rest of her life, and it was months before she could rally herself from the deep depression that accompanied her departure from him. She told no-one and suffered agonies in the hope that he would write to her. Her letters to him became more and more desperate but he, perhaps rightly so, did not reply and did not raise in her any hope of even a continuing friendship. Charlotte's suffering was awful and lasting and, like many of her experiences would find its way into her novels.

Charlotte had unwittingly fallen in love with a married man and then, as now, this was an impossible dilemma. Charlotte's faith and her upbringing would mean that she knew her situation was hopeless. Keeping her feelings secret, as she must do, caused her enormous distress. It is unlikely that her affection was reciprocated. Monsieur Heger had a wife and five children and his wife owned the school properties. He was not in a position, even had he wanted to, to abandon his family and surrender his responsibilities or his reputation. Charlotte's love included feelings of despair. She was aware of the impossibility of a relationship even though she longed for some small comfort and assurance from him long after she returned home. She wrote ill-judged letters to him which became more and more desperate saying,

Day and Night I find neither rest nor peace.... If I sleep I have tormenting dreams in which I see you, always severe, always gloomy and annoyed with me ... all I know – is that I cannot – that I will not resign myself to lose the friendship of my master completely – I would rather undergo the greatest physical sufferings than always have my heart torn apart by bitter regrets.

(J.R.V. Barker, 2010) p. 523.

And later when she began to realise that he may never correspond, the frantic nature of her distress is evident. She writes,

I have tried to forget you ... I have done everything, I have sought out occupation, I have absolutely forbidden myself the pleasure of speaking of you – even to Emily ... this is humiliating – not to know how to be master of one's own thoughts, to be slave to a regret, a memory...

(J.R.V. Barker, 2010) p. 557.

Charlotte's anguish dominated her life for the next two years. It may well have blinded her to some degree to the sufferings of both Branwell and Anne. Branwell, following his dismissal from the railways due to a discrepancy in the accounts, had taken up work as a tutor with the Robinson family for whom Anne worked. Having put his name forward and recommended him for the position, Anne was later horrified to discover that he had begun an illicit affair with Mrs Robinson. Anne resigned her post before the affair was discovered but when it was, Branwell was promptly dismissed by his cuckolded employer. Charlotte was preoccupied by her own heartbreak, but when she discovered the way that Branwell had behaved and his obvious inability to keep his sordid behaviour a secret, she was very angry. For eighteen months Charlotte had borne her grief in silence and now her brother was telling anyone who would listen of his love for a married woman. Charlotte had no sympathy for Branwell and his behaviour drove them irrevocably apart.

Unrequited love is a very sad state and it is both a wonder, and a huge shame, that neither Charlotte nor Branwell confided in, or empathised with, the other in a way that could have helped and supported them through their emotional turmoil. Both had fallen irrevocably for a married person completely out of their financial and social grasp. Branwell turned to opium and alcohol for relief and escape, whilst Charlotte internalised her longing and suffered physical and mental stress; often alone and with no possible hope of a happy outcome. Of the two, Charlotte was the most realistic as she was fully aware that she would never see Monsieur Heger again and that her love was as much for his masterful approach and his intelligent mind, rather than for his personal looks or attributes. Charlotte's love held no hope for a romantic attachment. Alternatively, biography suggests that Branwell believed Mrs Robinson to be in love and pining for him, and that as soon as her ailing husband died she would send for him and they would be married. Charlotte had no such delusions about Monsieur Heger. She knew that he was unattainable and she possibly realised that with her plain looks and old-fashioned ways he might never have been attracted to her even if he had been free.

When life becomes too hazardous or too painful, people deal with it in different ways. Each of the Brontë siblings suffered various catastrophes in their lives but only Branwell had the access to comforting alternatives like alcohol. Freud describes this need for an escape in the following words, which explain Branwell's dependency:

Life as we find it, is too hard for us: it entails too much pain; too many disappointments; impossible tasks. We cannot do without palliative remedies... powerful diversions of interest, which lead us to care little about our misery; substitutive gratifications, which lessen it; and intoxicating substances, which make us insensitive to it. Something of the kind is indispensable.

(Lane, 1980) p. 19.

For people who had no access to alternative substances for their pain, and this would include most women, they had no means of escape and often suffered enormous stress with accompanying mental and physical illnesses. Whereas Branwell could walk down to the Black Bull and 'drown his sorrows', his sisters had to bear their pain silently and stoically. It is little wonder that they hung on to the escapism of their creative world for much of their lives.

In her novels one sees Charlotte using her characters, to examine the notion of unrequited love and relationships that cannot be fulfilled. What Charlotte shows is often a belief in respect and a 'love' for the strengths and abilities of a man rather than a romantic ideal. Her heroes are always flawed or disfigured in some way that avoids them becoming the fantasy characters of Glasstown and Angria. Charlotte accepted human failings and her books express this. There is a reality in them that highlights people's inability to sustain a false image. Glamour and sophistication are often confounded. Her realism accepts that men and women cannot always live happy and fulfilled lives.

Branwell had possibly the opposite view to his sister. He appears to have been thoroughly overwhelmed by Mrs Robinson and unable to distinguish between her good and bad traits. It would not be fair to describe him as amoral but he does not appear to have exercised restraint, or questioned why Mrs Robinson would choose to have an affair with her son's tutor; a man of absolutely no means or prospects who could only bring her disgrace if their affair became public knowledge. Where Branwell appears to have let his heart rule his head, Charlotte's head ruled her heart and she knew that what she wanted was not only unattainable from Monsieur Heger, but possibly from any man. Whereas Branwell believed himself to be attractive, talented and erudite, Charlotte knew that she was small, plain and ugly, and that realisation was already a huge barrier to her from a very early age. Whilst it did not stop her dreaming of love, it realistically prevented her from believing that she would ever find a fulfilling relationship.

It has long been speculated by many biographers that Anne Brontë was in love with, or at least attracted to, her father's popular curate, William Weightman, the sender of Valentine cards and the flirt of the village. In a letter to Ellen, Charlotte had observed the way that they looked at each other in church, which, in those days, was intimate enough to cause speculation. The Rev. Weightman was a dedicated and much loved man who was amiable and popular. He was the only curate to be admired and welcomed by all members of the Brontë family. Weightman died suddenly from cholera in September 1842 at the age of 28. The Brontë girls were all away from home and only Branwell and Patrick could represent the family at his funeral, which the distraught Patrick conducted. Anne was working for the Robinsons at Thorpe Green and we do not know when or how she learnt of the curate's death or how much it affected her.

What of Emily? Did she ever have a lost love or an unrequited heartache for a man that she could never have? We do not know for sure although some biographers have suggested possible names. If Emily did not have a lover, or a lover in mind, or a lost longing and a broken heart, she could certainly feel and express the emotions that such heartbreak engenders. In the following lines her words express some of the deepest of emotions surrounding the final parting of souls when one is dead and the other continues to live and to mourn. Emily's poem, *Remembrance* is reproduced here in full for its remarkable ability to describe loss and the bitter pain of memories.

> *Cold in the earth – and the deep snow piled above thee,*
> *Far, far, removed, cold in the dreary grave!*
> *Have I forgot, my only love, to love thee,*
> *Severed at last by Time's all-severing wave?*
>
> *Now, when alone, do my thoughts no longer hover*
> *Over the mountains, on the northern shore,*
> *Resting their wings where heath and fern-leaves cover*
> *Thy noble heart for ever, ever more?*
>
> *Cold in the earth – and fifteen wild Decembers,*
> *From these brown hills, have melted into spring:*
> *Faithful, indeed, is the spirit that remembers*
> *After such years of change and suffering!*
>
> *Sweet Love of youth, forgive, if I forget thee,*
> *While the World's tide is bearing me along;*
> *Other desires and other hopes beset me,*
> *Hopes which obscure, but cannot do thee wrong!*
>
> *No later light has lightened up my heaven,*
> *No second morn has ever shone for me;*
> *All my life's bliss from thy dear life was given,*
> *All my life's bliss is in the grave with thee.*
>
> *But, when the days of golden dreams had perished,*
> *And even Despair was powerless to destroy;*
> *Then did I learn how existence could be cherished,*
> *Strengthened, and fed without the aid of joy.*

Then did I check the tears of useless passion –
Weaned my young soul from yearning after thine;
Sternly denied its burning wish to hasten
Down to that tomb already more than mine.

And, even yet, I dare not let it languish,
Dare not indulge in memory's rapturous pain;
Once drinking deep of that divinest anguish,
How could I seek the empty world again?

> (E. Brontë, *The Complete Poems of*
> *Emily Jane Brontë*, 1941) p. 223.

Emily wrote this poem, as most of her extant poems, as part of the *Gondal Saga*. It is written from one of her characters to another but it could apply to anyone who has suffered the loss of someone they loved. If Emily did not have somebody specific in mind, she had the enduring loss of her mother and two sisters to mourn and this poem could well apply to them.

Patrick and aunt Branwell also suffered loss and frustration, both mourning for a lost person or a lost time when they were young and happy with everything to look forward to. It should be recognised that whilst many happy and exciting things happened to the Brontë family, they all suffered tragedy and loss to a greater or lesser extent. This was, and is, a part of life and the longer we live the more likely and inevitably we will suffer. All-consuming disaster does not have to be an inevitable outcome of this bleak truth. Some people are challenged and strengthened by adversity. For the Brontë siblings their early sufferings led them into their fantasy world and their later trials added to their poetic outpourings. For the three sisters, their lives and loves turned into their novels in a way that allowed them to turn life into literature and express the human condition from a feminine perspective that had not been thoroughly exposed or examined before.

Chapter Ten

Publication and Disappointment

Charlotte tells us that she was looking through some papers one day when she 'came across' some poems by her sister Emily. For years, Charlotte had wanted to write and to see her work published. Her letters to Southey and his reply are testament to her ambitions and to the barriers against her fulfilling this dream. The need to go out to work had further thwarted her hopes and compromised her leisure time. The discovery of Emily's verse and the quality of its content spurred Charlotte into action. She had poetry of her own which she felt was as good, if not better, than some of the published verse she had read. On seeing Charlotte's enthusiasm over Emily's work, Anne shyly offered some of her verses for Charlotte to see and the idea of publishing a joint book of poetry was born.

Whilst this became a joint venture, Emily was initially very angry with Charlotte for reading her private and personal papers. It may be that Anne offered her own poetry to help to calm the rift between the sisters. The *Gondal Saga* was a private world between Anne and Emily and even their brother and sister were not party to all of its characters and events. Charlotte and Branwell, who were by this time often away from home working, may not have even realised that Gondal still existed and it may have been the discovery of her and Anne's continued indulgence that especially upset Emily.

Eventually, all three sisters were reconciled and, as long as they were able to preserve their anonymity, a proviso especially urged by Emily, and the removal of reference to Gondal, it was agreed that they would use some of their own money inherited from their aunt to have the verses published. To both protect their real identities and to suggest male compositions, which were more likely to receive a favourable response, the girls chose ambiguous pseudonyms. Using their own initials, they chose the androgynous names: Currer, Ellis and Acton Bell.

Charlotte eventually contacted the publishers, Aylott and Jones of Paternoster Row, London, on the same street as the Chapter coffeehouse where they had stayed before sailing to Brussels. At a cost of over £30, an enormous sum from their joint savings, their book of poetry was eventually published in May 1846, complete with errors and misprints, at a cost of 4s. A year later only two copies had sold and the rest were distributed as gifts.

Charlotte's enthusiasm and hope for the venture was not totally crushed by this result. A reviewer for *The Critic* had described the Bells as having, 'the presence of more genius than it was supposed this utilitarian age had devoted to the loftier exercises of the intellect'. (J.R.V. Barker, 2010) p. 588.

Whilst readers were not forthcoming, these snippets of praise gave Charlotte optimism and whilst she could acknowledge that poetry was not going to make their fortunes, and she herself was no longer writing it, novels could possibly be the way forward. Charlotte's contribution to the poems were mainly works from Angria written in the 1830s, Emily and Anne's were more current and showed an on-going development. Charlotte was later dismissive of her contribution and admitted that it had been a 'rash act' to rush in to print. The loss to their finances was heavy and they each realised that if it were possible to earn money through their writing it must be good enough to be accepted by a publisher, and be printed and distributed by that publisher, with no expense to themselves.

Within two weeks of the publication of *Poems by Currer, Ellis and Acton Bell.* (May 1846), Branwell suffered the blow that was to bring about his final decline. Mr Robinson, the husband of his former lover, fell ill and died at their home at Thorpe Green. News of his death roused Branwell into an ecstasy of expectation as he waited to be summoned by Mrs Robinson. As the new squire of Thorpe Green his life would be completely turned around and he would once again be loved and admired by his family and friends and move into a higher social class.

It may be that Mrs Robinson used Branwell for her amusement as a mild interlude whilst her ailing husband was confined. Whatever her motive, when Mr Robinson died, Branwell was told in no uncertain terms never to contact her again and his spirit was finally broken. Mrs Robinson sent her coachman to Haworth to inform Branwell that they must never meet again due to certain conditions in her husband's will which would leave her destitute if not complied with. This was in fact a lie designed to finally free Lydia of this troublesome young man who had written to her for money on occasion and whom she had probably indulged to keep him quiet about their affair.

Branwell was summoned to meet the coachman in the Black Bull and was later found on the floor in a state of fit and frenzy following the departure of this messenger of doom. For the next two years, he suffered appallingly and depended more and more on alcohol and the drug, laudanum. This substance was a common panacea for all manner of ailments, both physical and psychological, at a time when there was little alternative medication for treating disease. Laudanum is a mixture of alcohol and tincture of opium which contains morphine and codeine. It has sedative and painkilling effects and was freely available from shops, public houses and druggists. Whilst it had properties that could dull physical and mental anguish and still allow the person the ability to function, it had terrible withdrawal symptoms. Once addicted, it was almost impossible to become free of it. It was especially used by artists and writers who believed in its ability to enrich the imagination and enhance creativity, but it could also dangerously affect personality and promote aggression in addicts.

This breakdown in Branwell's physical and emotional health was witnessed acutely by his father and his sisters, and his behaviour and inability to rouse him from the deep torpor he felt, brought enormous stress and embarrassment to his family. His once adored sister, Charlotte, his ally and companion in childhood, practically abandoned him. She despised Branwell's weakness and inability to overcome loss or failure to make good. Charlotte had forced herself to do this regarding Monsieur Heger and she scorned Branwell for his lack of strength and moral fibre. Patrick fretted over his son continually and gave him advice, money, and hours of his time and affection, but it had little effect on Branwell's behaviour.

Branwell appears to have despised his father at this point and showed little respect for Patrick's age or his health issues and the demands of his parish. It is fair to say that Branwell wallowed in his sorrows and allowed addictions to replace any efforts to work or occupy his time fruitfully and constructively. He showed little regard or affection towards his siblings and sought out the company of friends who would help him to drown his sorrows rather than deal with them. Those genetic traits and personal strengths that had steered Patrick and fed his ambitions were not apparent in Branwell who seemed to give up too easily whenever confronted by a problem or a setback. Whereas his sisters showed drive and fortitude, Branwell appears weak and childish. Perhaps the pressure of early expectation was too much and the man who had been predicted to excel found himself unable to fulfil the hopes of others and collapsed under the pressure.

Branwell's death certificate, written in September 1848, described his death as due to 'Chronic Bronchitis'. It is more likely that he had the same tubercular disease that killed all of his sisters and lay dormant in each of the siblings. They had bouts of sickness, headaches, gastric flu, persistent coughs, bronchitis and low spirits that affected their abilities and their moods. None of this was helped by the environment in which they lived. Haworth and the whole country still had seasonal epidemics of such diseases as typhus fever, cholera and tuberculosis, all of which weakened or killed the sufferer. With an often-contaminated water supply and no effective sewage disposal, the town was a very unsafe place to live. Dr Wheelwright, the local surgeon, had no antibiotics to dispense and had to rely on many old fashioned and largely ineffective remedies.

Another influence on health was the climate and conditions. The weather dictated much of how people lived; where and when they went out and how they travelled, what they wore and how they coped with extremes of cold and heat. The poorer your circumstances the less clothing you would possess, or money to pay for heating and cooking. If you had no means of transport or little money to hire a coach, you walked everywhere no matter what the conditions. The Brontës walked a great deal, especially Patrick and Branwell who could walk and travel unaccompanied without raising comment. If Branwell walked to Halifax, as he often did, and it came on to rain or snow, he would get wet and his clothing would probably stay wet until it dried naturally in a warm room or was hung out to dry. This constant exposure to the elements affected everyone, but those with delicate lungs or inherent diseases would suffer especially.

In *Jane Eyre* Charlotte described her own experience of the actual journey taken every Sunday from the Clergy Daughters' School to the church at Tunstall two miles away, where the girls had to endure three sermons throughout the day as preached by their 'benefactor' the Rev. Wilson. The girls walked there and back in all conditions and stayed all day in the unheated church. This exposure resulted in chilblains, coughs, low fevers and chapped hands, feet and faces, and added to the misery of feeling perpetually cold and being undernourished. It further affected those whose constitution was already weakened.

In the Brontë novels, especially *Jane Eyre* and *Wuthering Heights*, the weather is a constant backdrop to the story, and so it was at the Parsonage. Each day the life and work of the house would be dependent on the weather and what could, or could not be achieved, according to the climate and the season. If you had no dry clothes to wear, you stayed in. A downpour on Monday may mean a two-day stay at home until your wool cloak was dry enough to wear. Fog and rain may keep you inside for many days if you had chest problems. Wet washing may be hung about the house in the winter months and bedding could be damp in a household where peat fires were the only source of heating a room. The temperature and the weather conditions were a constant and unrelieved irritant when inclement and a real danger to health.

In the Brontë novels these elemental issues govern the way some of the characters behave and affect how they deal with many of their challenges. *Wuthering Heights* is especially focused on the meteorological conditions and the ability of the characters to prepare for and deal with them. The book opens with Mr Lockwood lost and frightened in a snowstorm. *Jane Eyre* begins with Jane unable to take a walk because it is raining, and the consequences of this shape the whole of the rest of her story. These repeated references to the weather conditions in all of the Brontës' books reflect the reality with which it entered and occupied the lives and thoughts of the writers. It is only one aspect of their writing but it is noticeable and reflects one of the many influences on the sisters and the way in which their experienced environment found its way into their novels.

The disappointment of the sisters due to the poor reception of their book of verse did not affect them for too long. Even before the publishing of the poetry Charlotte had already informed Aylott and Jones, that the 'Brothers Bell' were preparing works of fiction described as, 'three distinct and unconnected tales'. (J.R.V. Barker, 2010) p. 590.

'Three distinct and unconnected tales'

The three novels which the Brontë sisters had begun to write around April 1846, were *The Professor*, by Currer Bell, *Wuthering Heights*, by Ellis Bell and *Agnes Grey*, by Acton Bell. After years of writing their juvenilia in collaboration, they now returned to this method of reading aloud to each other and discussing plot and narrative as they went along. Charlotte chose to write about her experiences in Brussels but to use a male narrator, possibly to further disguise her identity. Emily chose to write about the environment which she knew best but her story appears to have little autobiographical detail. Her tale occurs on the moorland above her home and she uses a variety of unreliable narrators to describe the events. Anne wrote a biographical story based on her experiences as a governess and used a first-person narrator to lend authenticity. It is interesting to note that Charlotte and Anne's time spent away from home as teachers and governesses meant that they had had less time for their make-believe worlds and when they came to write their novels they drew far more from their own experiences.

Emily was still immersed in Gondal and had unrestricted opportunity to live out her characters. *Wuthering Heights* has many elements of Gondal and yet it is also firmly set on the Yorkshire moors. It is a story with more than a passing nod to the works of Sir Walter Scott, a favourite of Emily's, and yet includes stories and fables from local history and journals. It contains Shakespeare's star-crossed lovers and is also a tale of the intensity of adolescent emotions. It is a timeless story of unrequited or unfulfilled love which also explores the notion of life after death.

It is recorded that Branwell boasted to friends that he had written some, if not all of *Wuthering Heights*. This claim lacks credibility due to his mental state but is also in question because of the efforts made by his sisters to hide their writing from both their father and brother. Patrick did not know of *Jane Eyre* until the published copy was placed into his hands by Charlotte in 1847.

Branwell was possibly unaware of his sisters literary output, at least until their true identities were uncovered. Branwell had, in the Angrian juvenilia written of characters like Heathcliff and Catherine, and also of the servant Joseph in the novel but so had Charlotte. Branwell may have, at some time, talked of the plot of *Wuthering Heights* or even transcribed parts for Emily, who was notoriously bad at spelling and grammar, but this is unlikely. Alternatively, Branwell may have been suggesting that some of the novel was based on his personal experiences and behaviour, which it would appear to have been. Emily was the only sister permanently at home during Branwell's deterioration and probably the only person in the house capable of dealing with his extremes of behaviour. The power of *Wuthering Heights* may well be nurtured in Emily's domestic experiences with her wastrel brother.

What Emily achieved in this work was a weaving together of many influences besides the reality of her brother's problems. The book explores the wider issues of genetics and heredity and how nature and nurture can influence and manipulate. It is about what can happen when the innocence of childhood is confounded by loss and change and it contains love and hate and extremes of violence and passion. It is, in other words, a huge exploration of the human condition.

Charlotte chose a tale where she could address some of her own issues of love and loss, but by choosing a male narrator and a male protagonist she failed to fully identify and describe the emotions and full experiences of her characters. *The Professor*, was rejected by many publishers before it reached the London publishing firm of Messrs, Smith and Elder. Their reader wrote to Charlotte to say that whilst they were not disposed to publish the manuscript, it had some merit and if she cared to submit a further work in three volumes it would be carefully examined. The book was eventually published in 1856, following Charlotte's death.

The Professor was an early attempt by Charlotte to work through some of her experiences in Brussels. She tried to do this by creating a male character, William Crimsworth, who suffers some of the trials she experienced herself. He is flawed by his reticence and inability to take matters into his own hands. He is a man who is led rather than a leader, and the use of a masculine persona does not allow its author to entertain or express identifiable emotions. Charlotte may have been trying to re-enforce the notion of a male author but it was not until she reworked the novel into *Villette* in 1853, with the female heroine, Lucy Snowe, that she produced a masterpiece.

Anne's first book, *Agnes Grey*, was different again from her sisters' first attempts, although it too had many elements of autobiography. It is a novel of manners with some similarities to the writing of Jane Austen, whom Anne admired. It is a book with a purpose to instruct its reader on all that is entailed in the life of a governess; a role that Anne herself suffered for nearly six years. It highlights a part of the dilemma of a surplus of unmarried women in the early nineteenth century who had little expectation or hope of marriage. The middle classes found such circumstances especially problematic as the onus often fell on the families of these women to support them. The only alternative was for the women to take up the very few respectable professions open to them, namely: a teacher, a lady's companion or a governess. Anne's experiences prompted her to highlight this problem and to show how the middle-class spinster had to live as an almost invisible part of society. She may be resented by her family as a drain on their resources. Or, if she did find suitable work, with a suitable family, she was often simultaneously alienated from the servants and denied admittance into the family of her employer or their social circle. She was, therefore, unappreciated, greatly undervalued and extremely lonely. Anne's dual aim was to publicise the plight of the governess, as experienced by a woman who had suffered it in all its guises and, perhaps even more importantly, to expose the truth behind the veneer of middle-class domesticity.

Anne had been greatly influenced by her aunt Branwell, whose religious piety she had absorbed possibly more than her siblings. Anne was aware of her status as the daughter of a clergyman and of her moral duty to serve her God and her family in any way that she could. Her novels are testament to her belief in a designated right and wrong and they highlight and examine the injustices between the sexes and those of the class system which re-enforces them. Anne's method in *Agnes Grey* is extremely intricate. On the surface, she follows a simple and straightforward chronology that contains no complicated human dynamics and no major incidents. The book has a single narrator, stating the facts as they occur and apparently leaving the reader to judge the results for themselves. Her aim is to instruct rather than to entertain. The novel can even become rather dull and repetitive until it is punctuated with snippets of colour that add to the portraiture and enliven the dialogue. Yet, it is in these sporadic moments of subjectivity that Anne can quietly voice her outrage. This first novel showcases an author who has something important to say and who wishes to expose injustice from her own perspective and she achieves this with impressive subtlety.

To say that Charlotte did this much better and with far more effect in *Jane Eyre* is true to a point. Anne's novel is written with less drama and passion but has closely observed detail, which highlights the wider social and political themes. Whereas Jane's story is a personal voyage of discovery, Agnes states how her life is and why it is unfair. By writing the story of Agnes as biographical, Anne is writing an exposé of female oppression.

At the time, none of these first three novels received the critical acclaim that their authors had hoped for and only two found a publisher, *Agnes Grey* and *Wuthering Heights*. These two books were accepted and published by the rather dubious Thomas Cautley Newby, a sole publisher with premises off Cavendish Square in London. *The Professor* was the weakest of the three and is still seen by many as an unfinished and crude first attempt to write *Villette*. Of the two published works, they were mainly lambasted by the critics, one as too coarse and passionate and the other as too unrealistic and idealised.

It would be many years before the brilliance of *Wuthering Heights* and its timeless appeal would be fully recognised for the giant work of literature that it is. *Agnes Grey* has lost the label of an inferior first novel and is now viewed more as an early feminist tract which alerted the reader to the impossible position of the unmarried, middle-class woman.

Chapter Twelve

Fame and Criticism

Messrs. Smith and Elders' invitation to Charlotte that they might look favourably on a three-volume work came just as she was finishing her manuscript of *Jane Eyre*. George Smith read the manuscript in one day and Charlotte was offered £100 for the copyright and a set of publishing conditions which included their first refusal on her next two books. This was not a large sum and though it would eventually yield around £500 for each of her four novels, Charlotte liked and stayed with Smith, Elder and Co. for the rest of her writing career.

Jane Eyre took the literary public by storm. Once again, this was a book that had a great deal of biography, but also showed the development and triumph of the plain, small and ugly Jane; the orphan child and overlooked governess. The story follows Jane's progress as she overcomes adversity and eventually meets her former rich and powerful chosen partner on equal terms. It is a novel that examines loss in many forms and deliberately exposes the harsh conditions Charlotte and her sisters suffered at the Clergy Daughters' School at Cowan Bridge (Lowood in *Jane Eyre*). It examines the role of the governess and her position in a large, middle-class home and environment, but it also highlights the faults and failures of the dominant and powerful male, Mr Rochester. In a reversal of roles, Jane is the moral leader; the character whom, despite falling in love with her master, can see and recognise his faults and will not be dominated by his will. She has a conscience and a self-respect that govern her ability to recognise right from wrong. In a notable scene, unusual in a Victorian novel, Jane stands up to the teasing and harassment of her employer. This is one of the first records of a female character challenging the power and dominance of her male counterpart. Jane forcefully implores Rochester in a speech where they have met in the garden and he has unmercifully tormented her that he is to marry someone else. She says,

'I tell you that I must go!' I retorted, roused to something like passion. 'Do you think I am an automaton? – a machine without feelings? And can bear to have my morsel of bread snatched from my lips, and my drop of living water dashed from my cup? Do you think, because I am poor, obscure, plain and little, I am soulless and heartless? You think wrong! – I have as much soul as you, – and full as much heart! And if God had gifted me with some beauty, and much wealth, I should have made it as hard for you to leave me, as it is now for me to leave you. I am not talking to you now through the medium of custom, conventionalities, or even of mortal flesh: – it is my spirit that addresses your spirit; just as if both had passed through the grave, and we stood at God's feet, equal, – as we are!'

(C. Brontë, *Jane Eyre*, 1980) p. 289.

This is trailblazing; this is a woman in fiction who is brave enough and strong enough to state her case and stand up to a man who is deliberately trying to belittle and humiliate her. Rochester is intentionally upsetting Jane to find out what her feelings are towards him, without being honest and open enough to declare his feelings for her. He plays games with her emotions but she stands up to him and can rise above his behaviour. Is he any better than Heathcliff? I suggest that at times he is far worse. He uses his position of power and class to hurt Jane and to confuse her. He is unkind and duplicitous. He even offers her marriage knowing that his first wife is alive and living two floors above them in Thornfield Hall. This is not a man of honour or moral fibre; he is weak and prone to lies and deceit. One could argue that Heathcliff, despite all his malevolence, is not false or subversive; he is as you see him and never pretends to be anything else.

It is interesting to compare the 'heroes', or 'anti-heroes' of the sisters' novels. They all write of violent, damaged men, destroyed or chastened by the love of a woman who is too good or too bad to deserve them. Charlotte solves the issue by allowing her hero to suffer physical and emotional destruction. In the fire at Thornfield Hall he loses his power and dominance and this aligns him with Jane in a social and physical bond that equalises them. Emily resolves the dilemma in her novel by allowing Catherine Linton to die and the saga to continue for twenty years whilst Heathcliff works out his anger and pain on everyone around him.

The way in which both Emily and Charlotte deal with men and their relationships with women was further explored by Ann in her next and final novel, *The Tenant of Wildfell Hall*. Each of the sisters' three novels, *Jane Eyre*, *Wuthering Heights* and *The Tenant of Wildfell Hall*, highlighted the role and the repression of women and the cruelty and conditioning of children at the hands of powerful men. They further demonstrated the dangerous excesses of men who have no guide or guard on their behaviour and emotions. The books also examined education, the class system, the obsession with wealth and status set against an immoral and frivolous world that had turned its back on nature and the natural. Each book addresses religion as both a personal and universal influence, but also showing that it can be corrupted and exploited by the rich and powerful or the ignorant and misguided.

The Tenant of Wildfell Hall, like *Wuthering Heights*, is seen through the eyes of a narrator; Gilbert Markham, who is intrigued by the lady who has taken up the tenancy of the Hall. Unlike Lockwood, the male narrator in *Wuthering Heights*, Markham has an affinity with the land and nature and displays more empathy and understanding of it. Helen Huntingdon, the female protagonist, is fleeing a brutal and loveless marriage. Her husband Arthur is a violent alcoholic who is determined that his son should follow the same decadent path as himself. Unable to bear the corruption of her beautiful and adored child, Helen runs away, taking the child with her, and hides in the obscurity of Wildfell Hall and the countryside.

As with *Agnes Grey*, Anne was determined to expose what she saw as the 'truth'. That truth was an exposure of the cruelty that many women had to endure against a system that allowed them to be abused by the very people expected to care for them: husbands, employers, fathers and brothers. This is not as simple as men versus women, or Anne wishing to show that women were better or stronger or morally less corrupt than men, but more that the whole system was wrong. The moral guidance of the church that preached a doctrine of love and equality for Anne, was being eroded and spoilt because of a lack of respect between the sexes. This was further condoned and perpetuated by laws that gave man complete control and possession over women, especially their own wives and children.

As was the case with her first novel, Anne's book received much criticism and critics warned readers, especially women, against it. Anne defended her subject and content by continually explaining that her novels had a morality that needed to be upheld against the evils of the day. Anne takes the high moral ground here and one is reminded of her father's religious tracts and sermons on the evils of sin and the didactic role of preaching and writing.

Each of the sisters display and expose the plight of women of all classes and status when used and abused by their male counterparts, but they further examine why people behave as they do and how easily they can be corrupted. This begins in childhood, and children and their parents or guardians are particular themes in the first parts of all the Brontë novels. Whether orphaned and abused like Jane Eyre and Heathcliff, or cosseted like Adele or Edgar and Isabella Linton, conditioned like Hareton, spoilt like Catherine Earnshaw, ruined like the children of the Murrays in *Agnes Grey* and those of Jane's aunt Reed in *Jane Eyre*, or abandoned like Lucy in *Villette*, or lonely like Caroline in *Shirley*, they all grow up under the influence of the parent or guardian in whose 'care' they are reared. They can sometimes alter the damage done to them as children, and this happens in a series of moral experiences where they chose the right and moral path. Jane Eyre triumphs after her many setbacks, whereas Heathcliff uses his rejection as a weapon and excuse to treat everyone with loathing.

By showing the development of the characters, often from childhood or teenage years through to adulthood, the authors can expose the problematic issues around childrearing, but also the effects of upbringing and why some adults develop good and useful traits and others do not. For Charlotte, there appears to be an emphasis on intelligence and the ability of her characters to suffer but to learn from their suffering and rise above it. For Anne, her characters develop from an understanding of reality and a belief in an alternative which, if they remain true to their faith and their innate goodness, will triumph over adversity. Emily's characters are simplistic and complicated in varying degrees. The inhabitants of the Heights are far more attuned to nature and animalistic instincts where the veneer of civilisation is very thin and their behaviour is more emotional. Down at the Grange the people are more refined and influenced by social conditioning and expectations.

Charlotte wrote two more novels after *Jane Eyre*, which were both published after the deaths of her siblings, *Shirley* completed in 1849, and *Villette* in 1853. *Shirley* is a novel with two heroines, Caroline Helstone, a woman who has been apparently rejected and abandoned by her parents, is in love with a mill owner, Robert Moore. Her unrequited love is a central theme of the book. Shirley Keeldar, possibly based on some of Emily's character and attributes, is a strong, almost masculine, figure: headstrong, domineering and with a rejection of conventional 'feminine' traits and qualities. This novel is not just about the heroines' personal biographies, although they are important, but also highlights some of the industrial conflicts of the day. It is an historical as well as a social account of life in west Yorkshire around the first ten years of the nineteenth century. For this reason, the novel is in the hands of a third person narrator who can comment on events rather than feel the action.

Patrick Brontë had lived through, and had experience of, the Luddite riots in the north of England and with her knowledge of these events, Charlotte focused part of *Shirley* on the rising of the millworkers against the loss of their jobs due to the introduction of machinery. At times violent and uncompromising, the novel places the role of women against the social unrest of the times and exposes them as representatives of the two sides of femininity. Caroline is trapped in her place as the niece of a vicar, smothered and controlled in her uncle's vicarage whilst Shirley is outspoken and aggressive, mocking Caroline's timidity and inability to stand up for herself. One can detect the characters of Charlotte's school friends, Mary Taylor and Ellen Nussey, seeping into the novel.

Although Charlotte knew the history of social unrest in Britain and was very aware of political debate on various social issues, she did not have overall insight into the actual plight of the labouring or working classes insofar as she could identify with them or describe their cause from their perspective. Charlotte held Tory and middle-class views about issues which affected her personally and does not express empathy with the lower classes. She observes and comments but appears to uphold the views of the mill owners rather than the workers. Shirley Keeldar does rebel against those with the means of production and power in the land who use their control to the detriment of others: the poor, women, children, and the working classes, and she symbolically chooses to marry a man who has little wealth or status. The fact that she marries at all, however, does place her back in a conventional arrangement but in her case, she marries the man she loves rather than someone 'suitable'.

Charlotte uses her characters, Shirley and Caroline, to voice many opinions about women and the role of women, in nineteenth century England and she also uses the narrator's voice to describe and explore some of the misguided opinions and beliefs of the male characters. Describing Mr Helstone's relationship with his wife, Charlotte wrote that,

> *Nature never intended Mr Helstone to make a very good husband, especially to a quiet wife. He thought, so long as a woman was silent, nothing ailed her, and she wanted nothing. If she did not complain of solitude, solitude, however continued, could not be irksome to her. If she did not talk and put herself forward, express a partiality for this, an aversion to that, she had no partialities or aversions, and it was useless to consult her tastes. He made no pretence of comprehending women, or comparing them with men: they were a different, probably a very inferior order of existence; a wife could not be her husband's companion, much less his confidant, much less his stay.*
>
> (C. Brontë, *Shirley* 1982) p. 82.

Whilst many marriages were not as abject as this, it is very much the male opinion of the times. Women and wives were inferior to their husbands, fathers and brothers; they had no legal rights and could not vote. Their role of wife and mother was based on an inherent belief that women were the nurturing homemakers who had charge of maternity and housekeeping but little else. Working class or poorer women had almost no say in any area of their lives and little or no influence on the men around them. Whilst other classes had the protection or backdrop of a level of financial security, the female lower classes had no such safety net and their lives and health were often destroyed by hard work, childbearing and poverty.

Charlotte did not have direct experience of the lives of the lower classes and she, as an author wanting to tell the truth as she saw it, does not try to emulate their distress. She does, however, continue to attack the middle classes who either admire or despise the layer of class above and below them. Thus, Charlotte's own experiences, those weeks spent in the houses of the affluent and her observations of the friends and families she visited and knew well, were transferred into her novels because she had watched and felt their friendships as well as their prejudices.

Sewing symbolised much of the art and usefulness of women and was a particular bane to Charlotte, not least because of her poor eyesight. The Brontë girls spent thousands of hours sewing and mending garments under the watchful eyes of their aunt. Understandably, aunt Branwell appreciated this skill as both an attainment and a necessary accomplishment in a household where there was little money to spend on clothes. In *Shirley*, Charlotte lets Caroline Helstone describe the boredom and waste of time she felt in much of this labour,

> *The afternoon was devoted to sewing. Mademoiselle, like most Belgian ladies, was especially skilful with her needle. She by no means thought it a waste of time to devote unnumbered hours to fine embroidery, sight-destroying lace-work, marvellous netting and knitting, and, above all, to most elaborate stocking-mending. She would give a day to the mending of two holes in a stocking any time, and think her 'mission' nobly fulfilled ... and when she first discovered that Caroline was profoundly ignorant of this most essential of attainments, she could have wept with pity over her miserably neglected youth.*
>
> (C. Brontë, *Shirley*, 1982) p. 107.

Similarly, Caroline's uncle, Mr Helstone, encourages his niece to, 'stick to the needle – learn shirt-making and gown-making, and pie-crusting, and you'll be a clever woman some day. Go to bed now: I'm busy with this pamphlet here.' (C. Brontë, *Shirley*, 1982) p. 122.

It is this constant moulding of women of a certain class into a certain type which Charlotte finds so irksome. There is no room for independence of thought or spirit for Caroline because she is surrounded by people who think she must always be led by others. She can only be allowed to perform certain menial tasks that will not attract attention or make her different to others.

Difference was to be feared because difference, especially in women, was too closely linked to bad manners or bad breeding, which was seen as perverse and perhaps indicating psychological disturbance. Female disturbance of behaviour was closely linked to hysteria and even to insanity. This linkage was feared and, unfortunately, sometimes associated with a lack of morals and a wayward and over-familiar disposition. Charlotte had introduced the madwoman issue in *Jane Eyre*, with very little sympathy or empathy towards Bertha Mason, Rochester's mentally sick wife. Insanity was feared and has been misunderstood throughout history. Only when medical research and intervention began to occur in the mid-nineteenth century and the first two Lunatic Acts were introduced, did changes in attitude and treatment occur. Before this, mental illness was viewed as either an ungovernable and untreatable state or, by some doctors, as an illness or weakness that could be controlled by the person themselves. A link was established between the power of unrestricted emotions and passions and types of insanity. Therefore, any inability to control one's emotions was viewed as dangerous. People who 'gave in' to their emotions were less controllable, less stable and a possible threat to the rest of the society. As women had little or no control over their choices and their lifestyle, their moral and psychological behaviour could be easily misunderstood or deliberately misinterpreted by people with an ulterior motive such as men who wanted to be rid of their wives. Others chose to ignore genuine frustration and boredom and allowed their partners to sink into depression and death. Mr Helstone in *Shirley* assumed that his ailing wife must be alright because she did not complain. This unwritten and unspoken expectation that women should suffer in silence or risk being viewed as troublemakers, and possibly mentally unstable, was a recurring topic in Charlotte and her sisters' writings.

There has long been speculation that the Brontë siblings may all have suffered from various forms of mental illness, to a lesser or greater degree. Did Branwell suffer from epilepsy and schizophrenia? Was Charlotte a manic depressive, or Emily psychotic and prone to phobias? Did Anne suffer from crises of religion which made her morbidly preoccupied? They may have suffered from none or all of these conditions and we cannot know at this distance in time. If they did, then the family would have gone to great lengths to disguise the shame of mental illness. Charlotte researched medical opinion of the day and was interested in the new science of phrenology which claimed to know the moral and psychological wellbeing of a person by studying the contours of their head and face. Charlotte writes a lot about the physiognomy of her heroes and heroines as a way of revealing their inner sensibilities. There is little doubt that fear of 'nervous disease' also worried Mr Brontë and he wrote copiously in the margins of his *Domestic Medicine* on this as much as on physical illness.

In all of the Brontë novels, the main characters suffer various moments of mental distress and doubts about their own capabilities and emotional wellbeing. Overwrought feelings and disturbed imaginations occupy all the protagonists at some time and, as we know from Charlotte's letters, she was often laid low by her own nervous disposition which was accompanied by nauseous headaches and morbid torpor. Knowing the Brontës' history, both the deaths and their romantic losses, is to understand a certain amount of this depressive mood. Charlotte and Branwell both had months, possibly years, of heartache and pain caused by their love of unattainable partners. This unrequited longing must have driven their emotions to a precarious mental state. Branwell's behaviour in his last months is not that of a man with a stable and healthy mind. How much of his demise was based on mental anguish and how much on his addictions is hard to tell as each probably fed the other in a chaotic downward spiral. As stated, both Anne and Emily may well have been in love with men who died young. Evidence comes mainly from Anne and Emily's poetry and the strength of feeling they express over the loss of a loved one but this has never been authenticated. The loss of their family members was surely enough to produce such dramatic verse.

In *Shirley*, Charlotte allows Caroline to succumb to a prolonged illness that affects both her mind and body and in many ways, it is Charlotte's statement about how easily the neglected and unhappy female can sink into a depression from which she may never recover. Caroline has been told by her uncle that her father was a drunkard and her mother abandoned her. Caroline is secretly in love with the mill owner, Robert Moore but, when she believes that he loves someone else and she will never marry him, she becomes so despondent with her life that a fever takes hold of her and for many days she hovers between life and death. Charlotte wrote these chapters during the last illnesses and deaths of Branwell and Emily, and named the chapter, *The Valley of the Shadow of Death*. In her novel, she did what she had done as a child and made her heroine rise up and live again. After her brother died, Charlotte takes us through the horror and the heartache of Emily's slow and harrowing death in *Shirley* by describing Caroline's illness as though the outcome will be fatal. She then allows Caroline's nurse, Mrs Pryor, to reveal to Caroline that she is, in fact, her long lost mother; this knowledge revives Caroline and she is eventually restored to health.

This theme of orphans and missing mothers is inherent throughout the Brontë novels and is an obvious reflection of their own motherless state and demonstrates that it is an abiding memory. One feels that they all believed that if only they had had a mother, their lives would have been so much better. The restoration of close and loving family members to both Jane Eyre and Caroline Helstone helps them to overcome their loneliness at crucial times in their lives.

The Brontë sisters each wrote what they believed was the truth as they perceived it and that included personal emotional trauma. This was not the usual way of presenting a story at this time in the history of English Literature and was especially avoided by the male writers of the times. It was not seen as necessary or desirable to put too much of one's personal feelings into writing intended for public consumption. The novel was designed to tell a story, to entertain and possibly instruct but always to describe in the physical and social sense. It was not seen as a platform for personal psychoanalysis and in this area the Brontës were offering a very different and often critical view of the world. Their characters are examined in terms of the inner conflicts and emotional dramas of the human condition which are separated from the civilised mantle that normally shields them. It was this exposure to 'reality' which caused many critics to describe the Brontë novels as 'coarse', 'vulgar' and 'not fit for decent people to read'. It was this scratching away at the surface of middle-class manners and class distinctions that the critics disliked and possibly feared. Novels which were emotionally involved and dealt with feelings which were normally hidden from public gaze were not welcome. Where would such exposure lead? It was dangerous, subversive, and therefore needed to be kept hidden from the eyes of people with taste and the ability to control their emotions.

It is here especially that the Brontë sisters are regarded as original. They exposed the plight of unhappy and neglected children as well as those who were pampered and spoilt by highlighting the twin evils of cruelty and indulgence. They tackled the dilemmas surrounding the role and fate of women, especially those of their own lower middle class who had very little alternative than to marry and be subjected to their husband's views and wishes. They further exposed the horrors of life as an old maid; a spinster who had to either work in other people's homes or be at the mercy of her family's benevolence. They examined the sanctity of marriage, the issue of bigamy, and the role that the husband and wife were expected to play in both public and private. Anne Brontë in *The Tenant of Wildfell Hall* even allowed her heroine to flee from her violent husband, taking her son with her. The sisters described the destructive power of neglect and isolation and the overwhelming emotional trials that could break the human spirit, even to death.

As well as their intimate examination of individual characters, they also display the ability to tackle leading political and social issues of the day.

Understandably, as well-educated and intelligent women themselves, women's education was a topic. Industrial changes, some of which they experienced, was a further issue and led to discussion on the causes and effect of both poverty and wealth and the influence of revolution in Europe. The changes from a predominantly agricultural to an industrial age lends the background to many of their stories and these changes are linked to a change in religious faith and the role of the church. They are writing at a time just before Darwin publishes *On the Origin of Species,* but one feels the questioning and the doubt about religion and long-held social beliefs, especially in *Wuthering Heights,* is already challenging the status quo.

These and many more issues are contained in the Brontë novels and it is the fact that they were written by women that many people, on discovery of that fact, found especially objectionable. These subjects were not the business of women and they had no right to expose the faults and prejudices of society at a time when war and revolution abroad was already causing excessive worry and disquiet amongst the government and business leaders. The rise of the Luddites, and later the Chartist movements, threatened revolution at home and frightened many of the upper classes who feared a working-class uprising. They did not want, or need, a similar revolt by the female sex highlighting their lack of status and disenfranchisement on top of the current unrest.

Chapter Thirteen

Recognition and Loss

Not everyone found the Brontë novels coarse and threatening though and after a slow start they began to sell and to enter the circulating libraries. It did not take long for the people of Yorkshire to recognise places and even people in the novels; rumour soon spread that not only were the writers female, but also the daughters of a clergyman. Confusion over the actual authorship of each book and, because of the success of *Jane Eyre*, the suggestion that Currer Bell had written all of the novels, meant that Charlotte and Anne hurried down to London to pacify Charlotte's publisher. These rumours may well have been introduced and fuelled by Thomas Newby in the hope that *Agnes Grey* and *Wuthering Heights* would sell more copies. When the sisters presented themselves at the offices of Smith and Elder to show that they were women and separate writers, Emily stayed at home, not wishing to expose herself to publicity. Charlotte convinced Smith and Elder of the existence of three separate writing 'Bells'.

As the fame of the sisters spread, one wonders at the reaction of their father and brother. It is said that Patrick's first realisation of his daughters published works was when Charlotte handed him a printed copy of *Jane Eyre* to read. He told his children that Charlotte had written a book and that it was 'better than likely'. This suggests that he was oblivious of their other novels with a naivety that is hard to believe, although it is often thought that the sisters wrote more often at night time after their father had retired to bed. Patrick's poor eyesight and health issues, and his worry over Branwell may also have contributed to his lack of insight and knowledge of his daughters' prolific writing.

Branwell was by now in a very delicate and unhappy frame of mind and just when he realised their literary success is hard to establish. It is possible that the sisters tried to keep their novels from him in a way of protecting him because of his own lack of literary achievement and failure to earn a living. He was by now deep in debt and his father and sisters often had to bail him out of trouble.

Charlotte was furious with his behaviour and whilst Anne and Emily tolerated him, it is thought that only Emily and Patrick had any genuine sympathy towards him. When, as previously stated, Branwell did learn of his sisters' success and boasted at the Black Bull that he was the author of *Wuthering Heights*, it may be that he recognised himself in parts of it or related some of the characters to his own creations, but it could also mean that he could not bear to lose face. For years, they had all written together and Branwell had displayed as much talent and enthusiasm as his sisters. To contrast their success with his failure must have been especially hard for him to bear.

Success is a difficult word to quantify. Success for Emily brought her a little extra money, a lot of criticism and the reality of exposure. One feels that none of these would have pleased her. Her novel was published in June 1847, along with Anne's *Agnes Grey*, but neither received much praise or positive publicity. Emily died eighteen months later, three months after the death of Branwell. Anne died in May of 1849, her second book, *The Tenant of Wildfell Hall*, having been published eleven months earlier. Charlotte wrote *Shirley* whilst the decline and deaths of her siblings were taking place and it was published in 1849. Her last novel, *Villette*, was published in 1853, three years before her own death in 1856, and her first novel, *The Professor*, was finally published posthumously in June 1857.

During these ten years, 1847 to 1857, the sister's works became famous and the contents widely read and discussed. Of the seven novels, *The Professor* is perhaps the lesser work and the least read. It is seen, even now, as the preliminary first efforts of a gifted novelist who followed it with *Jane Eyre*, *Shirley* and *Villette*. *Agnes Grey* was viewed for a long time as a quaint tale of a downtrodden governess. A deeper reading shows a strong and sustained story of adversity which is overcome by hard work and determination; a moral tale but one that also examines the role of women, female exploitation and problems with moral education. *Shirley* is a tale which again highlights the position of women in the context of the early nineteenth century and the growth of the industrial revolution. Of the remaining four novels, each has been described as a work of genius. Three of them have been lauded by feminists as championing the cause of women and the oppressed. Only *Wuthering Heights* defies its readers and critics. It is, no doubt, a work of brilliance like very few others in English Literature. It has its influences and origins in Shakespeare, Byron, Scott and

Wordsworth, but its content and characters, its plot and sub-plots, are very different from most other novels.

It is interesting to ask what Emily had in mind when she wrote the book. Did she intend to offer a moral tale, a descriptive story of moorland life, an entertainment or was she exploring her own faith and doubts? It is almost impossible to tell. There are no clues to this book and unlike her sisters, Emily does not state her purpose. What is known is that she wrote one of the most powerful and disturbing novels ever published.

Wuthering Heights has been described as a love story and the emphasis in most films of the book focuses on the lives of Heathcliff and the first Catherine. The original Hollywood version of the film, featuring Laurence Olivier and Merle Oberon, ends with the death of the first Catherine and does not even venture into the second half of the book. That it is a book of two halves is evident but the lives of the characters of the second part are inextricably linked to all that happens in the opening chapters. To see the book as a mere love story is to do it a grave injustice. It is a simple story but with multiple layers of disturbance and intrigue provided by a relatively small cast of characters. The moorland setting and the extremes of weather help to give it a harsh and gothic content where people seek revenge and death is a constant threat. The book is still difficult to decipher and not an easy read. One can understand why it was not welcomed by the majority of readers and critics. There are faults in the structure of *Wuthering Heights* and there are gaps and missing information which would have helped the reader and explained more about the plot, but it is, nevertheless, an amazing first novel.

The acclaim for *Jane Eyre* and the largely damning response to *Wuthering Heights*, and later to *The Tenant of Wildfell Hall*, led Charlotte to evaluate both of her sisters' novels. Siding to some extent with the literary critics she felt that, knowing the characters and personalities of her sisters, they had chosen their subjects badly. What she possibly failed to accept and acknowledge was that these books were part of the lived experience of her sisters, who had had far more contact with Branwell in his later years than she had. They had dealt with his ravings and his lack of self control and his abuse. Emily especially had suffered the reality of her brother's condition. Charlotte was sometimes at home, but Emily and Anne was there permanently.

Charlotte's response to Branwell's behaviour was scorn and a need to absent herself from him. Charlotte had suffered heartbreak in silence and saw no reason why her brother could not do the same. Branwell, her childhood partner and staunch supporter, was effectively cast aside by his elder sister at a time when he needed her the most.

Anne had suffered the embarrassment of knowing of Branwell's affair with their employer and of feeling obliged to resign from her post because of it. She, too, had little sympathy for Branwell's plight, but she watched and suffered from his absurd and violent behaviour, his bouts of wild drinking and his days of hangovers and lazing in bed. She witnessed his constant begging for money from their father and the effect that this had on the now elderly and ailing man who had had such hopes for his only boy. Anne saw what alcohol and drugs could do to a man and how, without moral guidance and fortitude, he could sink into an abysmal existence.

Emily also witnessed Branwell's sad deterioration but appears not to have judged him as harshly as her sisters did. Emily was a strong woman, but she did not necessarily apply the strict rules that she herself lived by, to the lives of others. Emily seems to have taken life as it happened without trying to alter anything or anybody. She would challenge many things but did not try to impose her views on to other people. In *Wuthering Heights* she relates a story as she sees it and leaves the reader to make their own decisions and judgements.

There is little doubt that *Wuthering Heights* and *The Tenant of Wildfell Hall* were influenced to some extent by the effect that Branwell was having on the household. From July 1845, when he received his dismissal notice from Mr Robinson, Branwell lost his ability to work or conduct his life in any meaningful way. His death in September 1848 ended three years of torment both for him and his family. It is natural that his plight would be expressed in his sisters' novels and in *The Tenant of Wildfell Hall*, Anne uses what she has witnessed at home to tell a cautionary tale of the destructive nature of alcohol. She shows how it can lead to violence and abuse and how the family, especially the wife or sister, can suffer at the hands of a husband or brother, who has lost control.

Sadly, the peace which should have followed Branwell's death was filled with anxiety, illness and the rapid decline of both Emily and Anne. The sisters had little chance to enjoy or benefit from the success and income that their work would eventually generate. The Brontës were all carrying the tuberculosis virus and the stresses of life and their many physical and emotional bouts of illness allowed the disease to take hold. It is a disease that flares up especially when the body is weakened by coughs and colds or the more severe ailments of bronchitis, influenza or pneumonia; little could be done to either cure or even alleviate the symptoms. Only Charlotte survived that terrible sequence of deaths but she too succumbed to tuberculosis in 1856 after being severely weakened in early pregnancy by excessive sickness.

Their tragic deaths add a poignant epitaph to their early promise, but they managed to leave a strong and lasting legacy. The Brontë sisters burst onto the literary scene at a time when there was very little female authorship and much of it was written for the drawing room and not the bedroom. The novel was intended as a source of amusement and entertainment and not meant to arouse emotions or indulge in passionate moralising. By examining each of the sisters in turn and the writings which made them so famous, one can see how and why they became such literary giants.

Chapter Fourteen

'Dear, Gentle Anne'

In July 1833, Charlotte's school friend, Ellen Nussey, made her first visit to Haworth Parsonage and met all of Charlotte's family. She described Anne as follows,

Anne, dear gentle Anne, was quite different in appearance to the others. She was her aunt's favourite. Her hair was a very pretty light brown and fell on her neck in graceful curls. She had lovely violet blue eyes, fine pencilled eyebrows, a clear, almost transparent complexion.

(J.R.V. Barker, 2010) p. 227.

Anne was 13 when this was written and she had never left home, except for the occasional visit to her godmothers. Her position as the youngest in the family is important as she was probably overprotected and well loved by her parent, aunt and older siblings but also, at times, dominated and patronised by them.

Anne was 3 months old when the family moved to Haworth and 19 months old when her mother died. Her only childhood recollections centred on the Parsonage and her mother substitute, aunt Branwell. Elizabeth Branwell, as described, was removed from the comfortable surroundings of her family and home in Penzance to take care of her sister's six young children. She had no experience of motherhood and had led a rather sheltered and pleasant life in the milder climate of Penzance. She had strict moral views and was probably averse to the noise and commotion of lively children in the confines of the house and spent a lot of time in her own room. She was in the awkward position of being neither wife nor mother, but was duty bound to provide for her nieces and nephew.

There is no doubt that the children respected their aunt and that she was a steady influence on them. She was a year older than their father and not at all used to the ways of a young, growing family. It is not unlikely that, rather than devote herself to them all, she undertook, subconsciously or otherwise, to align herself with the only boy and the youngest child. Anne was young enough to be moulded and cosseted by her aunt whilst Branwell's gender set him apart from the five girls and he would have been a favourite with the entire family. Certainly, Branwell loved and missed his aunt following her death in October 1842 and described her as 'the only mother I ever knew'. Branwell also witnessed his aunt's painful illness and suffering whilst the three girls were all away from home.

Although Anne was at home by the time Charlotte and Emily arrived back from Brussels following their aunt's funeral, we do not know how much her death affected them all. Anne appears to have been more influenced by her aunt than her siblings and this is possibly because her aunt had shown her more affection and spent more time with her than with the older girls. Anne appears to have been more compliant and obedient to her aunt's wishes and her whole character and personality is portrayed as quiet and gentle, as described by Ellen Nussey.

We know from the many letters, diary papers, juvenilia and other documents, that Anne was reared in a way that many youngest children are: as if needing to be especially sheltered and protected. Anne was not sought out for her opinions and would have had little sway over her elder siblings. When Charlotte became the eldest she appears to have taken the role very seriously and tried to dominate the others somewhat. Charlotte was often the lead in their adventures and it was she who wished to travel abroad. Charlotte wanted them to set up their own school and it was she who pushed for them to publish their writings. She was the driving force behind many of the events in the Parsonage and her sisters followed. Although one suspects that Emily was not a woman who could be pushed around or prevailed upon, it seems likely that she would go along with Charlotte at times to keep the peace or to carry out her father's wishes. It is quite remarkable that someone as home-loving, and possibly agoraphobic, as Emily went with Charlotte on her nine-month long, first trip to Brussels and yet Anne seems not to have been considered.

Anne therefore suffered the fate of many 'youngest' who are treated as too delicate to forge ahead like her older sisters, too young or inexperienced to make decisions, and too immature to lead the others or to be taken seriously. As children, Branwell once described Anne as, 'nothing, simply nothing at all'.

Whilst this was probably spoken with humour, it is a telling indictment on how she was viewed at times by both her brother and Charlotte.

Anne was only eighteen months younger than Emily, her nearest sister in age, and the two of them, whilst very different in looks and personality, did have a special bond. As the two youngest they shared a common ground against the two eldest which was mainly good humoured. There is no suggestion in childhood that there was anything other than normal sibling rivalry but as they grew older the division into two distinct pairs became more evident. As Branwell and Charlotte wrote more and more exclusively, Emily and Anne created their own world of Gondal.

Little of the Gondal story remains but we do know that after Charlotte left home for Roe Head School in June 1831 the writing and inventing partnership of the four children, which had concentrated on Glasstown and Angria, was finally severed. Emily and Anne were somewhat liberated and could now create their own lands and stories without the domineering influence of Charlotte and Branwell. They did this by inventing the North Pacific Island of Gondal and its neighbouring rival Gaaldine. There is surviving poetry from the *Gondal Sagas*, written as though by, and to, its main characters. This paradise island, which included a very Yorkshire and moorland landscape, produced many characters whose lives and loves are graphically described in some very beautiful and moving poetry. There are central themes throughout of loss and sadness, broken hearts and the loneliness of life and landscape. The heroine, Alexandrina Zenobia has a long and complex love affair with the hero, Alexander Hibernia. They are often separated and the poetry echoes their unhappiness and constant returning to a time when they were youthful and carefree. Death is also a theme in the saga and imprisonment and abandonment feature throughout.

These writings occupied Anne and Emily throughout their teens and into adulthood, Emily, with more time to indulge, never really let go of this 'other' world. Although Anne became more occupied with the reality of her work as a governess and the long hours of toil that it involved, she could still dip in and out of Gondal and indulge it when she and Emily were together.

Even at 15 years old Anne had never left the Parsonage for school or work, but in October 1835 she accompanied Charlotte to Roe Head School, where Charlotte was now a teacher. Emily had previously attended as a pupil but severe homesickness had caused Charlotte to insist to the headmistress, that she should be allowed to return home and Anne to take her place. Patrick had been reluctant to let Anne go, but the opportunity for her to gain a wider education and to socialise was now of major importance for her future employment. How much Anne was consulted or wanted to go remains a mystery, but some of the following effects on Anne suggest that she was just as homesick as Emily and that she suffered a major physical and emotional breakdown as a result.

As in all other areas of her life, Anne was patient, sensible and resigned. She had an inner strength which was not always recognised or regarded in her to the extent that it perhaps should have been. The portrait of Emily as the fierce and independent woman belies her disability when away from home and her inability to socialise or to even make herself amenable. At Roe Head, Anne was regarded as no-one very special. Charlotte had little time to spend with her and did not, in any case, wish to be accused of favouritism. There were few pupils of Anne's age and background so she made only a couple of friends who were much younger than herself. Anne does not complain about her situation. She would have been aware of the expense of her education and the opportunity it afforded her; knowing the family's precarious financial situation she would have stuck to her role and done all she could to benefit from the experience. This and other matters wore down Anne's health and her faith and caused her to question many of her previous beliefs.

Whilst Anne, like the others, had been raised in a liberal household they had all been brought up with strict Protestant beliefs which included complete faith in the Bible and the teachings of Christ. Elizabeth and Maria Branwell had had a Wesleyan Methodist upbringing in Cornwall but with possible leanings towards the doctrine of Calvinism. Patrick sympathised with most other religions and was a strong supporter of John and Charles Wesley and heard them preach. Methodism was not a popular religion in Haworth until it officially broke away from the main Protestantism of the times. Anne, who was greatly influenced and directed by her aunt, faced a religious crisis during her stay at Roe Head when she was away from home and the moral support of her father and aunt Branwell.

Calvinism was a doctrine which preached that only certain people, as pre-ordained by God, could enter Heaven and that all others, no matter how good and pure a life they lead, would be banished to the fires of Hell. This was contrary to the Protestant belief in a forgiving deity that welcomed all sinners if they repented. At Mirfield Church, where the pupils of Roe Head mainly worshipped, there were various visiting ministers including two with Calvinistic beliefs. Their preachings caused both Anne and Charlotte concern and added to their religious doubts.

Anne spent her whole life trying to do what was best for others, often at great sacrifice to her own health and wellbeing. She was fiercely devoted to her family. She was determined to do her best and suffer whatever trials she had to face. In this sense she was, in some ways, the strongest and the most resilient of the Brontë children. Anne never let her family down, never evoked controversy or scandal, and never doubted that she must follow a path of goodness and truth. Doubts about her faith blighted her stay at Roe Head and troubled her thoughts to the point that her health began to suffer. Anne was never as physically robust as her sisters and suffered from asthma and frequent bouts of fever, possibly a form of typhoid. It took Charlotte some time to realise that her sister was ailing as she was dealing with her own anger and her own reaction to the new religious thoughts which were also troubling her. She wrote at this time, 'I abhor myself – despise myself – if the Doctrine of Calvin be true, I am already an outcast' (Holland, 2016) p. 85.

At Roe Head, Charlotte had made the discovery that she disliked teaching, despite the kindness of the Misses Wooler and the pleasant house and gardens. Charlotte did not have the patience or the ability to teach children for whom she had little or no respect. She had become so wrapped up in her own misery that she failed to recognise Anne's until it was almost too late. Her sudden reaction to her sister's health brought doctors to Anne but they could only offer minimal assistance. Anne was physically and psychologically affected by extreme concern that when she died, she would die a sinner and go to Hell. This would mean that she would never see her mother and sisters again. The torment was too much for Anne to bear and she had to know the truth. At this point in her illness she requested the help of a priest. The man who came to her aid was neither Protestant nor Catholic, but a local Moravian minister, James La Trobe. The Moravian's creed had no time for the Calvinists preaching of hell and damnation believing instead in a loving and forgiving God similar to that of the Protestants and the Methodists. The Moravians understood God as very much a personal deity with whom each person had their own relationship.

James La Trobe's kindness to Anne, and his insistence that God was benign and that all sinners would eventually be forgiven, was a huge comfort to the troubled girl and his visits did a great deal to restore her to health. Charlotte, somewhat guilt-ridden that she had failed to recognise Anne's crisis and done little to help her, turned her fury on to Miss Wooler for not getting medical assistance for Anne much sooner. Miss Wooler was shocked and hurt by Charlotte's accusations and wrote to Mr Brontë explaining what had happened. Patrick, now ever fearful for his children's health, summoned them both back home.

Back in the safety and protection of the Parsonage and her family which she now needed both physically and morally, Anne's crisis subsided and she could dispel the religious doubts that had so affected her. Her happiness at being back home with Emily and the familiar routine of study, work, and walking on the moors, eventually restored her. Anne had been at school from October 1835 to December 1837, with only a few holidays at home or visiting family friends. Despite her setbacks at Roe Head, Anne had matured and was no longer the pliable and amenable youngest child. She had gained experience and knowledge enough to allow her to go out to work. She had studied a variety of different religious ideas and was more settled and determined in her own faith and beliefs. She would not fit back easily under her aunt's influence and routines, or even be quite so overshadowed by her closest confidante, Emily.

Anne's eighteenth birthday fell on 17 January 1838 and she had been willing and eager for some time to seek work. Even so, it was a year before she was allowed to leave home again and not before a suitable position could be found. This led Anne back to the Mirfield area to a rich and prosperous family, the Inghams, who had made money for many years from coal and wool manufacturing and lived at the imposing Blake Hall. Anne probably gained the position with the help of references from Miss Wooler and James la Trobe and possibly the Nussey family. Although young, Anne was regarded as kind, studious and morally sound. She had talent in music, singing and art, and was proficient in many academic subjects including French. Unlike her siblings, she also had a great fondness for children.

With high hopes and determination Anne set out for Blake Hall in April 1839, at last her own person and an independent working woman. It was, regrettably and through no fault of her own, a disaster. The Ingham children were totally different from the Brontë family. The four children under Anne's care were, Cunliffe aged 6 years, Mary, 5, Martha aged 3 and Emily aged 2. Unfortunately, the children had never been chastised or made to behave and their new and shy governess was no match for them. These children had many material possessions, but their lack of respect for others and selfish indulgence in play meant that they had little inclination to learn. The younger ones copied the elder ones and they copied their parents. Joshua and Mary Ingham appear to have had no time or inclination to spend on ensuring that their children were well-behaved or even educated, and Anne found them sadly lacking in the most elementary reading and writing skills. The behaviour and cruelty of the Inghams was represented in her novel, *Agnes Grey*. Renamed as the Bloomfield family much of their selfish and brutal activities were exposed.

Anne tried her utmost to control and contain the children using every method in her power. They were rude and nasty to her, showed her no respect, and Anne was instructed by the parents not to punish them. Naturally this led to a constant stress where the children fought a daily, and sometimes nightly, battle with their governess. In her determination to prove her worth, Anne continued in her post to do her duty and fulfil the trust placed in her by her own family. She tried to be patient and she tried to reason with her young charges but her perseverance and endurance was in vain and nine months after her arrival, Mrs Ingham informed Anne that her services were no longer required.

Although Anne must have felt a sense of failure and was upset over her dismissal, she would also have felt an enormous relief to be going home for Christmas and to be forever free of the obnoxious family. *Agnes Grey* was her way of writing out the memory of the misery that she had felt at Blake Hall and of examining how and why some children behaved in the way they did. She wanted to show how an upbringing with a lack of boundaries and moral guidance could ruin a child's later development. This was early child psychology and it was further developed in the treatment of young Arthur in *The Tenant of Wildfell Hall*. Anne had seen at first-hand how the spoiling of children with too many possessions and not enough discipline had led them to lose sight of the value of everything and everyone around them. The Ingham children had not been shown the importance of respect, friendship, manners or the sharing and caring for others. This was not the children's fault but a repeated pattern of behaviour passed down through generations. It was shown by Anne to be one of the dangers of a society based on wealth, where the possession of money and objects took precedence over the morals of the individuals, and greed and selfishness became the overriding attributes.

On her return home, Anne was welcomed back by her family who admired her for enduring her long and trying employment and she was soon immersed in the regular routines of Parsonage life. Anne and Emily continued to write their Gondal works and, except for a short while when Emily suddenly took up a post for three months as a teacher at Law Hill School, with equally disastrous consequences, the two worked and wrote well together. Both were growing older and wiser and had gained some experience of life outside of their home. As they matured so did their writing.

In the August of 1839 and following concerns about Patrick's eyesight and general health, a new curate was employed to assist the 62-year-old with his heavy workload. The Rev. William Weightman was a 25-year-old graduate of Durham University. He was intelligent, handsome and confident with a sense of humour and he completely charmed the residents of the Parsonage. Patrick came to look on him as a son and everywhere he went he was loved and respected by the parishioners. His frequent visits to the Parsonage brought him in close contact with the family and Branwell and his sisters all grew very fond of him. In an act of kindness, and on hearing that they had never received a Valentine card, Weightman walked ten miles to post anonymous cards to each of the sisters as a surprise. There is no doubt that this man could charm the ladies and his good looks and easy manner turned many a girl's head in Haworth. It is possible that he was especially fond of Anne. Charlotte comments in her letters about their closeness and sideways glances at each other in Church. How much of a romance or an understanding existed between William and Anne no-one knows for sure? Anne was shy and reticent and Weightman had a position to keep as her father's curate. Anne had no experience of men and would find it difficult to start a relationship even if the opportunity arose.

Around this time, Charlotte, perhaps because she herself had feelings for Weightman, began to ridicule him slightly and to exaggerate his fondness for the ladies. Whether this was to warn Anne or done through jealousy is unknown and it could have made Anne even less able to discuss what feelings she had for him. Again, it is not until she writes *Agnes Grey* and relates the story of Agnes's love for the young curate, Mr Weston, that one can compare her possible real life with the fictional one. Whether there could have been a romantic outcome for Anne is impossible to say. If she did have any understanding with Weightman it was to be a slow and measured affair because Anne deliberately set out to procure another governess post, as ever putting duty before her personal happiness.

Anne's new post was forty miles away from Haworth, a very long distance when travelling was so difficult and expensive. The post offered double the salary she had received from the Inghams and it was with the Robinson family of Thorpe Green Hall. The Hall was a rather isolated country house on flat country located two miles from the village of Little Ouseburn, some twelve miles north of York. Edmund Robinson had taken holy orders but was not a practising priest. He was also related to the Marquis of Ripon. His wife, Lydia, was the daughter of the Reverend Thomas Gisborne, the Canon of Durham. These facts would have comforted Anne and her family and they would have been happy for her to work for such a prestigious household.

Anne's hopes for a warm welcome and the respect of her new employers were soon shattered. Social status was at least as important to the Robinsons as it had been for the nouveau riche Inghams. Edmund was a country squire intent on following country pursuits and his wife was as much a social attribute as his lands and possessions. She, in turn, relished the wealth and status of her position and instilled in her children the need to pursue matters of financial rather than emotional importance.

When Anne arrived in May 1840, the Robinson children under her care consisted of Lydia, aged 14 years, Elizabeth (Bessie) aged 13 years, Mary, aged 12 years and Edmund, aged 8 years. Taking older charges would perhaps have pleased Anne as she would expect them to be more mature and better educated. What Anne found was that the girls had deliberately been kept from any serious study or education. Their mother felt that they needed only the few attributes that would ensure a good marriage and instructed Anne to teach them in the feminine arts of music, needlework and singing, possibly a little French and the art of letter-writing. Expecting the girls to be quiet and sober, Anne was shocked to discover them to be totally self–obsessed, frivolous and noisy. Only young Edmund appeared to have had any formal education and Anne was expected to teach him Latin in preparation for his examinations to a private school.

The first few months must have been very trying for Anne, and whilst she was not treated particularly cruelly by the children, as she had been at the Inghams, they were in charge and were difficult to bring to any sort of order. Luckily, there were some compensations. Anne could visit York and she especially enjoyed York Minster, a building that she truly marvelled at. She also spent time with the family at their house in Scarborough and that town became a special and beautiful place to her where she loved to watch the sea. Again, much of her experiences of this time are recorded in *Agnes Grey* and whilst it is always difficult to match fiction with reality, the parallels between Anne's life and those of her characters are recognisable.

Anne, as ever, persevered with her work and gradually she began to make some headway. Mr and Mrs Robinson were aloof from their governess but pleased with the progress she had made and the children were beginning to warm to her. She was, nevertheless, unhappy and one wonders whether that unhappiness had anything to do with William Weightman, who was so far away from her. In her diary paper of July 1841, Anne wrote, 'I am a governess in the family of Mr Robinson. I dislike the situation and wish to change it for another.' (Holland, 2016) p. 113.

Around this time, Anne spent a month's holiday at home, and as Charlotte and Emily were at that time in Brussels, it is possible that Weightman and Anne did spend some time together without the all-seeing eyes of Charlotte. Weightman had been curate for two years by now and was an invaluable help to Patrick. He worked unflinchingly and had time for all the parishioners and was especially noted for visiting the sick.

It was his compassion and care for the sick that brought about Weightman's death. The following summer brought an outbreak of cholera to Haworth. Visiting a sick parishioner, Weightman contracted the disease and by 6 September he was dead. None of the Brontë girls were at home at the time and knew nothing of his death or funeral. It was Branwell who sat weeping by the coffin of his friend and it was not until days later that Anne finally received a letter telling her that Weightman was dead.

Isolated and possibly heartbroken at Thorpe Green, Anne must have suffered enormously. She had no-one with whom to share her grief or to help and comfort her. For the rest of her life Anne would write heartfelt poetry of the loss of a man that the poet has loved. It is not unrealistic to assume that that man was William Weightman and that she loved him. The following is an example,

A Reminiscence

Yes, thou art gone! and never more
Thy sunny smile shall gladden me;
But I may pass the old church door,
And pace the floor that covers thee
May stand upon the cold, damp stone,
And think that, frozen, lies below
The lightest heart that I have known,
The kindest I shall ever know.

Yet, though I cannot see thee more.
'Tis still a comfort to have seen;
And though thy transient life is o'er,
'Tis sweet to think that thou hast been;

To think a soul so near divine,
Within a form so angel fair,
United to a heart like thine,
Has gladdened once our humble sphere.

(A. Brontë, *The Brontës Selected Poems*, 2003) p. 92.

In *Agnes Grey*, Anne continued the method that the Brontë children had adopted in childhood, she created a happy ending. So, Agnes marries the curate for whom she has waited so long but in reality, Anne may have mourned her own loss for the remainder of her life.

Another death was also imminent. Within five weeks of Weightman's demise, Anne was called home to the bedside of her dying substitute mother, aunt Branwell. After two weeks of suffering, Elizabeth Branwell died on 29 October 1842 with Anne and Branwell beside her. Charlotte and Emily were summoned home from Brussels but took many days to return.

In these few short weeks Anne lost two of the people whom she may have loved the most. She and Branwell had possibly been their aunt's favourites and they had both loved William Weightman, one as a brother and the other as a possible soulmate. For a while the brother and sister were united in their grief and it is perhaps because of Branwell's distress and his recent dismissal from his latest job on the railways, that Anne took the decision to approach her own employers for a position for him. It was a logical and sensible idea; it would take Branwell away from the public houses of Halifax and Haworth and the friends who encouraged his dissolute lifestyle. It would also give Branwell some purpose and position, and he would be company for Anne at a time when she felt lonely and vulnerable.

Mr and Mrs Robinson were guided by a growing faith in Anne and the way that she was having a positive effect on the children, who had begun to treat her with greater respect and fondness. They approved her brother as sole tutor for Edmund and would have been especially pleased with Branwell's knowledge and abilities, especially in the classics.

Throughout the next eighteen months, life at Thorpe Green improved for Anne as she and her charges grew closer and they became easier to manage. Anne was ever an eyewitness on life and these years at Thorpe Green gave her enormous insight into the lifestyle of the upper classes. Like Charlotte, Anne could acutely observe people and discover how and why they behaved in a certain way. Anne was, in her work as a governess to people of a higher class and wealth than her own, able to spend time in the drawing rooms of the rich and influential without having to take any part. The governess was ideally situated to silently witness the lives of others from a unique perspective. She could be ignored yet see and hear without being dismissed like a servant, or included like the family or visitors.

It was always Anne's belief and intention that fiction should mirror the truth as near as possible and in her novels she relates what she experienced whilst working for the Inghams and the Robinsons. She highlighted them in all their domestic situations when they were separated from the social outside and behaving in ways that they assumed were unobserved. Although Anne is making the point that people behave differently in private than in public, she becomes fully aware that the behaviour of her own family was no better at times than that of anyone else. In fact, it was towards the middle of 1844 when Anne was appalled to discover that her brother and her employer's wife, Lydia, were having an affair. Whilst their liaison was currently a secret from Mr Robinson, it was at times in full view of the servants and staff.

The knowledge of her brother's dalliance must have been a terrible challenge to Anne and left her in an impossible situation. As the affair developed it became more blatant but Anne felt she could neither betray her brother nor stand back and continue to watch it happen. After much heart-searching, Anne decided that her only choice was to resign from her post. Mrs Robinson was probably relieved to see her go but, ironically, the girls were greatly upset and begged her to stay.

Anne had become a mentor and comforter to the three girls even though she disapproved of some of their ideas and behaviour. Each, guided by their mother, was set on making a wealthy marriage where neither love, not even affection, seemed to take priority. This was anathema to Anne, whose romantic views of love and marriage were based on mutual respect and deep emotions. It grieved Anne that they would be wealthy but unhappy, and this certainly proved the case for at least one of them.

Anne had certainly influenced her pupils and to show their appreciation they had recently presented her with a charming puppy named 'Flossie' which Anne kept with her until the end of her life. Watching the adolescence and adulthood of the girls had shown Anne the dangers and pitfalls of children who were pressured into behaving in a gender-set way and who mirrored their parents to maintain a class respectability which was, underneath, far from happy and harmonious.

When Anne wrote *Agnes Grey*, her acute observations of children, their education and their psychological development, forms a major part of the story and is a new area of fiction designed to highlight some of the problems that occur when children are misguided and misinformed. Anne felt that children needed love and discipline in equal measure and within the families where she had worked, this had been sadly lacking. Each child had been both over-indulged and under-developed. The inevitable results worried Anne and her books attempted to show how a child could be moulded and manipulated into almost any shape or personality, depending on their early influences.

Anne returned to Haworth in June 1845 too ashamed to tell even her family what was happening back at Thorpe Green. She had no need to; a month later Branwell himself arrived home in disgrace having been dismissed by an enraged Mr Robinson who had finally realised what had been happening. It was the end of Branwell's career and happiness, and the beginning of his long slide into alcoholism and opium addiction, which would henceforth become the major part of his life. He raged against a fate that had separated him from the woman he loved, and whom, he was convinced, loved him in equal measure. His three sisters witnessed his shocking loss of self-control as he sank into deep depression and substance abuse. Their broken nights and unhappy observations would resurface in their novels.

Around this time, Charlotte 'discovered' a book of Emily's in which she had been writing private poems that were separate from the Gondal verses. Charlotte was deeply affected by the power and musicality of the works and begged Emily to allow them to be published. As indicated, hours of violent argument and stony silences ensued as Emily railed and fretted against her sister for invading her privacy. Despite this extreme reaction, Charlotte was not to be thwarted and had no intention of missing this opportunity to realise one of her burning ambitions: to see her work in print and to judge how the publishing world may deal with any further written works.

It is important to remember that Branwell had, over the years, had many of his poems published in various newspapers and journals; at least a dozen in the *Halifax Guardian*, one, named *Penmaenmawr*, as late as December 1846, and others in the *Yorkshire Gazette*, *The Leeds Intelligencer* and the *Bradford Herald*. He had also embarked on a novel entitled *The Weary are at Rest* based on his love for Mrs Robinson in her role as the neglected wife. Despite this, none of his sisters invited him to share in their publishing ventures, a measure of the distance which had grown between them.

The book of poems was rejected by various publishing houses over the next few months, but after the sisters agreed to pay for the publication, it was accepted by Aylott and Jones of London. The book was published in May 1846 and was favoured by some of the leading critics and the girls were delighted. The fact that the book did not sell was less of an issue to its authors. It was in print, they were, at last, published authors and their anonymity was intact. They were spurred on to each complete works of fiction that they had been engaged with for some time, and they were soon ready to offer their first three novels to the rounds of publishers.

Chapter Fifteen

Agnes Grey

Anne Brontë informs her readers from the very beginning of the purpose and nature of her book. The opening paragraph states that,

> *All true histories contain instruction; though, in some, the treasure may be hard to find, and, when found, so trivial in quantity, that the dry, shrivelled kernel scarcely compensates for the trouble of cracking the nut. Whether this be the case with my history or not, I am hardly competent to judge. I sometimes think it might prove useful to some, and entertaining to others; but the world may judge for itself. Shielded by my own obscurity, and the lapse of years, and a few fictitious names, I do not fear to venture; and will candidly lay before the public what I would not disclose to the most intimate friend.*
>
> (A. Brontë, *Agnes Grey*, 1988) p. 61.

Anne says a lot in this first paragraph. Her story may seem trivial to some readers who do not have the time and patience to discover the inner core of the tale, but she has something to say and she thinks it important and necessary for people to read her story. She wants others to learn from her experiences so that they are more aware and more empathetic to the sufferings of the armies of 'invisible' women who labour for years in the homes of others with little or no recognition or reward. She needs the public to know the 'truth' about suffering, about obscurity, about rejection and about love that is linked with inevitable loss and separation.

The book is clearly based on some of Anne's personal experiences and she tells us here that she has merely altered a few names to protect herself and others. She believes that she has the knowledge and the ability to expose her story to a world that needs to know how different life can be for people with wealth and status and how they may use their privileges for good or evil. She seeks to

A view of Church Street and the narrow lane that led the Brontës past the church and up to the Parsonage in 1820. It remains very much the same today but has more buildings on the North side.

The Parsonage as it looks today. It has different windows and an extra wing was added in the 1880s. However, the main body of the house is still laid out as it was at the time that the Brontë family lived there.

A view of St Michael and All Angels church from the garden of the Parsonage. The church was rebuilt in the 1880s but the lower part of the 1655 tower still remains.

This view of Haworth Moor is taken from Haworth looking west across the moors. It is the scene that the Brontë family would see from the upstairs windows at the back of the Parsonage.

This photograph shows the hallway of the Parsonage. Four rooms and the staircase lead from this area and it still retains its flagstoned floor.

This photograph shows part of the kitchen with a Victorian range. The costume in the corner is from the film, 'To Walk Invisible'.

This picture of the front parlour shows the recently acquired original dining table on which the sisters wrote their novels and many of their poems, sagas and letters. At night the sisters would often walk around the table reciting their work. Eventually only Charlotte was left to continue the ritual.

This room was originally Branwell's bedroom art studio. The room has been recreated using items from the film, 'To Walk Invisible' and with the help of our current artist in residence, Simon Armitage. It reflects Branwell's chaotic lifestyle during his last years before the fire which motivated his father to share his own bedroom with his son to observe and protect him.

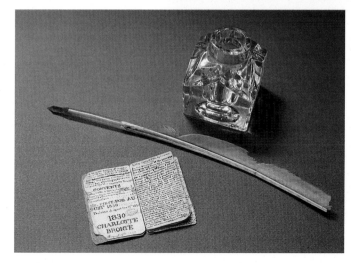

In childhood the Brontës imitated their favourite journal, Blackwood's Edinburgh Magazine, in miniature books with minute script, containing many stories, articles, pictures and poetry.

This is a picture of Top Withins Farm as it looks today; a safe ruin standing high on the moors a few miles above Haworth and beside the well-used Pennine Way. The building goes back to Elizabethan times and many families lived and worked here until the middle of the twentieth century. The location may have been in Emily's mind when she described the moors surrounding Wuthering Heights.

This shot is taken through one of the deep set windows on the south side of Top Withins, overlooking the moors.

Some of the only trees on the moors grow beside the old ruin and bend according to the prevailing west wind.

The view looking back eastwards towards Haworth from Top Withins. A walk often taken by the Brontë children.

Many moorland paths and old drover routes criss-cross the moors and have been used for centuries to carry people and goods safely across these sometimes treacherous routes between Yorkshire and Lancashire.

A photograph of the church from the Parsonage which shows the Sexton's House and part of the school room, which was raised by subscription organised by Patrick Brontë.

Another view of the moors as seen by the families living at Top Withins Farm. The stone window frames and thick walls protected them and their animals from the wildest weather.

Top Withins and Moorland. A view from the valley of Sladen Beck looking up to Top Withins to the north west. The moors are running with streams, springs and becks that nourish the land and the wildlife.

A view of the Parsonage from the graveyard, which surrounds two sides of the house. The picture shows the unhealthy habit of table top graves which prevented the natural decomposition of bodies.

The crowded graveyard which finally had to be closed after the interment of many thousands of bodies, which were the cause of water contamination in the village.

In Memory of

MARIA, WIFE OF THE REV? P.BRONTE A.B.MINISTER OF HAWORTH;
SHE DIED SEPT? 15TH 1821, IN THE 39TH YEAR OF HER AGE.
ALSO OF MARIA, THEIR DAUGHTER; WHO DIED MAY 6TH 1825, IN THE 12TH YEAR OF HER AGE.
ALSO OF ELIZABETH, THEIR DAUGHTER; WHO DIED JUNE 15TH 1825, IN THE 11TH YEAR OF HER AGE.
ALSO OF PATRICK BRANWELL, THEIR SON; WHO DIED SEPT? 24TH 1848, AGED 31 YEARS.
ALSO OF EMILY JANE, THEIR DAUGHTER; WHO DIED DEC? 19TH 1848, AGED 30 YEARS.
ALSO OF ANNE, THEIR DAUGHTER; WHO DIED MAY 28TH 1849, AGED 29 YEARS;
SHE WAS BURIED AT THE OLD CHURCH SCARBOROUGH.
ALSO OF CHARLOTTE, THEIR DAUGHTER; WIFE OF THE REV? A.B.NICHOLLS, B.A.
SHE DIED MARCH 31ST 1855, IN THE 39TH YEAR OF HER AGE.
ALSO OF THE AFORENAMED REV? P.BRONTE A.B.WHO DIED JUNE 7TH 1861, IN THE 85TH YEAR OF
HIS AGE; HAVING BEEN INCUMBENT OF HAWORTH FOR UPWARDS OF 41 YEARS.

THE STING OF DEATH IS SIN, AND THE STRENGTH OF SIN IS THE LAW. BUT THANKS BE TO
GOD, WHICH GIVETH US THE VICTORY THROUGH OUR LORD JESUS CHRIST." 1 COR.XV.56, 57."

The memorial tablet to the Brontë Family. It was erected to commemorate the lives of this remarkable family in the church where the Rev Brontë preached for over forty years and where all of his family worshipped.

IN MEMORY OF
EMILY JANE BRONTE
WHO DIED DEC 19TH 1848,
AGED 30 YEARS.
AND OF
CHARLOTTE BRONTE
BORN APRIL 21ST 1816
DIED MARCH 31ST 1855.

The brass plaque which lies over the crypt in St Michael and All Angels church, where all of the Brontë family, except Anne, lie buried.

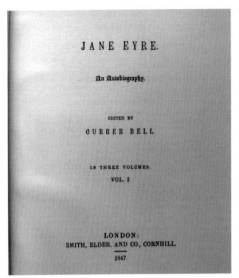

The front piece of Charlotte's famous novel, *Jane Eyre*, which was published in three volumes in 1847.

An assortment of the miniature books containing juvenilia produced by the Brontë children in their formative years and carefully preserved by friends and collectors and now in the care of the Brontë Parsonage Museum.

A selection of the Brontës' seven novels and a few of the many thousands of books written about their lives and works.

reveal the rich at play and expose those who use and abuse their children, their spouses, their employees and their friends and acquaintances.

Anne takes a moral stance when she describes behaviour. She examines truth, honesty, patience, integrity and suffering, but always with hope; the hope that by following one's duty and putting others before oneself, people can overcome their trials and will reap rewards, if not in their earthy existence then in the Heaven described by Christ. Anne's intention is to make the reader aware, and yet it is not a novel of strong and dramatic passages, but a rather simple and quiet story based on observation rather than action. In her Preface to the second edition of *The Tenant of Wildfell Hall*, Anne, in answer to the critics of both her books, states that,

> [W]*hen we have to do with vice and vicious characters, I maintain it is better to depict them as they really are than as they would wish to appear. To represent a bad thing in its least offensive light is doubtless the most agreeable course for a writer of fiction to pursue; but is it the most honest, or the safest? Is it better to reveal the snare and pitfalls of life to the young and thoughtless traveller, or to cover them with branches and flowers? Oh, Reader! If there were less of this delicate concealment of facts – this whispering 'Peace, peace', when there is no peace, there would be less of sin and misery to the young of both sexes who are left to wring their bitter knowledge from experience.*
>
> (A. Brontë, *The Tenant of Wildfell Hall*, 1982) p. 30.

In *Agnes Grey*, she also presents an overview of religion which exposes those who manipulate and falsify their faith. By comparing the kind and compassionate Mr Weston with the sour and hypocritical Mr Hatfield, Anne demonstrates the two poles of Christianity and lets the reader decide which one they should support. Throughout the novel Anne shows the reader, rather than trying to instruct them. She creates scenarios where the reader can judge for themselves what is happening and why. By using her experience Anne can describe scenes that offer an insight into the behaviour of the various children and adults in the two households. This allows the reader to see and understand what the problems are. The reader is expected to be astute enough to realise that the worst characters in the book can directly attribute their difficulties, their attitudes and their opinions to generations of poor parenting based on beliefs that have no moral guidance.

The novel reveals an overall sadness. It is not necessarily about Agnes, although her life is hard and lonely for much of the novel, but that of the child, any child, who even at a very young age, has no sense of purpose or direction and constantly imitates and replicates all the faults and misguidance of his or her parents and carers. Although in her novels Anne is talking about her own experiences as a governess and is, therefore, looking at a particular social class, she is not equating poor parenting as a particular fault of the wealthy. She is instead demonstrating that any child in any culture or social class needs some boundaries and morals if they are to have a chance of growing into valued members of their society. A childhood that promotes selfishness and the importance of possessions and status will not automatically bring happiness, in fact, more likely the opposite. Agnes's attempts to guide her charges and to demonstrate a better way of living where they can make informed choices and live more fulfilling lives is repeatedly thwarted because of social convention and gender stereotyping.

Unlike her sisters, Anne Brontë does not look for meaning in behaviour but rather allows her characters to expose their personalities for the reader to judge. She does not psychologically analyse behaviour but instead, puts it in its social perspective. She tends to show what happens rather than why it does. In this way, she is the observer relaying back to the reader what she has seen and heard and the reader can decide what to do with that information and also decide what is good and right and what is not.

Agnes Grey has more in common with Jane Austen's work than with other Brontë novels. It is domestic and undramatic but it highlights the manners and minutia of everyday life. There are instances when Anne describes a scene with such accuracy and feeling that one can wonder if it is based on personal experience. One such simple yet enormously revealing passage is the following, where Agnes has arrived cold and nervous at the home of her new employers, the Bloomfields, and Mrs Bloomfield watches over her whilst she attempts to eat a cold supper,

> *I really could not converse. In fact, my attention was almost wholly absorbed in my dinner, not from ravenous appetite, but from distress at the toughness of the*

beefsteaks, and the numbness of my hands, almost palsied by their five hours'
exposure to the bitter wind. I would gladly have eaten the potatoes and let the
meat alone, but having got a large piece of the latter on my plate, I could not be
so impolite as to leave it; so, after many awkward and unsuccessful attempts to
cut it with the knife, or tear it with the fork, or pull it asunder between them,
sensible that the awful lady was a spectator to the whole transaction, I at last
desperately grasped the knife and fork in my fists, like a child of two years old,
and fell to work with all the little strength I possessed.

(A. Brontë, *Agnes Grey*, 1988) pp. 74–75.

Anne does not have to show the reader this scene but it demonstrates the realism and the acute observations that she uses to impart information. The reader can feel Agnes's embarrassment; can blush as she is watched in all her incompetence by the overpowering Mrs Bloomfield, the very person she had hoped to impress. It is in these short, colourful domestic scenes that Anne is so accomplished as a writer.

Although it is tempting to see some of the work as autobiographical, the reader is being shown in Agnes a young, rather childish woman who is inferior to Anne Brontë in knowledge and experience. Agnes is not even the main interest of the story. The whole idea is that the reader is seeing things through her eyes as if they were there at the time. Agnes is the conduit standing between the characters and the reader. The role of the governess allowed this 'fly on the wall' documentary and from her unique position Agnes can narrate the story, often with no personal comment. The story focuses especially on the children of the Bloomfield and Murray families and are based on Anne's experiences in her two employment situations in the homes of the Inghams and later, the Robinsons. Through the mouthpiece of Agnes Grey, Anne can expose the character of the children she had to deal with and the attitudes of their parents.

The behaviour of the Bloomfield children is shocking and the encouragement by their parents to indulge in violence is especially appalling. The children spit, kick and torture their way through three chapters of the novel, yet the reader is presented with behaviour which is fully condoned by their parents and this understates the actual horror that is being described. Killing and torturing young birds in their nest is not viewed as offensive. The 7-year-old Tom Bloomfield tells Agnes that,

Papa knows how I treat them, and he never blames me for it: he says it is just what he used to do when he was a boy. Last summer, he gave me a nest full of young sparrows, and he saw me pulling off their legs and wings and heads, and never said anything; except that they were nasty things and I must not let them soil my trousers: and Uncle Robson was there too, and he laughed, and said I was a fine boy.

(A. Brontë, Agnes Grey, 1988) p. 78.

This level of cruelty is hard to reconcile even with the child's age and ignorance, but it is the pleasure and encouragement by the adults which the boy is innocently exposing. It is also what Anne Brontë is hoping her readers will recognise and condemn. The Brontë sisters believed that all living things were God's creation and deserved the same care and respect as people. Anne shows that children can be cruel but that this trait can and should be discouraged and be replaced with a sound moral responsibility to all creatures. By using this seemingly small incident, which some people may see as children just messing around and experimenting, Anne exposes something far more sinister and perverse.

The Murray family, Agnes's next engagement, are older than the Bloomfield children and Agnes is expecting a higher standard of both morals and behaviour. These children are less violent but equally obnoxious and badly behaved. Again, the parents take little or no role in their moral guidance and when they do concern themselves with their children, it is to encourage them to be as frivolous and shallow as themselves.

Rosalie Murray, the eldest of the Murray children, has no thoughts outside of her mother's intent to see her married to the richest and most powerful man she can find. When Rosalie hears that Agnes's sister is to be married, her comments are a summing up of her attitude towards men and marriage. In an exchange with Agnes she asks,

> '*Who is she to be married to?*'
> '*To Mr Richardson, the vicar of a neighbouring parish.*'
> '*Is he rich?*'
> '*No – only comfortable.*'
> '*Is he handsome?*'
> '*No – only decent.*'

'Young?'
'No – only middling.'
'O mercy! What a wretch!'

(A. Brontë, *Agnes Grey*, 1988) p. 131.

Rosalie has her head filled with romantic notions of handsome wealthy men and little or no interest in love and respect. Agnes knows that this will lead to Rosalie's unhappiness but is helpless to stop the cycle of loveless marriages. As predicted, Rosalie's marriage is a sham and she is seen eventually as unable to express love, even to her own child, of whom she is already jealous. She asks Agnes,

What pleasure can I have in seeing a girl grow up to eclipse me, and enjoy those pleasures that I am forever debarred from? ...it is only a child: and I can't centre all my hopes in a child; that is only one degree better than devoting one's self to a dog. And for all the wisdom and goodness you have been trying to instil into me – that is all very right and proper I dare say, and if I were some twenty years older, I might fructify by it: but people must enjoy themselves when they are young: and if others won't let them – why, they must hate them for it!

(A. Brontë, *Agnes Grey*, 1988) p. 238.

The exposure of the cruelty and sadness of children and childhood is possibly Anne's greatest achievement in this work. Children were not, and had not, been considered as particular subjects for novels and very little heed was paid to their needs or their status, in fact they mostly had no status. Whilst the children in this novel are mostly bad mannered, disruptive and selfish, Agnes's acute observation of them demonstrates all the reasons why. *Agnes Grey* is a cautionary tale on how not to treat young children and the monsters that they can become without careful training. The Victorian adage that children should be seen and not heard was a way of denying children their rights, but also of pretending that they were someone else's problem. That someone else could be the teacher, the governess, the servants, the employees, the nursemaids or anyone with whom they came into contact. The novel shows that in Anne's experience, when the parents were involved, and in these times the higher up the social scale the more distanced children were usually kept from their parents, there was little positive or quality influence over them.

This parental separation contained an acute lack of care for the physical and psychological welfare of the child and Anne goes a long way to expose the harm that adults were consciously, or unconsciously, inflicting on their children and wards. Alongside this theme, Anne further highlights the solitary and insidious role of the governess. She can do little to remedy the situation where she finds children who need moral and social guidance. Without the support of the adults in the family the governess can only watch and hope that her limited discipline and attempts to show kindness, will eventually produce results.

In this first novel, Anne uses poetic license to bring about a happy ending for Agnes when she is reunited with Mr Weston and they are married. She marries the only man suitable for her, a clergyman, but if neither he nor a teacher had been available, she would most likely have had to remain a spinster. Anne quietly expresses in her tale an undercurrent of social dysfunction and a lack of female choices and rights. By the time she moves on to her next novel she has fully got to grips with her subject and is far more ready and able to step confidently out on to the political and social platform.

Chapter Sixteen

The Tenant of Wildfell Hall

As noted, Branwell Brontë's life became more and more unhappy following the end of his affair with Lydia Robinson and his sisters had to observe much of his painful reaction. During this time, they were all writing and in June 1848 Acton Bell's novel, *The Tenant of Wildfell Hall*, was published, less than three months before Branwell succumbed to the effects of tuberculosis, alcohol and opium.

Having been forced to observe Branwell's behaviour and being often called upon to assist him in his daily activities during the last months of his life, it is understandable that his sisters were horrified and disgusted by his degeneration. Branwell appeared to have no self-control. His addictions had taken a stranglehold and his constant bemoaning of the loss of Mrs Robinson must have pushed the efforts of anyone trying to help him to the limits. By now creditors were a regular feature at the Parsonage door as Branwell owed substantial amounts of money to many people. He had sunk to exhorting money from friends and family but was unable to meet his debts.

In a household where the other adults all had a degree of faith in God and who lived by a strict moral code, Branwell's behaviour was intolerable. He had become an embarrassment to everyone and it was more acute because of his early promise of great intellect and talent. Patrick must have felt especially for his son and deeply mourned the loss of his bright and optimistic boy and the wretch he had become. Branwell was now, in every way, the direct opposite of his father, physically, emotionally and morally.

Yet one could argue that this did not follow the pattern of a child ignored or undisciplined. Branwell's behaviour was not born of a lack of love and care. He had been both morally tutored and allowed to freely develop his talents. In *The Tenant of Wildfell Hall,* Anne identifies three major areas where the raising of a boy or young man can go wrong.

The first is if his needs and wants are raised above those of his female family members, in other words where he is spoilt or over indulged, and it can be argued that Branwell's needs and his talents and desires were placed, at times, above those of his sisters purely because he was male. Yet, in the case of the Brontës, it is true to say that Patrick was very liberal in the amount of time, money and care which he spent on all of his children and this was unusual. Anne also shows that over-indulgence can include encouragement in, and abuse of, any substance which alters the mind and behaviour. The second area is the social expectations of males at that time. Middle-class boys were reared to be educated and go out into the world and create wealth which they then passed on to their heirs in an unending cycle. It was the natural order. Anne's argument was that this male dominance not only suppressed the intelligent and creative female, but it gave men a higher status which they naturally enjoyed and did not want to relinquish. It made them believe themselves to be superior human beings. Anne demonstrates that this superiority allowed men to become selfish and self-indulgent. The men in her novels did not see themselves as answerable to wives, females or children, and this caused them to turn a blind eye to their sufferings. Lastly, and perhaps most importantly, Anne viewed the lack of moral guidance, especially when combined with some or all of the above, as a fatal flaw which could only lead to corruption.

Anne saw in Branwell the promise of youth turned upside down because he could not meet the expectations placed upon him and he did not have the self-discipline or confidence to hold down work. He broke at least five of the Ten Commandments, namely: 'thou shalt keep the Sabbath Day holy' 'thou shalt not covet thy neighbour's wife', 'honour thy father and thy mother', 'thou shalt have only one God', and 'Thou shalt not commit adultery'. He indulged in alcohol and opium which affected his ability to behave in a moral, social and caring manner. He had, in effect, turned away from all that he had been taught and all that his family believed in.

In many ways, Branwell was the man who wished to remain a child. The fantasy world of his childhood was immense and overpowering, but when he had to face the reality of growing up, of working for his keep and fulfilling his obligations, he was unable to rise to the demands. He was a man who could not face the reality of adulthood or deal well with adult relationships. By carrying all the splendour and escapism of his early imagination into his adult life he was unprepared and unrealistic in his view of reality and therefore almost bound to fail.

Branwell's spectacular failure was certainly meat to his sister's novels but there is much more to their stories than Branwell's downfall. Anne, especially, struggled to overcome the religious fervour of the Calvinists and those members of the church who believed in eternal damnation for all sinners. Anne dearly wanted to believe that no matter how dissolute or violent her brother behaved, and no matter how much he hurt his family, he would eventually repent and be accepted by God. This doctrine of universal salvation was Anne's greatest hope and it is what she wishes for in her fictional character Arthur Huntingdon.

In her new novel, Anne examined some of Branwell's behaviour in the portrayal of Arthur Huntingdon and the effect that his dissolute lifestyle had on his wife and child. Huntingdon was wealthy but a gambler who drank and womanised. He was cruel to his wife and he tried to bend his young son's natural kind and caring nature so that he would become as nasty and evil as his father. (This is reminiscent of Heathcliff in *Wuthering Heights* where he also tries to brutalise young Hareton to make him grow as twisted and violent as his father, Hindley.) Whilst Huntingdon is not Branwell, many of his traits can be compared to Branwell's especially his alcohol addiction and his anger and violence towards his family.

Anne allows Arthur Huntingdon to fall but then to eventually repent and allow his wife to nurse him in his final weeks. Helen is shown as a woman who can forgive and who is willing to accept and acknowledge her husband's failures whilst also recognising that he is the father of her son. Helen wants Arthur to show repentance and display the moral characteristics that her son will inherit. Apparently, on his deathbed, Branwell did repent his wasted life and his family were comforted in the belief that he would enter heaven and be reunited with his mother and sisters.

Anne's new novel brought mass disapproval from the critics and was deemed unfit for the eyes of young ladies with its, 'profane expressions, inconceivable coarse language and revolting scenes and descriptions by which its pages are disfigured' (Spencer, 2000) p. 13 (from *Sharpe's London Magazine*, August 1848).

Surprisingly, one of the books greatest critics was Charlotte Brontë, who suggested that its author was unqualified to handle the subject matter. She felt that Anne had chosen the wrong subject and that she could not have picked anything so far from her own nature and sensibilities. Charlotte was attempting to defend the accusations of coarseness and to deflect her own memories of Branwell's drunkenness. Charlotte still viewed Anne as the little sister and the one least likely to succeed. She may have been right to say that the novel broke Anne's health and that its content did not reflect the characteristics of its author, but Charlotte failed to understand Anne's experience as a governess or appreciate the lessons Anne had learned whilst silently watching the lives of those around her, including her own brother. It is ironic that Charlotte was unable to separate the author from her story and failed to appreciate that Anne had done what she herself was doing. By turning life as she observed and experienced it into literature, Anne was remarkable in her ability to show human frailty and she needed only to be an observer, not an active participant, to understand the extremes of human behaviour. This indicates how much of Charlotte's own writing was autobiographical and how far she failed to realise that both of her sisters could step away from their characters and their stories to examine the deep psychological effects of social interaction.

Anne was happy to defend herself against the critics and once again stated that she was merely telling the truth and saw her novel as a warning; a parable that could assist others from falling into the paths of evil. She wrote a similar defence to the one she had written for *Agnes Grey*, insisting that,

> *I know that such characters do exist, and if I have warned one rash youth from following in their steps, or prevented one thoughtless girl from falling into the very natural error of my heroine, the book has not been written in vain.*
>
> (A. Brontë, *The Tenant of Wildfell Hall*, 1982) p. 30.

In many ways Anne appears unaware that, as with Emily, her writing may be seen as shocking and coarse. She has witnessed these people and their behaviours and so she wants to truthfully record it. If it shocks others who have a different point of view, or who simply do not believe that people are so violent and immoral in their own drawing rooms, then Anne insists the opposite. She did not realise that by writing about such characters she was indirectly suggesting that *she* was coarse and lewd and that the critics are condemning her as much as her writing. Again, as in *Agnes Grey*, Anne relays the story for the reader to interpret as they see fit. She cleverly states her case but one does not see Helen Huntingdon as Anne, they are two distinct characters; again, Helen is Anne's mouthpiece, just as Agnes was.

The central character and purpose of the novel is the downfall and death of Arthur Huntingdon and it is his behaviour which dictates the actions of the other individuals. Anne shows that he causes Helen's dilemma and the loss of his wife and child, he causes the loss of his fortune and his property and worst of all he may lose Christian forgiveness. In a similar way to *Wuthering Heights* and possibly more so, Anne can set 'the monstrous in the ordinary'. She relates her story of domesticity and rural, gentle farming life against the contents of Helen's journal which describe the horrors of her married life. There is again a similarity with Jane Austen; an ability to describe the most extraordinary idiosyncrasies and immoral behaviours, yet hide it in the ordinary and the domestic in a way that is not always apparent on first reading.

One can argue that Jane Austen did not display the addict, the drunkard and the violence as obviously as in Anne's work; in fact it was often seen as 'normal' and therefore more shocking. Jane Austen is subtle and clever and uses humour and satire to state her case. Anne is more straightforward and less sophisticated as a writer, but she is just as capable of placing 'the monstrous in the ordinary, whereby making it more monstrous and less ordinary' (Daiches, 1965).

The tenant of *The Tenant of Wildfell Hall*, is Helen Huntingdon, a woman who had been duped into falling in love with a wastrel who, after their marriage, sank into the depravations of many of the men of his class who had the time, money and opportunity to waste their wealth on gambling, drinking and womanising. When Helen sees that her husband, and her mother-in-law, accepts this behaviour as part of the male role, and that they wish her son to grow up in a similar dissolute fashion, she runs away and hides herself and her child in a different part of the country where she tries to support herself, anonymously, as an artist. The book contains Helen's diary which relates the history of her marriage and explains why she had to leave. The main theme of the novel exposes the abuse that husbands and fathers can inflict on their wives and children and that their behaviour is sanctioned by the law and upheld by the class and gender structure of society.

Helen is eventually courted by a local gentleman farmer, Gilbert Markham, who believes her to be a widow, 'Mrs Graham', and much of the novel examines his gradually coming to see her as the woman she really is, the dispossessed and fugitive escapee from a violent marriage. In a similar role to Lockwood in *Wuthering Heights*, who never grasps the concept of reality because of his social expectations and misconceptions, Markham must go through various trials before he can understand Helen's position and cast off his own self-delusions and superior attitude. Both Arthur Huntingdon and Gilbert Markham are shown as the products of a male-dominated social structure that has created men who, in their own way, can be both violent and cruel and both have the concept of ownership whether it is their land, their money, or their female relatives.

Anne does not just target Arthur Huntingdon, although he is the main protagonist and the most cruelly excessive. Markham's attack on Lawrence, who unbeknownst to him is Helen's brother, is particularly brutal and unprovoked. It is the attack of a man who has lost self-control through jealousy and misunderstanding but it is as inexcusable as much of Huntingdon's behaviour.

In this way, Anne is exposing more than just a straightforward equation of male debauchery equalling female oppression. She is using a whole range of male behaviours from the subtle dialogue between brother and sister, to the all-out assault, to show that most men value power and dominance before equality. Gilbert Markham is not as debauched as Arthur Huntingdon but he has many traits that are unattractive and narcissistic. Anne was highlighting that everyone makes bad decisions and behaves unreasonably at times, whether male or female. Her mission was to expose the hurt and fear caused when actions take place without regard to others and without moral and social boundaries. This is not a straightforward male versus female argument; Arthur's mother is as vicious and uncaring as her son. It is a matter of each gender understanding the needs and wants of the other and showing respect and tolerance through each generation. In her novel, Anne is insisting that women are equal to men and should be shown all the respect and legal protection given to their male counterparts, but also that the female is not perfect and nor is she better than the male.

Anne showed that despite the law and social convention, there was a cause and a reason why a woman should be allowed to leave a husband who was unable to care for her and cherish her and their children, in the way that perhaps challenged the Christian marriage vows which insisted that a wife should, 'Love, Honour and Obey'. For Anne, any relationship that was not based on mutual respect and admiration was doomed. As she watched her brother's fall it was even more obvious to her that illicit love, immoral behaviour and the betrayal of trust could only bring heartbreak.

Published during the first twenty years of Queen Victoria's reign, *The Tenant of Wildfell Hall* highlighted some of the secrecy and horror that took place behind the façade of Victorian gentility. It exposed the violence borne of suppression and the hidden. In his essay on 'The Uncanny' (Freud, 1917–19), Sigmund Freud described the German words, 'heimlich' and 'unheimlich', and uncovered a linear association where 'heimlich' the German for homely and familiar can be drawn out through various interpretations until the homely and familiar become the opposite, the secret and the unfamiliar. He associated the homely with being part of a withdrawal from external affairs, of things hidden behind closed doors and away from the eyes of the crowd.

I suggest that what one witnesses in *The Tenant of Wildfell Hall* is Anne Brontë's attempt to lift the veil of Victorian middle-class propriety and expose some of the hidden secrets and lies that lay behind its carefully maintained social structure. The Victorian home was not necessarily a place of civilised respect; it could be a place of extreme violence and cruelty and it was invariably the wives and children who suffered. Even worse, those who suffered had no outlet or escape, no law to protect them and no wealth or employment to rely on. They were helpless, and as such were victims of a system that held them in little or no regard unless they had a husband, father or brother who could shelter and protect them. Until changes in the law, which did not occur until 1891, wives and children were the legal property of their husbands or fathers.

In the character of Helen Huntingdon, Anne creates a modern woman who is intelligent and talented but has the misfortune to fall in love with a man who flattered and courted her when she was vulnerable and naïve. She believed that he would settle into marriage and honour and love her. Helen is, in some respects, everywoman; she is betrayed but is also misguided in her own choices. She makes wrong decisions and must pay the price for them. She is vaguely aware of her husband's faults but misguidedly believes that she will be able to influence him and change his ways. Helen has an honesty and a morality which never wavers. She has made, and continues to make, mistakes, but she is self-aware and knows right from wrong.

Anne demonstrates how women can easily fall into a trap from which they are unable to escape. The law on marriage was absolute, but Anne demonstrates how no-one should expect their partner to be anything less than faithful and mature. It is Huntingdon's choice to behave in the way he does, certainly at first. Once he has become addicted to drink, he is, as all addicts are, a slave to this vice and eventually no longer able to alter his behaviour, even should he wish to do so. This was Branwell's dilemma and the dilemma of all who are caught in the vortex of addiction. In Branwell's case it was the culmination of a ruined love affair that was amoral and should never have been allowed to blossom. For Arthur Huntingdon, it was the result of a lifestyle passed from father to son in the conviction that it was manly and necessary to behave as the dominant and aggressive alpha male.

Anne is one of the first writers to dare to bring these issues to the fore and it is little wonder that the critics found her work highly disturbing, almost anarchistic, in its suggestion that women should rebel against men whom they were unable or unwilling to obey. It is ironic that in the twenty-first century, any woman who deliberately stays with a man who has used and abused her and her children would be vilified.

Once again Anne defended her work against her critics and in her preface to the second edition of her novel she wrote,

> *I wished to tell the truth, for truth always conveys its own moral to those who are able to receive it. But as the priceless treasure too frequently hides at the bottom of a well, it needs some courage to dive for it, especially as he that does so will be likely to incur more scorn and obloquy for the mud and water into which he has ventured to plunge, than thanks for the jewel he procures...if I can gain the public ear at all, I would rather whisper a few wholesome truths therein than much soft nonsense.*
>
> (A. Brontë, *The Tenant of Wildfell Hall*, 1982) p. 29.

It is thanks to the courage of writers like Anne Brontë, who were prepared to challenge the status quo, that the lives of women gradually improved. In *The Tenant of Wildfell Hall* and in *Agnes Grey*, Anne subverts the class values that promote violence and injustice under the guise of propriety. Anne does more than just expose the 'monstrous in the ordinary', she actually employs the very same layering of monotony over monstrosity in her novel-writing to turn this sinister trope of the middle class back upon itself.

What happened in these middle–class households? The culture was to keep up appearances and to cover atrocity with banality. Anne exposed this hypocrisy by fictionalising her real experience of it. Yet she did more than just this. Anne recreated banality within the text itself. She hid her own outrage between the predictably straight lines of her unembellished narrative. She wrote novels that claim only to instruct yet simultaneously, silently, she appals her reader. In *Agnes Grey* particularly, Anne masquerades just like the ordinary 'normal' family does. She constructs a conformist vehicle in which to cover her disgust just as the middle classes constructed a palatable exterior to hide their profanities. Anne turns the sinister method of the monster on the monster itself and thus gives it unprecedented exposure. Ultimately, the success of her secret agenda as an author means that the perpetrator's own clandestine behaviour implodes. Semi-invisible, seemingly obedient, altogether unambiguous, the governess exploits her anonymity to the full.

Chapter Seventeen

'The poor little woman of genius'

In a letter of March 1853, the distinguished author, William Makepeace Thackeray described Charlotte Brontë in the above quote and went on to say,

> *... but you see she is a little bit of a creature without a pennyworth of good looks, thirty years old, I should think, buried in the country, and eating up her own heart there, and no Tomkins will come ... a noble heart longing to mate itself and destined to wither away into old maidenhood with no chance to fulfil the burning desire.*
>
> (Thackeray, 1974) pp. 196–7.

Harsh as Thackeray's description appears it was sadly, mostly accurate. Charlotte was the smallest and the plainest of the sisters and regarded herself as ugly. On writing *Jane Eyre*, she expressed the desire to write of someone as plain and insignificant as herself. This was an important part of Charlotte's worldview and part of her anger and dissatisfaction with the gender issues she wrote about. She constantly asks why the rich and beautiful are recognised and fêted whilst the ugly and poor are dismissed as unworthy or, at worse, invisible. It is a constant theme of her novels and she continually examines the reasoning behind it. It appears to both Charlotte and to her heroines that education, honesty and stoicism are paramount, and these are lasting attributes that cannot alter with the vagaries of time and fortune.

Critics and scholars have tried for nearly 200 years to analyse and understand the Brontës' lives and works, and too often have managed to mix up the two. Thackeray thought that he knew Charlotte as much through her works as in his meetings with her and many critics have followed this lead. Elizabeth Gaskell's biography of Charlotte was written as much to defend her friend from the critics as to explore the biography of her life. Hundreds of biographers have followed these early writers but one would expect that those who met and knew the Brontës would have a much better knowledge and understanding of them. This has not always been the case. Eyewitness accounts of their lives have been prejudiced or out of context and sometimes told more about the writer or teller than about their subject. Many myths about their lives still abound. Modern researchers and academics have looked more to the Brontës letters, essays and diary papers to gain insight into their lives and thoughts and then examined their books for the historical and social fiction which was based on their experiences. The enormous thirteen-year research on their lives by Dr Juliet Barker, published in 1994 and revised in 2010, has given scholars the most comprehensive study to date.

Current knowledge of the Brontës comes from detailed research done, especially by Juliet Barker and Margaret Smith, on the hundreds of letters that formed Charlotte and Ellen's correspondence over their twenty-five-year friendship, and Christine Alexander's work on the Brontë juvenilia. There are many others. The Brontë letters are possibly the most accurate records of their daily lives. It is always dangerous to assume autobiography in novels, even when there appears to be obvious parallels with the author. The Brontës did not write autobiographies, but they did write stories based on people and events of which they had both knowledge and experience. Furthermore, they could convey their own beliefs and emotions into their work as part of the plot and characterisation.

We do know from Charlotte's letters to Ellen, and from Ellen's own description of her friend, that Charlotte was concerned at her lack of good looks and sophistication, but we also know that whilst this is a theme of her work, she did not let her appearance interfere with her ambitions. It may, in fact, have been the spur that caused her to rise and demonstrate against the unfairness of a world that valued false attributes.

We do know that when she found herself in the role of eldest child, Charlotte responded with seriousness and fortitude. This may have led to a certain superiority over her remaining sisters and at times a rather dismissive attitude towards their talents and needs. She was always the loved and much loving sister, but she was very much the person who wanted to be in charge. In childhood, Branwell also wanted to dominate and the two often sparred as each fought for pole position. In her letters one sees the Charlotte who thought she knew what was best for herself and for those around her, and was not afraid to say so. This self-confidence and self-control in her writing was not always to her benefit and it could make her stubborn and unsympathetic to the needs and feelings of others. At times, she was very rude to Ellen and quite dismissive of her friend's illnesses or unhappiness. Charlotte was always very hard on herself and expected others to control their behaviour and their emotions to the same extent that she did. Her looks and her small stature, her short-sightedness and her shyness, linked sometimes to a lack of empathy and a superior attitude did not make her attractive to many, but she had some remarkable talents and abilities.

In childhood, whilst aligning herself with Branwell in particular, the 7-year-old Charlotte shouldered the role of eldest child with some mental and physical stress. Her father and aunt now relied on her and expected far more of her than she was possibly able to give. Charlotte always took her responsibilities seriously and had amazing strength of character and durability even under the most extreme circumstances. This did take its toll on her health and throughout her life she had long periods of depression and sickness with repeated headaches, possibly migraine, and various debilitating aches and pains. It is impossible to know when and how the Brontë children all became infected with the Tuberculosis virus. It was possibly brought home by the girls from the Clergy Daughters' School, or it may have been from more local sources. Certainly, repeated infections of the lungs, coughs, asthma, influenza and bronchitis plagued them all throughout their teens and adulthood and weakened their systems and affected their mood. Charlotte especially suffered agonies from toothache and also repeated sick headaches possibly linked to her extreme myopia.

Despite these afflictions, Charlotte was ambitious and could be strong when necessary. It was Charlotte who encouraged her siblings to write and to study and it was she who took studying to enormous lengths to fit herself as a teacher and governess. Charlotte was undoubtedly highly intelligent and very studious. Her poor eyesight was a burden but did not stop her from spending hours poring over newspapers, letters and books. Like her siblings, she learnt to play the piano but had to stop when it became too difficult for her to read the music. Alternatively, she excelled at drawing and here her poor sight influenced her ability to produce delicate and intricate copies and miniatures as she peered closely at her subject.

Charlotte once wrote to Ellen that she just wanted to write. Writing was lifeblood to her and what had been an escape route for her and her siblings in childhood evolved into a need to express herself and examine the world through written language. Like Anne, she wished to enlighten and educate her readers. Charlotte wanted to tell the truth as she saw it, based on her own experiences. It was also cathartic and helped Charlotte to understand the world and her experiences in it. For years, the children had written their fantasy tales and poetry and Charlotte felt that they had the talents to get their work into print, just as their father had before them. She even wrote to the poet Southey, asking for his advice and sending examples of her work. His reply, as noted, was a resounding negative when he told her that, 'Literature cannot be the business of a woman's life…'.

Fortunately, Charlotte did not follow his advice, but his words have echoed down the centuries from many men who went before and after him. Women had enough to do with their husbands, families and domestic chores. It was felt that they were not fitted or educated enough to express their views in print.

Like her sisters, and all other women of their social class, Charlotte's choices in adulthood were very limited. The choice was basically between marriage, teaching, becoming a governess or being a lady's companion. Charlotte probably doubted her ability to attract a husband. Whilst she was a believer in romantic love and possibly longed for it she had no delusions about her looks and position. Despite this she received four marriage proposals!

Charlotte had tried teaching when she was invited back to Roe Head School by Miss Wooler but hated it and especially resented the lack of time she had to herself or to spend on her own writing and musing. Children never seem to have attracted Charlotte in the way that Anne had such a fondness for them. Charlotte possibly had little patience with children and her own childhood was so different from the pupils she had to teach that she found it hard to empathise with their needs.

In 1839, when Charlotte was 23 years old, she took temporary work as a governess. This was with the Sedgwick family at Stonegappe and she soon realised that it was not anything like she had imagined. It is hard to know what Charlotte had expected, but it confirmed her belief that children annoyed her rather than provided a pleasure or a challenge. Her employers found Charlotte to be awkward and unhelpful, whilst Charlotte found them to be proud and unsympathetic. When Charlotte was unhappy or disillusioned she often became ill and it is possible that this was why she was unable to carry out her duties and soon left. For a while the Brontë family were together and that Christmas was a pleasant one. The weeks that followed were some of their happiest times with the help of the ever-eager William Weightman to amuse them.

In May, possibly because Charlotte too had fallen under the spell of the Rev. Weightman, she felt obliged to warn Ellen, who was currently being courted by a clergyman, that she must only marry a man whom she respected. Whilst Charlotte may have harboured the idea of a passionate and romantic love, her head ruled her emotions and she was probably resigned to the fact that romantic love was not likely to be a part of her life.

By March 1841 Charlotte had taken the position of governess to the White family of Upperwood House, Rawdon, where she had charge of two of their children, Sarah, aged 8 and Joshua, aged 6. Whilst Charlotte tried to make this placement work, the hours were long and the amount of sewing she had to do weakened her already damaged eyesight. Once again, she became thoroughly miserable and after nine months she gave her notice.

These attempts to gain and keep work say something about Charlotte's needs and characteristics. She was aware of the necessity to contribute to the family financially but realised that this was work for which she was ill-fitted. She had neither the patience nor the tenacity of her sister Anne. Charlotte could display anger and frustration in a way that Anne never did. Charlotte could be sharp and dismissive whereas Anne was kind and considerate. Anne liked children, Charlotte did not. Anne was endlessly selfless whereas Charlotte's ambition and drive meant that she could and would, at times, put her own needs before those of others.

This became evident when, in the September of 1841 and whilst still a governess, Charlotte wrote to her aunt with the proposal that the sisters should open their own school and that she and Emily should go to a good finishing school on the continent where they could refine their education and accomplishments. Charlotte argued that this was a necessary move which would increase their chances of successfully teaching in their own establishment. They could then all work and live together without ever having to go out into other people's houses again. This was Charlotte's idea and was discussed with her sisters but she was the driving force behind the scheme and it was she who decided what, where, when and if it would take place.

The idea to open their own school was a good one although it lacked the possibility of an initial large investment. Had it been realised, it would have given them both commitment and freedom as they would share the work and have time to spend on their own simple pleasures in much the same way as the Wooler sisters had at Roe Head. They would be together in close harmony and would be providing for themselves. It was Charlotte, influenced by Mary and Martha Taylor's attendance at an expensive finishing school in Brussels, who saw the opportunity of studying abroad as part of fulfilling some of her own ambitions to seek new experiences and to travel.

The circumstances surrounding the Brussels venture and the time spent there are important because two of Charlotte's novels are set in the city and examine her experiences there. Both *The Professor* and *Villette*, explore the contrast between life in Belgium and the Belgians with their British counterparts. On a much deeper level, *Villette* explores the social and psychological effects of being abroad and away from the familiar, on the life of a lonely and isolated young woman.

Aunt Branwell must have received Charlotte's letter with misgivings. To fund the Brussels project, Charlotte asked her aunt for around £50, a substantial sum at that time. After such a long period of time it is difficult to know why Charlotte pushed so hard to go abroad. She was certainly the driving force, for only a few weeks before, Miss Wooler had offered her own school to Charlotte; a most generous proposal that would have given the Brontë girls an excellent start. This proposition would have resolved most, if not all, of the sisters' problems and established them as teachers with the lease of a decent property. It is hard to understand why they did not grasp this kind offer with alacrity. One suspects that it could only be Charlotte's sudden and new idea of copying the Taylor's lead and fulfilling her own ambitions that caused Miss Wooler's generous offer to be rejected.

To undertake a journey from Haworth to Brussels in February 1842 was no easy feat. It shows how determined and pioneering Charlotte was in her drive and ambition and belies the myth, first suggested by Mrs Gaskell, that they were isolated spinsters in a backwater of the Yorkshire countryside. The Brontës were active, intelligent and determined young women with modern ideas and exceptional courage. This was a difficult journey to a foreign and unknown place but both sisters, whatever their misgiving, took up the challenge.

It is also notable that both their aunt and their father had the confidence in the girls to support this scheme. Patrick, with his liberal views on education and his eagerness to assist and accompany his daughters had encouraged them on this venture with little or no thought to his own safety and health en route. He was now a 64-year-old man with failing eyesight and would have had to make the long trek back home on his own. It was a remarkable accomplishment for him and tells us a lot about his dedication and commitment to his family. Aunt Branwell financed the scheme which encouraged her nieces to set out on this venture. Charlotte showed that she was not content to sit at home or in other people's drawing rooms, she wanted experiences and that journey to Brussels, despite sea sickness, must have delighted her.

Charlotte and Emily lived and studied at the Pensionnat for the next nine months and they worked hard and gained the approval of the master, Monsieur Heger, a strict but highly accomplished teacher who urged the English girls to speak and write in French. Their language skills improved enormously and their teacher was very struck by their abilities. Monsieur Heger had been married to his wife for some years and they had five children. Madame Heger owned the school and the boy's academy adjoining it where her husband taught for most of the time. In a letter to Ellen, Charlotte described her 'master' as,

[A] *man of power as to mind, but very choleric and irritable in temperament; a little black ugly being, with a face that varies in expression. Sometimes he borrows the lineaments of an insane tomcat, sometimes those of a delirious hyena; occasionally, but very seldom, he discards these perilous attractions and assumes an air not above 100 degrees removed from...the mild and gentlemanlike... Emily and he do not draw well together.* (Palmer, 2002) p. 54.

Despite her description this small, dark, married man had the most profound and lasting effect on Charlotte, which altered her thoughts and actions for many years. Monsieur Heger recognised in Charlotte an intelligent woman who loved to learn. He was an intelligent man who loved to teach and he must have found, in both sisters, minds ripe and eager to absorb knowledge. Emily he found difficult because she was very reserved and her shyness meant that she made no efforts to mix with the other pupils, but he recognised her qualities, describing her some years later in the following words,

She should have been a man – a great navigator. Her powerful reason would have deduced new spheres of discovery from the knowledge of the old; and her strong imperious will would never have been daunted by opposition or difficulty; never have given way but with life.

(J.R.V. Barker, 2010) p. 460.

With regard to Monsieur Heger's opinion on Charlotte, we do not have a direct description. They argued and they bantered, their opinions and ideas often in dispute, but Charlotte learnt a great deal from him both directly and indirectly. They appear to have recognised qualities in each other which drew them together intellectually and, as far as Monsieur Heger was concerned, this was their only and entire relationship. Charlotte was soon captivated by this man who could reason and argue with her on an equal footing and who encouraged her studies whilst aiding and advising her progress.

Both Charlotte and Emily developed and progressed during their stay in Brussels, especially in French, German and Music. Emily was teaching music to some of the younger girls, although she hated the chore, and Charlotte was giving lessons in French. It was only a letter from home advising them of their aunt's terminal illness that necessitated their early return to Haworth in November 1842.

Once more the two sisters underwent the long and hazardous journey, but they carried a letter with them from Monsieur Heger to their father which reveals a great deal about their time there and his opinion of the sisters. The two men had never met as Monsieur Heger had been away when Patrick had taken his daughters to Brussels. In a touching and affectionate letter Monsieur Heger wrote,

I have not the honour of knowing you personally and yet I have a feeling of profound admiration for you, for in judging the father of a family by his children one cannot be mistaken and in this respect the education and sentiments that we have found in your daughters can only give us a very high idea of your worth and of your character. You will undoubtedly learn with pleasure that your children have made extra-ordinary progress in all the branches of learning, and that this progress is entirely due to their love of work and their perseverance.

(J.R.V. Barker, 2010) p. 475.

Monsieur Heger may have wanted both of the girls to return but Emily had no such plans and was very happy to be back at the Parsonage. It was decided, probably by Charlotte herself, that she would return alone as a teacher on a small salary. This arrangement would have been suggested by the Hegers' and it is a measure of Charlotte's eagerness to return that she journeyed back to Brussels alone in late January 1843. For a young lady to travel such distances unchaperoned was unusual, almost scandalous, but there was no aunt Branwell to voice disapproval and the money she had left in her will for her nieces gave them an independence that they had not previously enjoyed. One can imagine Charlotte setting off this time with confidence and assurance and high expectations. She was returning to her studies, her teaching and her 'master'.

The journey was difficult and when Charlotte turned up at London Bridge Wharf late at night, the sailors on the packet at first refused to let her on board. This incident could have had serious consequences for an unaccompanied woman at night on the River Thames but fortunately she persuaded them to allow her to stay overnight ready to set sail the following morning. In many ways, this whole journey and the following months were a foolhardy venture that had little chance of ending successfully. Charlotte had underestimated living at the Pensionnat without Emily and she soon realised that she was different from the other teachers in language and culture, and her new position separated her from forming friendships with her pupils. Her only friends were the Hegers but she was aware that they had a growing family and their own busy lives and could not be expected to seek, or need, her company. She still revered Monsieur Heger and was now teaching English to him and his brother-in-law. In return, Monsieur Heger set Charlotte essays and translations in French and German. It is in these essays that we find Charlotte's remarkable ideas about her own views on genius, what it entails and where it comes from.

Monsieur Heger felt that art and genius could only be expressed in study and knowledge whereas Charlotte believed it to be a gift from God, an inspirational gift that was handed to a few and could not be acquired or studied for. Charlotte wrote,

> *The nature of genius is like that of instinct; its operation is at the same time both simple and marvellous; the man of genius produces, without labour and as*

if by a single effort, results which men without genius, however knowledgeable, however persevering, could never attain.

(J.R.V. Barker, 2010) p. 487.

Whilst Monsieur Heger agreed that the gift came from God, he argued that it must be linked with knowledge. He railed back at Charlotte saying,

Without a voice there is no singer – undoubtedly – but there will be no singer either without art, without study, without imitation. Nature makes a painter – but what would he be without study of perspective – of the art of colour? ... Genius without study and without art, without knowledge of that which has already been done, is Force without a lever ... it is the sublime musician, finally, who has only an out of tune piano to make the world hear his sweet melodies which he hears ringing out inside him. Certainly the gem-carver does not make the diamond, but without him the most beautiful diamond is a pebble.

(J.R.V. Barker, 2010) p. 488.

It is at this level of intellectual argument that Charlotte and her teacher fought and wrangled over their views and ideas. Charlotte relished the stimulation of his teaching and his counter arguments and became more and more dependent on his approval and goodwill. With few alternative distractions and no other company she valued, Charlotte became isolated from everyone else whilst growing obsessively aware of her tutor. Inevitably, this led to her estrangement from Madame Heger who now found her new teacher awkward and taciturn. Charlotte had always been unwilling to socialise and was generally morose, but as it worsened it was perhaps Madame Heger who first recognised that Charlotte's behaviour and symptoms could be those of a woman in love.

Constantine Heger was a married man and a Catholic with moderate wealth. He had a kind and intelligent wife and five children. The family were respected and admired in their social circle and in the city itself. There are few people of less suitability whom Charlotte Brontë could have lost her heart and reason to. Charlotte, the strong and stoical woman with high morals and high opinions, the shy but determined parson's daughter who believed in Christianity and all the doctrines of her faith, who could endure almost any trial and any pain, gradually and disastrously fell in love with the man whom she had come to see as her equal and her inspiration.

Charlotte wrote out the emotional turmoil which she experienced during this time in her first and last novels. In *The Professor* she partly hides her Brussels experiences and emotions by creating a male protagonist, but in *Villette*, one sees a painful and honest study of unrequited love complicated by isolation and depression. This was trailblazing; a woman writing about a most painful subject from her own acute experience which conveyed all the confusion and emotions that she felt at the time. Like Anne, she strove to tell the truth by using a female heroine, Lucy Snowe, to relate the story and parts of the novel are particularly distressing as Lucy's health and mind gradually collapse.

Charlotte arrived home from Brussels in the first week of 1844, hopelessly depressed, telling Ellen that,

> *I think however long I live I shall not forget what the parting with Monsieur Heger cost me – It grieved me so much to grieve him who has been so true and kind and disinterested a friend…*
>
> (J.R.V. Barker, 2010) p. 502.

Whilst Monsieur Heger may not have realised the depths of Charlotte's feelings towards him, he became more and more aware when he received increasingly unguarded letters begging for his friendship, or even a word of comfort. Sensibly, he maintained a complete silence.

Inevitably, Charlotte learnt from this experience, but there is no doubt that she suffered appallingly from the total loss of Monsieur Heger's former friendship and support. Unfortunately, the years of suffering that followed, when Charlotte could not speak to her family of what was ailing her, seem to have hardened her in some ways.

Charlotte kept control over her feelings at great personal cost to her physical and mental health but there is no doubt that Monsieur Heger had mentored her well and her skills and her writing had greatly improved. She could now appreciate far more the many influences and experiences that drew people together and when she wrote her novels, it was with the extra insight that her whole Brussels experience had provided. Her heroes did not have to be dashing and handsome as they had been in the juvenilia. They could be frail, physically unattractive and ordinary men with all the faults and all the perplexities of their race.

The lack of interest shown in their school project over the next few months led to its abandonment and it was never revived. Charlotte now stayed at home, suffering bouts of headaches, sickness and general malaise. She was well enough to visit Ellen and work around the house but had no energy or heart to take up outside employment. The leaving of Mary Taylor, the most bold and intrepid of Charlotte's friends or acquaintances, on the six weeks' sea journey to New Zealand may have helped to stir Charlotte from her lethargy. In some ways Charlotte envied Mary's spirit whilst recognising her own limitations. She wrote, '[She] is on that path to adventure and exertion to which she has so long been seeking admission. Sickness, hardship, danger are her fellow travellers … while we have been sleeping in our beds' (Palmer, 2002) p. 63.

Mary's pioneering spirit helped to spur Charlotte's creativity and drive and made her realise that to accomplish her dreams she must recover her health and ambition and move forward.

Chapter Eighteen

The Professor

When Charlotte began to write her first novel, *The Professor,* she had returned from Brussels and spent many months of heartache desperately waiting for a letter from Monsieur Heger that would never arrive. His silence and his withdrawal of their friendship was more than she could bear and she was slowly losing her self-control. As with much of Charlotte's life, her only way of dealing with loss and disappointment was in sickness or to write out her distress. In writing she could create the happy endings which she and her siblings had been practising for most of their lives.

Unfortunately, Charlotte faltered over her first novel and made mistakes that she would later remedy but which made it hard to find a publisher. It was rejected nine times and was only published after her death. The book is, in many ways, Charlotte's letter to herself and a way for her to analyse and make sense of her experiences in Brussels. It is semi-autobiographical but uses a male hero and narrator. Charlotte's attempts to be authentic are hampered by her use of William Crimsworth and his first-person narrative. She was a much better writer than this book suggests but one can see that this was her way of bringing the Brussels episode of her life to a conclusion. She was attempting to move forward whilst trying to protect her anonymity. Charlotte was still hurt and distressed when she was writing her first novel and it was not until she rewrote and restyled it as *Villette* that she gained full control over her writing and her emotions.

The Professor does however have merit and is a brave attempt to analyse isolation and love. William Crimsworth is a teacher at a small French academy trying to make his way in the world where his lowly position and lack of funds make him rather contemptible to his peers. Writing under her pseudonym Currer Bell, Charlotte may have been trying to offer a male view of life whilst distancing herself from any accusations of autobiography. In this version, it is Crimsworth, the professor, who falls in love with one of his female pupils,

Frances Henri. Crimsworth is an odd character who does not elicit sympathy from the reader, in fact he has very little in the way of virtues. He is a hard and disciplined man, at times boring or foolish, who never really captures the reader's imagination. He is also a man alone in a hostile world who has the courage to rise from his humble beginnings to achieve a level of success and to marry the person he loves. He is, therefore, the embodiment of his creator's fantasy.

Where Charlotte excels in this novel is partly in her portrayal of Crimsworth as a realistic character with all the faults and perversions of his type, which allows her to wipe away that veneer of respectability and to almost make fun of it. She exposes Crimsworth as a man who is awkward and socially inept and she does not try to make him handsome or sophisticated. This takes careful and considered restraint in an author and it is not always recognised as one of the merits of this novel.

Acknowledging one's faults and striving to better oneself is a maxim which Charlotte tried to maintain, and one sees in Crimsworth this determination to be independent, both socially and financially. Like Charlotte, her hero recognises that money is essential and that affairs of the heart can rarely be satisfied unless there is financial security. This was another major issue for Charlotte, who knew the fear of always being beholden to others for her abode and her needs, and this includes the Parsonage and her father's income. Had Patrick died, they would all have had to leave the Parsonage for the next incumbent and only their education and skills would have served to keep them solvent.

Crimsworth, as Charlotte's persona, travels to Brussels to enhance his teaching experience and to earn more money. In this he follows the 'self-help' ideas of the times and the requirement for people to provide for themselves and their families. Crimsworth knows that he has only his own merits to fall back on but he is both realistic and, at times, naïve. For a man who has determination and drive he does not always display an understanding of the world around him. He makes a series of mistakes and is only able to develop and mature with the help of Frances. She is his strength even though she refers to him as *'Monsieur'* or her 'master'.

It is in her treatment of Frances Henri that Charlotte can voice her concerns and demonstrate the changes in female attitudes and demands that would gradually become recognised and discussed. Charlotte is one of the first female writers to allow her heroine to work after her marriage as part of a new idea of earning her own keep whilst standing side-by-side with her husband. This echoes Charlotte's own feelings about both marriage and independence. She did not value, or wish for, the dependency that women had to adopt when they married and abhorred the type of attitudes expressed in the following article from *The Manchester Examiner* of 1848, which proposed that, 'Married life is woman's profession; and to this life her training – that of dependence – is modelled.'

This type of sentiment was very far from Charlotte's view of marriage which she saw as a mutual partnership and a linking of ideas and shared experiences. Through the character of Francis Henri, Charlotte can expound on the issues of marriage itself and on the dilemmas facing women both within marriage and those unfortunate enough to be 'left on the shelf'. Frances echoes Charlotte's mixed feelings on these matters as she struggles with the need for a husband as an equal partner but also as her 'master'.

Charlotte uses Crimsworth to goad his wife into admitting her thoughts about marriage. He asks her three times what she would do if her husband was a profligate or a drunkard, and each time Frances replies that she would try to endure it for a while and if there was no hope of cure she would leave. Crimsworth asks her what she would do if the law forced her back to him. The following is the revealing exchange between them,

'Monsieur, if a wife's nature loathes that of the man she is wedded to, marriage must be slavery. Against slavery all right thinkers revolt, and though torture be the price of resistance, torture must be dared: though the only road to freedom lie through the gates of death, those gates must be passed; for freedom is indispensable...Death would certainly screen me both from bad laws and their consequences.'

'Voluntary death, Frances?' Crimsworth asks,

'No, Monsieur. I'd have courage to live out every throe of anguish fate assigned me, and principle to contend for justice and liberty to the last.'

'...supposing fate had merely assigned you the lot of an old maid, what then? asks Crimsworth.

'...An old maid's life must doubtless be void and vapid – her heart strained and empty. Had I been an old maid I should have spent existence in efforts to fill

the void and ease the aching. I should have probably failed and died weary and
disappointed, despised and of no account, like all other single women.'
(C. Brontë, *The Professor and Emma a fragment*, 1983) p. 226.

By using Crimsworth to draw out his wife's views, perhaps the reader eavesdrops on Charlotte's own fears. It is interesting that Charlotte objected so much to *The Tenant of Wildfell Hall* partly because Helen Huntingdon leaves her husband. It is, for Charlotte, against the laws of Christian marriage but Charlotte is also saying that marriage should never be for titles and riches. A woman must first get to know the man and know his faults and his weaknesses and decide whether she can tolerate or change them. For Charlotte respect comes first; a mutual respect which may or may not deepen into love. In her letter to Ellen Nussey written in 1840, she had advised Ellen on this very point, stating that she must marry a 'man you respect,' then 'moderate love,' may follow. 'Intense passion' was not desirable. In *Agnes Grey* it is Mrs Murray's intent on marrying off her daughters to rich husbands that Anne/Agnes objects to and she demonstrates that these loveless and contrived marriages can often result in years of heartache.

Frances makes the statement that whilst she works just as hard as her husband, and their jobs and hours are the same, she earns only a fraction of his salary; 1,200 francs against her husband's 8,000. It is this discrepancy that causes her to want to work harder and for them to develop a school of their own. Frances wants equality and independence and to be with the man she loves, not necessarily three attributes that sit together in Victorian society. Charlotte makes her point though, and although it is not laboured she clearly exposes the discrepancy in their salaries. It is quite astonishing to note that in this country this issue was not tackled or fully unresolved, until the coming of the Equal Pay Act of 1970, the Equal Pay and Sex Discrimination Act of 1975, the National Minimum Wage Act of 1998 and the Equality Act of 2010, which stated that, 'men and women performing work of equal value should receive the same pay'.

Charlotte Brontë was highlighting this inequality 125 years before the first Act of Parliament attempted to address the issue and 154 years before the Equality Act of 2010.

Charlotte had many conflicting emotions when she returned from Brussels. One of these was probably anger to find herself back home with few prospects and the terrible weight of an unfulfilled and hopeless infatuation. Her last months at the Pensionnat must have been utterly miserable for her, and now the object of all her desires was 500 miles away. She probably began the writing of *The Professor* at some time in late 1845 or early 1846, having written her last letter to Monsieur Heger in November 1845. She is still upset and unhappy and one can see a pattern in the book where her mood pushes and pulls the characters in odd and confusing directions. Crimsworth can be irrational, stupid, angry, childish, racist and gauche, describing his pupils in terms of 'half-breed', 'dirty' and 'vacuous'. Charlotte's narrative jumps around from these nervous irrational assaults, to passages of calm and rational thought where Crimsworth is the model husband and friend.

The turbulence of Crimsworth's life is, we are told, linked to the loss of his mother, whose portrait is lost and then restored to him. The mother figure is here in Charlotte's first book and the missing mother is seen as the cause and reason for all of Crimsworth's problems. Charlotte still imagines that her own mother would have kept the family close and happy and been the person to whom she could have turned and who would have helped her to overcome her longing for Monsieur Heger. When a parent or child dies whilst still young, those who remember them recall them as when they died and they stay forever young and beautiful. They represent all that is good and by no longer being alive they can be cherished and no harm can ever alter them. Crimsworth has a portrait of his mother because a portrait will not age. Had her mother still been living when Charlotte was writing her first novel, she would have been 63 years old and far less the romantic angel which her children may have imagined her.

Charlotte explores some of this in *The Professor* and it is new and innovative because it is a deeper and darker part of the human psyche which she is exploring, consciously or possibly subconsciously. There is a searching for home and the fireside and the mother figure throughout the novel; it is not a fault, but part of Charlotte's exploration of human emotions and her own anxieties. Whereas most books of the time follow a linear story, this novel is erratic and jumpy and one is never completely sure in which direction it will go because its author was erratic and jumpy and lacked direction.

One can appreciate that this book has a lot more to offer than a simple tale of love and marriage or even of female emancipation. *The Professor* incorporates an examination and exposure of mental health, where the mind and body are placed in such an alien and foreign situation amongst people who are different, or even enemies, that it is in danger of collapse. Just as Charlotte's time at the

Pensionnat changed from a happy and industrious world of learning into a bitter and intense place of distrust and subterfuge, this book has many elements of the neurosis and melancholia that threatened to send Charlotte into breakdown.

In *The Professor*, the tension is below the surface and is only noticeable in behaviour that is irrational or abnormal. It is not until she writes *Villette,* that Charlotte is fully capable of describing the disintegration of the mind. In *The Professor* it is still under the surface, although barely so and Crimsworth is saved from complete mental breakdown by the love and support of his wife. Again, Charlotte writes what she wishes would have happened to her; the salvation borne of love and kindness to mend a broken body and soul.

There are many biblical references in *The Professor* which is understandable, with Charlotte's immense knowledge of the Bible and her Christian education but, like so many parts of this book, they are often camouflaged and can only be identified where the reader is also familiar with the Bible and is aware of their links and significance. In her excellent essay on the first three Brontë novels, Stevie Davies describes the linkage between Mademoiselle Reuter's garden and the Garden of Eden (Davies, *The Cambridge Companion to The Brontës*, 2002). When Crimsworth is shown around her garden by Mademoiselle Reuter, he savours the flowers and the scents and describes her cheeks as like 'the bloom on a good apple', Crimsworth fancies that he has found someone to love but, as the book progresses, Mademoiselle Reuter becomes the serpent in the garden; the venomous snake whose 'apple' tries to poison him.

Repeatedly, Charlotte uses an inverted metaphor by substituting male for female, and vice versa, to highlight the personalities of the characters. It is clever and it is unusual but it is only apparent to a reader who is well versed in Biblical stories and text. This makes *The Professor* a confusing and difficult book to understand and appreciate. It echoes, in reverse roles, the story of Charlotte and Monsieur Heger, but it is told at a time when its author is still hypersensitive about that relationship and lacking in the control she could apply in her later works.

Although the book was rejected by publishers and is still considered of lesser merit than the other Brontë novels, it is worth the effort to read it as a book that is trying to encapsulate the mental state of its author and to examine how she writes out her emotions in her novel. It is daring and it is one of the first books to explore the condition of the self-made man or woman and the treatment of anyone attempting to rise in a society that does not value their class or opinions.

Chapter Nineteen

Jane Eyre

By the time Charlotte came to write *Jane Eyre*, in the summer of 1846, she had received a letter from the publishers Smith, Elder and Co, who, whilst declining to publish *The Professor*, were encouraging her to write a three volume novel. Charlotte replied in August that she had such a work in progress which would be finished within a month. By September, the book had been sent, read, very favourably received and was published in October.

The immediate success of *Jane Eyre* and its effect on those who read it was profound. It was to some extent the *Harry Potter* of its day; it was new, it was different, it appealed to all ages and both sexes and it was about an orphaned child whose goodness triumphed over evil. In this book, Charlotte revealed herself as an author who had written out her anxieties in her first novel and could now settle to a far more interesting and mature work. She could write about emotions without becoming emotional so that the book moves along with speed and credulity even though it contains scenes of the gothic and the ghostly.

This time Charlotte stated that the book was an 'autobiography', and in it she wrote about her personal experiences, as a child and as a governess, in the fictional guise of her heroine, Jane Eyre. Both history and Charlotte testify to some of the events in the book and there are many examples of Charlotte's experiences in the first chapters. Later in the novel when Jane begins to fall in love with her employer, Mr Rochester, it is not with the nervous anxiety and crass behaviour of Crimsworth, but with quiet, good sense. This time Charlotte's views are expressed with deep knowledge and feeling because she has lived and felt some of it, but has now learnt to control her emotions and her narrative in a way that allows the reader to appreciate the events and to believe in them.

Jane Eyre describes the journey of a young orphaned girl who is being cruelly mistreated by her aunt and cousins. Her tyrannical cousin, John Reed, attacks her but Jane is punished for the fracas and locked in the red room where her uncle had previously died. The scene in this room is every child's nightmare and one that many children and adults can identify with. The child is helpless and terrified and the adults are imprisoning her in the dark where she dreads seeing the ghost of her dead uncle. Charlotte describes the child's terror whilst highlighting the cruelty of her aunt. The child is, as always, at the mercy of those who are older and more powerful and can do anything they wish to hurt and torment. There is a physical and psychological battle taking place in this scene, which sets the tone of the book. Jane is often in extreme circumstances, even life threatening, and she must overcome each obstacle with little or no outside help. What she does have, and maintains, is the moral strength to stand up to injustice. Even at this tender age, Jane knows that there is no justification for her aunt and cousins' behaviour towards her. It is only as she grows older that she realises that she was a misfit in their home, a child outside of their social order and, therefore, despised, feared and consequently mistreated and alienated.

It stirs the reader's emotions to see the child Jane suffer and this is further compounded when Jane is sent to the awful Lowood school where she receives more harsh and unwarranted punishments at the hands of ruthless teachers. The school's benefactor, the Reverend Mr Brocklehurst, is shown in all his malevolent greed. His misinterpretation of the scriptures justifies, to him, the mistreatment of the pupils in his care. As a bigot, with strict Calvinistic beliefs, he personifies the hellfire doctrine and preaches that punishment of the body purifies the soul. In a telling altercation between Jane and Mr Brocklehurst when he comes to visit her aunt to arrange her removal to Lowood, he tells the innocent and abused Jane,

> 'No sight so sad as that of a naughty child…especially a naughty little girl. Do you know where the wicked go after death?'
> 'They go to hell,' was my ready and orthodox answer.
> 'And what is hell? Can you tell me that?'
> 'A pit full of fire'
> 'And should you like to fall into that pit, and to be burning there for ever?'
> 'No, sir.'
> 'What must you do to avoid it?'
> I deliberated a moment; my answer, when it did come, was objectionable: 'I must keep in good health and not die.'
>
> (C. Brontë, 1971) p. 27.

This short interchange is an insight into Brocklehurst's bullying and religious fanaticism and Jane's reply enrages him. It also highlights Jane's wonderful childlike logic and truthful response. Throughout the novel, she resists religious tyranny.

In these early chapters, Charlotte is echoing the harsh treatment which she witnessed and suffered at school as a child; it is her way of both writing out her experiences and highlighting the school's awful regime. Charlotte insisted that Lowood was as accurate to her as her own experiences and despite threats from the school's former director and teachers, she did not alter this claim. Charlotte never forgave the schools benefactor and director, Rev. William Carus Wilson, for the treatment and deaths of her two elder sisters and her passionate description of Lowood was her way of letting the whole world know what had happened; in many ways, a just and perfect revenge. The reader feels, especially in the twenty-first century, the huge distance between schools and orphanages then and the social system in England today. Pupils died at the Clergy Daughters' School. They died of typhoid, cholera, and tuberculosis all exacerbated by the poor conditions, awful diet, lack of heating, poor light and inadequate clothing. Even worse, they suffered from the deprivation of love and care and kindness from many of the staff, who also exercised the belief that to punish the body would save the soul.

This oppressive religious education continues for Jane for six long years as a pupil and two more as a teacher. Her only adult guide is Miss Temple, the kindly superintendent who can occasionally stand up to Mr Brocklehurst, but even she is at her employer's mercy and must conform to his rules and regulations. Only when Miss Temple prepares to leave does Jane decide that she has the knowledge and experience to go to work as a governess. Although Charlotte hated being a governess, by letting her heroine take on the onerous role she is being realistic. Working as a teacher or governess are the only two reasonable alternatives for someone in Jane's situation. A lesser role would be as a servant, but Jane has received a lot of education and at 18 years old is the right age to take on one of these two occupations.

With no money and no friends or family to help or guide her, Jane advertises for a post and accepts that of governess to a young French girl, Adele, who is living at Thornfield Hall, a middle-class country house owned by Mr Rochester. In this second section of the book the reader is shown the lifestyle and behaviour of a country squire who has wealth and breeding. He has travelled widely and worked in the colonies. Mr Rochester is a 'man of the world' who has had mistresses and Adele, Jane's charge, is possibly his illegitimate daughter. The contrast in class and circumstance between Jane and Rochester is huge and their paths would never normally cross. Mr Rochester lives the life of a wealthy bachelor and it is the housekeeper who organises the Hall, especially during her master's long absences. When Rochester does come home there are balls and parties at which Adele is allowed to spend a little time. Jane, in her menial position, can watch but can never join in. Rochester is an experienced womaniser and flirt and greatly enjoys these events where all the various rich and marriageable ladies are invited.

As stated, as an observer of the middle and upper classes, the governess was in a unique position. She saw and heard a great deal of what went on but was hardly noticed by people in the house. Jane is largely an invisible person but she has by now grown into a young lady with her own opinions and her own moral views. She has talents and she has intelligence, but she lacks any pretence of beauty and has no wealth or connections. She is just plain Jane.

Occasionally, Jane does find herself in Rochester's company. He is handsome and playful and Jane soon warms to him even though she understands that he has many faults. When he speaks to her she is a little shy but she is not overwhelmed by him and is always able to stand her ground and can even argue with him. Jane realises that her feelings towards him are growing and she is wretched because she knows that she has nothing to offer him and that it is inevitable that he will marry one of the attractive women that surround him, probably the devious but beautiful Blanche Ingram.

Charlotte is making many statements about class, wealth and beauty in these chapters. Rochester can have anything he wishes and has all that most men could ever want, except a beautiful wife, but that will happen when he decides to marry. Of course, the twist in the plot occurs when Jane keeps hearing cries from the attic rooms and is told that it is an old housekeeper, Grace Poole, a drinker, who is now living up there apart from the household. Jane occasionally sees her on the stairs but, although alarmed, does not question her appearance. Rochester continues to notice Adele's governess and starts to tease her. Jane is drawn to her employer but is convinced that he will propose to Miss Ingram.

Events in the house take a dramatic turn when Jane is fetched in the middle of the night to a fire in Rochester's room and she helps to save his life.

This event brings them closer and eventually Rochester asks Jane to marry him. Although this marriage would be an unlikely scenario in reality, Rochester has recognised the innate goodness in Jane and her kindness and honesty. He is rather tired of the fatuous chatter and passing beauty of the women in his life and has seen in Jane a new and different kind of woman. She can match him in intelligence and knowledge if not in experience and travel, and she fascinates him with her strength and moral fortitude. This is the new woman, the woman who does not have to be rich and title-seeking, or beautiful and beguiling, merely honest and truthful. Rochester can at last see that a woman can have other qualities, more lasting and more important.

Unfortunately, Rochester is both a liar and a cheat. On their wedding day, as they take their vows, it is revealed that Rochester already has a wife and she is the one living in the attic and Grace Poole is her nurse. Mrs Bertha Rochester is insane and has been confined in the attic rooms at Thornfield Hall because her husband can neither control nor divorce her. Despite their aborted wedding and the revelation of a wife, Rochester still pleads with Jane to stay with him but his offer would make Jane his mistress not his wife and she refuses. Jane's principles will not allow her to be anything other than a wife to the man she loves; anything else is, to her, un-Christian and unacceptable. That Rochester makes this suggestion, and the fact that he was willing to go through with a bigamist marriage, is especially shocking and severely damages Jane's trust in him.

Charlotte cleverly reveals the issues that face people tied up in emotional conflict. She is not trying to condemn Rochester, although she exposes him. He is flawed and vulnerable and he too has been tricked into a marriage. Bertha Rochester, formerly Antoinette Mason, was a West Indian from the colonised islands where Rochester had gone to make his fortune. She was not a slave, but an heiress to the wealth of a sugar plantation. It is her wealth and beauty, combined with Rochester's class and background, that brings about their 'arranged' marriage. Her family are aware of a history of insanity in the family but choose not to warn Rochester. After their marriage, Rochester gains her wealth but she is increasingly unstable and he realises that he has been tricked. He is, naturally, bitter and although he brings his wife back to England with him and continues to provide for her, there can be no conventional married life.

Charlotte had knowledge of colonialism and of the creation of wealth using slaves and she could see the link between slavery and anyone who lacked personal freedom and choice. She recognised in the slaves of the British Colonies the total dominance of men, especially over women, and this included sexual conquest as much as the physical humiliation. Rochester would not have married a slave but he marries a woman who is being dominated and manipulated by her family. There are many undercurrents of sexual intensity in the novel and they are epitomised by Bertha Rochester as the mad, dangerous and uninhibited femme fatale. Charlotte's portrayal of Bertha is a clever and important one in which she is both highlighting and condoning the conventional belief that women must be subjugated and dominated, or else they become sexually deviant and hysterical. The twist here is that Bertha is also the victim. She is mentally ill and she was used by her family to entrap Rochester and then left to her own mental breakdown. She is 'deported' to England and incarcerated and isolated at Thornfield Hall. Charlotte is aware that Bertha is as much a victim as any other married woman who has no rights and no freedom and, in Bertha's case, an illness for which there is no cure and no sympathy.

Charlotte was also conversant with the law and religion in respect of marriage and its legal implications. Marriage for Charlotte was an unbreakable bond, sanctioned by both the church and the state, and could no be broken. The fact that Heger was married was as much a part of Charlotte's heartache as her unrequited love for him. There was never any question of an affair or of him breaking his marriage vows. Only death can separate a married couple in Charlotte's view and that is in the hands of God. It is why her anger against Branwell was so extreme. Branwell and Mrs Robinson had broken divine laws as well as secular ones. They had committed a cardinal sin and one that Charlotte had especially resisted. Jane Eyre, too, cannot allow herself to be compromised by Rochester into becoming his mistress as it is against her principles, but she struggles with the overwhelming urge to stay with Rochester stating,

Think of his misery; think of his danger – look at his state when left alone; remember his headlong nature; consider the recklessness following on from despair – soothe him; save him; love him; tell him you love him and will be his. Who in the world cares for you? Or who will be injured by what you do?

(C. Brontë 1971) p. 279.

This is a very sound argument. Who would be injured if the orphaned governess became her employer's mistress? The answer is clearly, no-one. Fortunately, Jane finds the strength and the resolve to say to herself,

> *I care for myself. The more solitary, the more friendless, the more unsustained I am, the more I will respect myself. I will keep the law given by God; sanctioned by man. I will hold to the principles received by me when I was sane, and not mad—as I am now. Laws and principles are not for the times when there is no temptation: they are for moments such as this, when body and soul rise in mutiny against their rigour; stringent as they are; inviolate they shall be ... there I plant my foot.*
>
> (C. Brontë, 1971) p. 279.

Jane's only option at this point is to leave, as Charlotte did when Brussels and Monsieur Heger became a hopeless and intolerable situation. Jane leaves Thornfield and the coach drops her at a crossroads in the middle of open countryside. This crossroad is a metaphor for Jane's position. She is at a crisis and a major turning point in her life. She is lost in all aspects of the word, physically, emotionally and environmentally. She remains 'lost in the wilderness' for some days, walking across moorland and dales with no compass and no notion of where she is or where she is going. She is a woman who is bereft of all that she had hoped for and in homeless destitution is near to death when she finally arrives at a cottage. Here, she is eventually nursed back to health by a kind family of two sisters, Diana and Mary Rivers and their brother, St John, a clergyman.

This trial by homeless wandering is of course an echo of Christ in the wilderness, searching for answers and resisting temptation. It is a baptism back to sanity and to sound moral judgement which allows Jane to earn her rest and recovery with the Rivers family. She has resisted the devil and can now regenerate in the knowledge that she made the right decision. She has not surrendered to Rochester, she has not broken his marriage vows and she has not morally compromised herself. It does not mean that she does not still love Rochester but she now cares as much for herself and her own spiritual wellbeing.

People have argued that it is easier to be self-sufficient and self-aware when one is an orphan or separated from family and friends. There is a necessity to be self-reliant, to survive, and this can be an asset; a driving force that allows that person to take risks and have total choice by the very fact that they are not answerable to anyone. One can see some of this in Jane's case. Family, as Charlotte was aware, could be a wonderful and comforting support, but could also be the focus of extreme heartache and suffering. Charlotte got both from her family and she works through this dilemma in *Jane Eyre*.

In the end, she appears to bow to convention and allows Jane to discover that the Rivers are in fact her cousins and so she gains a family. She also gains wealth when she receives money from her uncle's will. Jane is, therefore, rising in class and respectability. She has moved from the lowly, unhappy and unwanted orphan to the settled, happy and financially secure woman. She is rising through the social ranks at a time when Rochester is falling.

Back at Thornfield Hall, Bertha has set the house on fire and died by leaping from the battlements and smashing her brains on the cobbled yard below; a death that is particularly descriptive and horrific. Her death is necessary to the plot for Rochester to move on. Thornfield is consumed by fire, and Rochester, in trying to save his wife from the rooftop, is hit by falling masonry and injured and blinded. In order for Jane and Rochester to get together again, Charlotte has to have them meet on an equal footing. Rochester 'falls' by losing his home, his wealth and his physical attractiveness, whilst Jane 'rises' in class, wealth and status. He will be dependent on her and not the other way around, and he is now a widower so there is nothing to stop a proper marriage.

Before that can happen, Charlotte has a further trial for Jane in the form of her cousin St John Rivers. St John wants to be a missionary in India and before long he asks Jane to accompany him. Once again, Jane's life is at a crossroads. She can go to India with St John as his helpmate and have a useful and fulfilling life helping others and spreading the word of God but St John wants her to go as his wife. Jane is aware that they do not love each other and their lives would be sterile although purposeful in the service of the church. Jane has known love and she is aware of passion and she has none of these feelings for St John. Furthermore, there are links between St John and the strict doctrine of Mr Brocklehurst. Both believe in hellfire and predestination, and their creed is one of condemnation rather than salvation. Jane describes St John's religious character after hearing him preach,

Throughout there was a strange bitterness; an absence of consolatory gentleness; stern allusions to Calvinistic doctrines – election, predestination, reprobation – were frequent; and each reference to these points sounded like a sentence pronounced for doom. When he had done, instead of feeling better, calmer, more enlightened by his discourse, I experienced an inexpressible sadness...

(C. Brontë 1971) p. 310.

In these chapters at Moor Cottage with her new-found cousins, Jane again goes through a journey of self-discovery. St John opens a door for her to be a missionary in India, something that she had previously told Rochester she would do if he married someone else. Jane has all the attributes necessary to devote her life to God and to helping others but, convention dictates that St John cannot travel abroad with a young woman who is neither his sister nor his wife. Society will not allow it. Once again, Jane is torn between doing her duty and following her heart. She is fully aware of St John's coldness and his inability to express his feelings. She also believes that should she grow to feel affection, or even love for him, he would reject it and she would be even more wretched.

St John's rigid views and his attempts to overcome Jane's resistance are unfruitful because he dictates to her and makes demands of her. On the one occasion that he is kind and gentle with her, she almost gives in and agrees to go to India with him. She resists because she does not want him or anyone else to decide her destiny. She is still her own person and able to stand up for what she believes to be right, but she is unsure and is waiting for a sign to help her to choose the next path to follow. The sign arrives in the form of a disembodied but familiar voice calling her name, and Jane knows that her destiny lies with Edward Rochester, not St John Rivers.

Charlotte uses many plot devices to contrive and manipulate the story to bring about a happy ending. Yet it is happy only insofar as Jane and Rochester have been through the highs and lows of life before either of them can be suitably matched and deserving of their happiness. This echoes Charlotte's belief that you must work and suffer before you can gain your rewards and that by staying on the moral path, you earn your place and your happiness. She does, of course, say much more than this. By highlighting Jane's struggles, both physical and emotional, Charlotte is describing the role of women and children in a patriarchal society that has not stopped to examine the damage it may cause to its most vulnerable members.

Jane will not accept her allotted place in an uncaring society and will not respect anyone who does not recognise her for her strengths and beliefs. She resists some very powerful men: Mr Brocklehurst, Edward Rochester and St John Rivers. She also deals with some domineering and merciless women; her Aunt Reed, Miss Scatcherd at Lowood and to some extent, Bertha Mason; all women who affect Jane's perception of the world and cause her pain and suffering.

Jane Eyre is a book which examines people and their behaviour against a background of both wealth and poverty. By following Jane's journey through life, the reader is confronted with many questions about the way people live. The book has been especially adopted by feminist critics because it exposes the subjugation of women. Jane famously states during her early days at Thornfield Hall,

> *Women are supposed to be very calm generally: but women feel just as men feel: they need exercise for their faculties and a field for their efforts as much as their brothers do; they suffer from too rigid a restraint, too absolute a stagnation, precisely as men would suffer; and it is narrow minded in their more privileged fellow-creatures to say that they ought to confine themselves to making puddings and knitting stockings, to playing on the piano and embroidering bags. It is thoughtless to condemn them, or laugh at them, if they seek to do more or learn more than custom has pronounced necessary for their sex.*
>
> (C. Brontë, 1971) p. 96.

It was bold statements such as these that both excited and appalled the early readers of *Jane Eyre* and which highlight for the modern reader the kinds of confines and hardships that women have suffered and are still suffering. Charlotte Brontë was one of only a handful of women who were strong enough to identify and describe the underprivileged conditions of many women and children at that time.

Chapter Twenty

Shirley

The runaway success of *Jane Eyre* has overshadowed Charlotte's three other books. *Jane Eyre* was, and is, the most widely read and best remembered. Charlotte was in effect a biographer of fictional characters who used some of her own biography in her novels. For *Jane Eyre* and *Villette* this worked very well. When she came to write *Shirley*, she did not use this autobiographical approach and instead, began an historical work which was based in the 'Condition of England' genre.

It is important to remember two main things about this third novel. Firstly, by now Charlotte Brontë was a known and successful novelist fêted by the very cream of the literary world. Though still shy and reticent at times, she was moving in social circles where she was meeting famous writers such as William Thackeray, to whom she had been introduced at her publisher's dinner party. Her opinions were being sought and her ideas listened to. Her name and fame were spreading and her publisher was looking forward with anticipation for her next great work. To follow on from a runaway success is most difficult and Charlotte seems to have had trouble in choosing her subject, her setting and her characters. The second issue with the novel concerns Charlotte's domestic experience at the time. She was writing at home and the health and welfare of her siblings was becoming a grave concern. That summer saw Branwell's body and spirit completely overcome by his addictions. He wrote to his friend, J.B. Leyland, in June, 1848,

> *Mr Nicholson has sent to my father a demand for the settlement of my bill owed to him immediately, under penalty of a Court Summons ... I have also given John Brown this morning ten shillings ... If Mr N. refuses my offer and presses me with the law I am RUINED. I have had five months of such utter sleeplessness, violent cough and frightful agony of mind that jail would destroy me for ever.*

(Palmer, 2002) p. 79.

Having Branwell at home meant that every day and night was an increasing burden on his family. His father had taken his son into his bedroom after Branwell had accidently set his own bed on fire, but the vigilant old man got no rest. Emily and Anne did their best to keep Branwell safe; Emily often helped him up the stairs to bed when he was too drunk to walk. Charlotte could barely bring herself to communicate with him but would have seen and heard his extreme behaviour with exasperation and despair. It was not the most conducive atmosphere in which to write a novel.

In the end, Charlotte chose to move away from the autobiographical and write about political and industrial change, at least in the first chapters. She set the novel in the early 1800s at the time of the Luddite risings which were spreading through various Northern counties. With the jobs of millworkers already being threatened by the introduction of mechanical looms, the government, via its Privy Council, had also introduced a commercial war against Napoleon. Under a set of rules known as Orders in Council, they had instructed the Royal Navy to blockade French and allied ports to prevent goods, especially military weapons, getting to France. These measures affected the whole of European and American trade and it also affected the British home trade as the demand for goods, both import and export, fell. This fall in demand hit both the Yorkshire woollen mills and Lancashire cotton mills and meant workers were already losing their jobs. The introduction of automated machinery would make the situation a great deal worse for them.

The politically aware Charlotte was knowledgeable on these affairs but had not experienced them for herself. She based much of these themes in the novel on her father's experience of a Luddite attack by men from Nottinghamshire, championing the workers' cause much the same as modern day 'flying pickets', These men stormed Rawfolds Mill, near Cleckheaton in West Yorkshire in 1812. Patrick had stood firmly on the side of the law, against the mill workers, but had sympathy for their cause and understood the effects that the loss of their jobs would have on them and their families. He was at that time a curate at St Peter's church Harsthead, near Liversedge in West Yorkshire, an area where Luddites and their sympathisers were active.

Although *Shirley* was written and published around the same time as other industrial novels such as Dickens's *Dombey and Son*, Mrs Gaskell's *Mary Barton* and William Thackeray's *Vanity Fair*, Charlotte's work was not didactic. The true 'Condition of England' novel offered an insight into the working and living conditions of the working classes and exposed the causes of their poverty and distress. Charlotte does not attempt to gain the readers sympathy, and nor does she empathise with the workers or the unemployed and the poor in her tale. The political reality is a backdrop rather than the central theme of the book.

Charlotte may have set out to expose political unrest and its causes, but she does not stick to this early theme. There is a reason for this. As stated, Branwell's health had deteriorated alarmingly and on 24 September 1848, at the age of 31, he finally died. Charlotte was, naturally, deeply affected by the loss of the brother that she had once loved and admired, and for whom she had previously held such high expectations. The two of them had been a partnership throughout childhood and had bounced ideas and experiences between them in a way that had spurred each other on to greater things. For the last three years of his life, Charlotte had scorned him and deplored the way in which, in her opinion, he had wallowed in his suffering and made everyone else suffer along with him. Even so, his death was a terrible blow to her and one wonders if she suffered any guilt from her harsh treatment of Branwell and whether she, if anyone, could have helped to save him. She wrote to her publisher soon after his death, saying,

> *I do not weep from a sense of bereavement – there is no prop withdrawn, no consolation torn away, no dear companion lost – but for wreck of talent, the ruin of promise, the untimely dreary extinction of what might have been a burning and shining light ... I had aspirations and ambitions for him once – long ago – they have perished mournfully – nothing remains of him but a memory of errors and sufferings – There is such a bitterness of pity for his life and death – such a yearning emptiness for his whole existence as I cannot describe.*
>
> (*Selected Letters of Charlotte Brontë*, 2007) p. 120.

Charlotte was overcome with this loss of what Branwell could have achieved and took to her bed with all manner of physical and emotional ailments. Despite the shock of his loss and the sudden quietude in the Parsonage the family's mourning soon turned to further concern and worry. Emily had caught a chill at Branwell's funeral and began to display all the tell-tale signs of rapid consumption. The cough, the pain, the inflammation and the difficulty in breathing all worsened and Emily quickly deteriorated. Unfortunately, for Emily and her family, Emily refused help and insisted on doing her normal housework and following her daily routines. This stoicism may have been admirable, but it helped no one. As Emily's condition grew worse her sisters could only stand by helplessly and watch her drag herself around the house. This longing to help was, for Charlotte, exquisitely painful as all the love and care that she had withheld from Branwell was now available in abundance for her sister, but Emily rejected any assistance from those who so desperately wanted to help her. Charlotte wrote to Ellen towards the end of November,

> *I told you Emily was ill in my last letter...she has not rallied yet. She is very ill. I believe, if you were to see her, your impression would be that there is no hope. A more hollow, wasted, pallid aspect I have not beheld...God only knows how all this will terminate...I think Emily seems the nearest thing to my heart in this world.*
>
> (Palmer, 2002) p. 83.

Within three weeks, Emily, at the age of 30, was dead and her heartbroken sister wrote once more to Ellen and in her next letter her concern for her remaining sibling becomes apparent,

> *Emily suffers no more from pain or weakness now ... she is gone, after a hard, short conflict ... yesterday we put her poor, wasted mortal frame quietly under the church pavement ... we feel she is at peace. No need now to tremble for the hard frost and keen wind ... She has died in a time of promise. We saw her torn from life in its prime. But it is God's will ... I now look to Anne and wish she were well and strong, but she is neither.*
>
> (Palmer, 2002) p. 85.

Charlotte had spent six months writing and lost two of her three siblings, and her youngest sister was also showing signs of the fatal illness which heralded her death in May 1849. One can only speculate on how these three consecutive deaths affected Charlotte both as a sister and as an author. Although neither of her sisters had ever been robust in health, it is unlikely that Charlotte expected to lose them so soon. The industrial novel that Charlotte may have set out to write morphed into a tale where the industrialisation was still a strong theme, but it was overtaken by the tale of two women who partly resembled her sisters. The homes and families they lived in and amongst, also had many references to those of Charlotte's closest friends, the Nusseys and the Taylors.

Reading *Shirley*, one can note the disparities and the lack of flow as Charlotte's tale flits around, and one sees and hears bits of conversation with events and background loosely strung together. There is no first-person narrator to give explanation or cohesion. It could, at times, be almost seen as a very early example of a 'stream of consciousness' narrative.

It is also, by being set in the past and containing some of the author's experience of the death of her siblings, a novel about loss; the loss of childhood, the loss of simplicity and, especially, the loss of the pre-industrial world when Tabby's 'fairies' lived at the bottom of the valley instead of massive, smoke-belching, textile mills. It is the echo of six children racing across the open moors full of energy and hope. It is a book about the inevitability of change that must always take place over time both in people and in the environment.

Charlotte, with her amazing ability to observe and to imitate, does manage to create a novel where she portrays funny, sad and interesting characters, and where she examines again the role of women in a world dominated by rich and powerful men. There is humour in this work and it is witty and sharp. Unfortunately, there is also an understandable sentimentality and a contrivance to see the two heroines married off to the males of their choice in a way that belies the promise of the first few chapters.

Shirley is a book about two very different young women. Shirley Keeldar is a socially and financially independent young lady who is outspoken, strong, and can resist the bullying of the men in her life. Caroline Helstone is the vicar's niece and is dominated by her uncle. Caroline has fallen hopelessly in love with Robert Moore, the local mill owner. The opening chapters describing political issues, religious beliefs and the local families are some of the best and display Charlotte's humour and ability with characterisation. Her opening paragraphs prepare the reader for the tale but the words are spoken with irony,

If you think, from this prelude, that anything like a romance is preparing for you, reader, you never were more mistaken. Do you anticipate sentiment, and poetry and reverie? Do you expect passion, and stimulus, and melodrama? Calm

your expectations; reduce them to a lowly standard. Something real, cool, and
solid, lies before you; something unromantic as Monday morning.

(C. Brontë, *Shirley*, 1982) p. 39.

Charlotte does offer a tale of sentiment and romance and she does it whilst trying to place it in context and by offering some humour, some pathos and some insight into the lives of its characters. Her initial environmental scope narrows into the private and personal lives and relationships of her two heroines but not in any linear unfolding, rather in a series of sketches; a collection of scenes that are not necessarily linked.

Shirley Keeldar displays both feminist and masculine traits. She falls in love with a tutor, the male equivalent of a governess. The man, Louis Moore, has no means or status but she loves him and intends to marry him despite the objections of her family. Caroline begins as the opposite to Shirley as she is very feminine but she is also weak and browbeaten. The focus of her unrequited love, Robert Moore, is shown as a proud and rising industrialist who is insensitive and implacable. Caroline is the child abandoned by her parents, the enduring theme of a Charlotte Brontë novel, who becomes so trapped and unhappy in her uncle's house that she almost dies. The love that Caroline receives from Shirley and from the nurse, Mrs Pryor, who turns out to be her long-lost mother, and eventually from the man she loves, saves Caroline's life and also makes her a much stronger person. Whilst Caroline's strength and purpose increases, Shirley slowly loses her independence and succumbs to marriage and the dominance of a husband.

It is another story where good triumphs over evil and where the heroines get their men, but it goes through many different phases before this can be achieved and it does so at great cost to all the people involved. By using Shirley and Caroline as her main spokespersons, Charlotte can highlight some of her own arguments about religion, romance, male power and the role of women. Shirley can be viewed partly as a portrait of Emily with some of Mary Taylor's characteristics; two highly individual and intelligent women who were very different to anyone else Charlotte ever knew. The Taylor family are represented in the book as the Yorke family, and Rose Yorke is very similar in character to Mary Taylor. Similarly, one can identify in Caroline's character traits of Ellen Nussey and Anne Brontë. Charlotte always worked best with the familiarity of people whom she knew and could characterise. The book is not autobiographical but it is a study of people and events and behaviours that Charlotte knew and had observed at close quarters.

The lives of Shirley and Caroline are influenced by their different status; Shirley the wealthy independent woman, and Caroline the abandoned child. Both go through crises of illness and both suffer mentally as much as physically. Once again Charlotte gives a detailed account of the female psyche and the reasons why women may become unstable and depressed. She also exposes the real fear of madness, linked to women who are repressed and have to contain their emotions and their sexuality.

Caroline is Charlotte's study in female repression and it is a very intense and important early description of the internal pressures and external anomie that can unravel the mind. Caroline is starved both physically and metaphorically. She has no purpose and her uncle will not let her have any employment. She has fallen in love with Robert Moore but he is so occupied with his mill and his work that he takes no notice of her. She wonders to herself,

> *I have to live, perhaps, till seventy years ... half a century of existence may lie before me. How am I to occupy it? What am I to do to fill the interval of time which spreads between me and the grave? I shall live to see Robert married to someone else, some rich lady: I shall never marry. What was I created for, I wonder? Where is my place in the world?*
>
> (C. Brontë, *Shirley*, 1982) p. 190

Caroline sees herself as becoming the one thing that for many women was even worse than a bad marriage and that was to become an old maid. The old maid was depicted as a woman who was unloved and unwanted. She had failed to get a husband and was little use to the society except for performing charitable works. In this book, Charlotte highlights what was, for many, a rather sad existence. Caroline knows that these women also wonder why they were created and what is their purpose? She notes that other people decide for them, saying that their role is to do good and help others so that they can be happy in the knowledge that they are 'devoted and virtuous'. Caroline asks,

Is this enough? Is it to live? Is there not a terrible hollowness, mockery, want, craving, in that existence which is given away to others, for want of something of your own to bestow it on? I suspect there is. Does virtue lie in abnegation of self? I do not believe it. Undue humility makes tyranny; weak concession creates selfishness.

(C. Brontë, *Shirley*, 1982) p. 190.

It is the 'abnegation of self' that frightens Caroline and contributes to her illness. She has nothing of her own and no-one to love her. In contrast to Jane Eyre, who used her orphan status to rise, Caroline sinks into a dangerous state which is part feverish anxiety, part anorexia, and part deep depression.

On waking the next morning she felt oppressed with unwonted languor ... she missed all sense of appetite: palatable food was as ashes and sawdust to her ... her eyes were bright, their pupils dilated ... she felt a pulse beat fast in her temples ... her brain in strange activity ... hundreds of busy and broken, but brilliant thoughts engaged her mind ... now followed a hot, parched, thirsty restless night.... How had she caught the fever she could not tell ... probably in her late walk home some sweet, poisoned breeze, redolent of honey-dew and miasma, had passed into her lungs and veins, and finding there already a fever of mental excitement, and a languor of long conflict and habitual sadness, had fanned the spark to flame, and left a well-lit fire behind it.

(C. Brontë, *Shirley*, 1982) p. 399.

Caroline's years of neglect and hopelessness have, with the sudden physical infection of a summer cold, kindled and ignited a mental breakdown which could bring about her death.

Modern medical science understands and explains this internalisation of unhappiness, which can upset the mind and body and lead to many of the mental illnesses identified today; self-harming, eating disorders, depressive disorders and suicidal tendencies. At the time of writing *Shirley*, Victorian treatments and attitudes towards mental health were largely misunderstood and misdiagnosed, consequently many disorders were also mistreated. The Victorian male was very wary of the mental health of women, and part of the theory behind keeping them subdued and domestic was to prevent their 'unnatural urges' being allowed to blossom. Women were not meant to be sexually aware or permissive unless they were prostitutes. They had to be kept virginal until safely married and there was very little worse that could happen to a woman than to become an unmarried or 'fallen' mother. If marriage did not occur then they could be viewed as a threat to the moral health and safety of the society, their families and of themselves unless they were kept protected or, in some cases, incarcerated.

Caroline finds herself barred from occupation, unlikely to marry and unable to face the 'old maid' option. She metaphorically decides to turn her face to the wall and give up. Even the attentive nursing by Mrs Pryor does not make Caroline recover, even though she is tender and loving, two of the qualities of which Caroline is so in need. Once a week she asks her nurse to sit her by the window for an hour and it is during this hour that Mrs Pryor realises that it is because Caroline can see Robert Moore riding by the vicarage on his horse towards Whinbury market.

It is made explicit that Caroline is dying and she is, in effect, dying because she cannot have the man she loves and has no other person on which to place her affections. She is dying physically and emotionally. She cannot eat, she cannot walk, she has no energy and no reason to go on living. She loves a man who is barely aware of her existence and the pain of her separation from him is more than she can bear. Her response to her life is in many ways completely rational; her mind and body are reacting to an impossible situation in the only way it knows how. Caroline and Mrs Pryor discuss Caroline's illness and Caroline asks,

'Do you think I shall not get better? I do not feel very ill – only weak.'

'But your mind, Caroline: your mind is crushed; your heart is almost broken: you have been so neglected, so repulsed, left so desolate.'

'I believe grief is, and always has been, my worst ailment. I sometimes think, if an abundant gush of happiness came on me, I could revive yet.'

(C. Brontë, *Shirley*, 1982) p. 409.

It is at this point that Mrs Pryor reveals that she is Caroline's mother but also informs her that her father, now dead, was a cruel and vicious man whom she had to leave. He was, despite his treatment towards his wife, always kind to his daughter, who had inherited his good looks but not his bad character. It is an interesting piece of realism that Charlotte does not allow the father to be good and saintly, but a man whom his wife had to leave and the cause of their child's abandonment. In an extraordinary speech, Mrs Pryor explains why she did not come back and claim Caroline when she saw a picture of her. She says,

> *I had reason to dread a fair outside, to mistrust a popular bearing, to shudder before distraction, grace, and courtesy. Beauty and affability had come in my way when I was a recluse, desolate, young, and ignorant: a toil worn governess perishing of uncheered labour, breaking down before her time. These, Caroline, when they smiled on me, I mistook for angels! I followed them home, and when into their hands I had given without reserve my whole chance of future happiness it was my lot to witness a transfiguration on the domestic hearth: to see the white mask lifted, the bright disguise put away, and there opposite me sat down – oh God! I have suffered.*
>
> (C. Brontë, *Shirley* , 1982) p. 411.

This is reminiscent of the experience of Helen Huntingdon in *The Tennant of Wildfell Hall*; the happy bride who knows nothing of the true nature of her husband until after they are married. Mrs Pryor, or Mrs Helstone as she really is, was married to James, William Helstone's brother, and she left her child with her brother-in-law in the hope that he would look after her. It is interesting to find that Rev. Helstone was in many ways less kind to Caroline than her father was likely to have been.

Shirley Keeldar also suffers an illness that is linked to madness and, like Caroline, the illness is brought about by fear and the inability to share her worries with anyone else. Charlotte uses illness as a method of bringing out the characteristics of her heroines and to expose their weaknesses and faults, but she also uses it to allow movement in a particular direction. Caroline is strengthened and happier after her illness, Shirley is weakened insofar as her strong will and independence are shown as traits that do not help her and which actually separate her from others. This isolation is detrimental to her health and progress. Shirley's character and viewpoint must be modified to attract and marry Louis Moore. Society will not allow the marriage of a man and woman so diametrically opposite, so Louis must rise and Shirley has to fall, just as, though oppositely, Jane and Rochester did.

Shirley's illness is real to her, but psychosomatic in origin. She has been bitten by a possibly rabid dog in an incident which echoes one that actually happened to Emily Brontë. Like Emily, Shirley dashes into the house and cauterises the wound with a hot iron. Rabies, or hydrophobia, was a real threat to people; its progress and the death of the individual was a horrible, painful, and terrible way to die. Cases had been recently recorded in Haworth around the time that Charlotte was writing and she would have been aware of the symptoms. It may be that Emily worried silently about her condition for many weeks, possibly eventually sharing her experience when she felt that the danger was over.

Rabies takes two forms, but both attack the central nervous system. *Furious rabies*, which starts with flu-like symptoms of fever and muscle-weakness, insomnia, anxiety and agitation with a growing fear of water, eventually brings about the dreadful foaming of the mouth and the violent agitation of the brain that finally leads to death. *Paralytic rabies*, takes longer to develop but leads to a gradual paralysis, coma and death. The gestation period can be anything from four weeks to many months, even years.

Shirley was right to be worried, but feels that there is no-one she can confide in because they will fuss over her and pamper her and treat her as an invalid. Shirley does not want this and she naturally dreads the thought of dying as a raving lunatic, exposed and pitied by her family and friends. Although she is losing weight and cannot eat, she continually denies that she is ill. She does however rewrite her will and when Henry Sympson reports this to his tutor, Louis Moore, Louis finally confronts Shirley and she confesses her fears to him. At this point, Louis and Shirley are brought together and finally, as he realises that she is not as he had feared, in love with Robert Moore, they are able to come together. It is interesting that Charlotte cannot join the independent and wealthy female with the poor and honest man. She must hand Shirley's property and fortune over to her husband so that they can meet on equal terms. Shirley states that she wants Louis to 'master' her and be her strength. Shirley had tried to break the masculine boundaries but is herself broken back into becoming a dependent female.

This fits in with the Victorian idea that the man must be in charge of his family. Charlotte is very good at exposing the anomalies between the sexes and the fate of the thousands of women who are overworked and undervalued. But whilst exposing the hypocrisy, she cannot allow the total upset of the status quo. She does not allow the different classes to mix and this is part of her own lower-middle class and Tory beliefs. Whilst she may describe the plight of the Luddites, the mill labourers and the old maids, she does not align her heroines with them or do anything to further their cause. They are part of the historical background of the book rather than the focus, although she is a front-runner in exposing some of their problems.

The use of illness in this book is very apparent and can be seen to echo what was happening in Charlotte's life and home. Charlotte knew that illness and death were the great levellers, and that when people are gravely ill or greatly agitated, one sees them at their most vulnerable and exposed. Robert Moore is shot and must have his wounds nursed, during this time he begins a change that allows him to appreciate what is most important in his life. Although he is still very enthusiastic in expanding his mill and his wealth, he can now let Caroline into his life, but not before she has inherited money. Louis Moore has a short illness from which he is rescued by Shirley and when they marry he will, by law, inherit all of her possessions.

This contriving to create a happy ending is not as straightforward as it seems. Charlotte has grown as an author and is more aware of the reality of the human spirit. Whilst one can appreciate the rapid growth of industrialisation and the wealth and prosperity it brought, at the close of the novel Charlotte casts some doubt on a happy ever after ending. One sees this in the lifting of the Orders of Council which will make Robert Moore a very rich man. Despite this, one wonders at this progress when Robert describes to Caroline how he intends to destroy the valley and woods that Caroline so enjoyed. He declares,

The copse shall be firewood ere five years elapse: the beautiful wild ravine shall be a smooth descent; the green natural terrace shall be a paved street: there shall be cottages in the dark ravine, and cottages on the lonely slopes: the rough pebbled track shall be an even, firm, broad, black, sooty road, bedded with cinders from my mill: and my mill, Caroline – my mill shall fill its present yard.
(C. Brontë, *Shirley*, 1982) p.597.

Caroline pronounces these changes as 'horrible' but he continues to describe his plans,

I will pour the waters of Pactolus through the valley of Briarfield ... I will get
an act for enclosing Nunnely Common, and parcelling it out into farms.

(C. Brontë, *Shirley*, 1982) p. 598.

Whilst one can appreciate that this is the 'progress' of industrialisation bringing
jobs and homes to the unemployed, there is the age-old battle between beauty
and industry, and between the natural and romantic and the grind of labour
and growth of wealth. Other anomalies are also present which disturb the last
chapter. Mrs Pryor, Caroline's mother, is an important character who is very
aware that marriage can go wrong and she is wary of the marriage between her
daughter and Robert Moore. She has not liked him in the past and knows that
many a businessman can become greedy and selfish and she is naturally worried.
We have seen Robert brought almost to bankruptcy and this levelled him and
his ambitions but he is now on the rise again and one wonders if his business
drive will alter him.

Louis and Shirley have a strange pre-marital existence where Shirley
continually procrastinates over fixing a wedding date. For weeks, she refuses to
name a day but is finally,

[F]*ettered to a fixed day: there she lay, conquered by love, and bound with a*
vow ... thus vanquished and restricted, she pined, like any other chained denizen
of deserts ... she furthered no preparations for her nuptials; Louis was himself
obliged to direct all arrangements: he was virtually master of Fieldhead, weeks
before he became so nominally.

(C. Brontë, *Shirley*, 1982) p. 592.

This is a deliberate ploy by Shirley to make Louis the master; the man in charge
of her and her fortune. She abdicates from her possessions and her status until
she is the attractive plaything that she assumes she needs to be. Charlotte tells
the reader that,

[Louis] *would never have learned to rule, if she had not ceased to govern: the*
incapacity of the sovereign had developed the power of the premier.

(C. Brontë, *Shirley*, 1982) p. 592.

Shirley continues to be obtuse at times and rather an awkward and strange creature and one wonders when and if she will be happy in her marriage. Caroline describes their union when she returns one day from Fieldhead,

> *Shirley is as naughty as ever, Robert: she will neither say Yes or No to any question put. She sits alone: I cannot tell whether she is melancholy or nonchalant: if you rouse her, or scold her, she gives you a look half wistful, half reckless, which sends you away as queer and crazed as herself.*
>
> (C. Brontë, *Shirley*, 1982) p. 593.

There is much to like and admire in this third of Charlotte's four novels and plenty to irritate. Charlotte's insistence on showing off her ability to write in French and her constant reference to the Bible may have been more significant when first written but does little now to enhance the story or move it along. Her stopping and starting and her lack of insight into the plight of the lower classes is a fault, and her move from the political to the romantic is rather contrived. What she does offer is wonderful portraits of her characters and her appreciation of mental health and loss is especially notable and beautifully crafted. Her humour and perception is evident, especially in the chapters concerning the curates and the Yorke family. Charlotte had laboured on this book through some of the worst days of her life and it is to her credit that she achieved such a work of art.

Chapter Twenty-One

Villette

Charlotte Brontë finally finished the writing of *Villette* in November 1852 after a long and sporadic effort during which, at times, she was often unable to write. This was partly due to writer's block but also to her low mood and ill health. Charlotte knew that she had to endure the loneliness of home without her siblings for the rest of her life and, quite naturally, it brought her to a very low mood. She described the long, lonely days and sad nights in a letter to her friend Laetitia Wheelwright,

> *The solitude of my position fearfully aggravated its other evils. Some long, stormy days and nights there were when I felt such a craving for support and companionship as I cannot express. Sleepless, I lay awake night after night; weak and unable to occupy myself, I sat in my chair day after day, the saddest memories my only company.*

> (Palmer, 2002) p. 108.

Charlotte is naturally grief stricken. Grief is in effect a type of mental illness or disturbance; an anguish of the emotions and psyche that has no cure and little comfort. For someone with Charlotte's long history of a nervous and delicate constitution, it particularly overwhelmed her. For many months, it manifested in various physical disabilities. In her letters, she describes weeks of no appetite, sleeplessness, toothache and continuous sick headaches with fever and bad colds. She also had the threat of tuberculosis, her siblings' killer, to worry about.

That Charlotte could write at all in these months is due to her abiding belief that the only way out of grief, or any hardship, was to stay occupied and to work no matter how bad she felt. This had always been Charlotte's response to setback and disappointment. Her self-control was often at its strongest when she was under the most extreme pressures. She had decided that *The Professor*, still not published, needed to be revised and rewritten in the first person and by a female narrator. It was now eight years since Charlotte had last been in Brussels and she had learnt to contain and properly analyse her feelings and her experiences. She felt them too important to abandon and was now able to treat the story objectively and realistically.

Villette describes the life journey of orphan Lucy Snowe. It begins with Lucy living with her godmother, Mrs Bretton, where she helps to look after a little girl, Polly Home, who has been left in Mrs Bretton's care. Polly idolises Mrs Bretton's 16-year-old boy, Graham. Lucy moves on to be a lady's companion to a Miss Marchmont who, on the night before she dies, tells Lucy of her sad and lonely life following the death of her lover, thirty years before. Lucy then gains employment as a nursery governess at the school of Madame Beck in the town of Villette in Belgium. She becomes an English teacher at the school but the work is very hard and she becomes increasingly lonely and alienated. She is attracted to Dr John, who is actually Graham Bretton, the school's English physician, and following a long summer holiday when she is left alone at the school she suffers a mental breakdown. Dr John eventually comes to her aid and Lucy is reunited with her Bretton godmother who is now living in Villette. Dr John falls in love with one of the older English pupils at the school, Ginevra Fanshawe, who is a silly and fatuous young woman whom Lucy met on the boat crossing the Channel to Belgium and whom she greatly dislikes. It was their chance meeting that brought Lucy to Mme Beck's school

Eventually Dr John is reacquainted with Polly Home and falls in love with her. The scheming Ginevra falls for a penniless aristocrat, Alfred de Hamal. These two have secret meetings at the school and to cover their tracks, regale Lucy with stories of ghosts and a nun who haunts the premises. Alfred dresses up as the nun and his hauntings of Lucy contribute to her mental breakdown.

Mme Beck has a cousin, Paul Emmanuel, who is a master at the school. He and Lucy begin to spend time together and the more affectionate they become, the more Mme Beck tries to keep them apart, as she does not see Lucy as a suitable match for him. After many months of acquaintance and gradual acceptance, M. Paul pledges his intention to marry Lucy when he returns from family matters abroad. He has made arrangements for her to run a small school of her own. The novel is left open ended when M. Paul's ship is lost at sea. The reader is not told whether he survives and returns to marry her, or whether he drowns and she is left alone to fend for herself.

It is apparent that some of this book is biographical and at times, autobiographical, but although this allows Charlotte to guide the reader through the story and explain events along with their accompanying emotions, she does not always do this. Sometimes she uses an odd direct narrative where she talks to the reader, suggesting that the reader decides on how Lucy is feeling at times and how they should interpret her behaviour. Added to this, one often sees Lucy through the opinions of other people and through the statements Lucy makes about others. She is a rather elusive character. This elusiveness adds to her mystery and her ambiguities. Again, Charlotte is trying to write out her experiences whilst hoping to withhold some of her own personal identity.

This novel repeats Charlotte's need to highlight the limitations of the unmarried middle-class woman. Lucy is not working class and cannot, therefore, apply herself to manual labour. The roles of teacher, governess or companion are her only options. These options leave her unfulfilled and unrewarded. She is poorly paid with no prospects and has little rank and no direct friendship or companionship with her employers. In all respects, Lucy is an outsider in Belgium. She is a Protestant in a predominantly Catholic country and is therefore surrounded by believers in the Roman church; this in itself is enough to alienate her. She does not speak French and so thinks and talks in English before slowly learning and understanding the new language and culture of the Belgians. She has no money and is very much at the mercy of her employer and the girls she must teach, many of whom are confident, wealthy and attractive young ladies.

Understandably, Lucy withdraws into herself but this act of self-preservation causes her to become somewhat paranoid about the behaviour of others towards her, especially Mme Beck. Lucy begins to feel watched and spied on and believes that people are trying to cause her trouble. This is partly true of Mme Beck, who jealously guards the men who work in or visit the school. Whenever Dr John or M. Paul show any interest in Lucy, Mme Beck investigates the reasons why. Yet, neither of them communicates with Lucy for her good looks or feminine charm, they are genuinely trying to be either her friend or her teacher.

When the summer holidays arrive and the pupils and teachers go away for the long break, Lucy has nowhere to go. The school closes and she is left behind to wander about the empty schoolrooms and silent corridors. For the whole of the eight-week break Lucy is practically the only person left at the school and the solitude plays on her fraught nerves. She states,

> *How vast and void seemed the desolate premises! How gloomy the forsaken garden...my spirits had long been gradually sinking; now that the prop of employment was withdrawn, they went down fast. Even to look forward was not to hope: the dumb future spoke no comfort, offered no promise, gave no inducement to bear present evil in reliance of future good. A sorrowful indifference to existence often pressed on me.*
>
> (C. Brontë, *Villette*, 1984) p. 228.

Lucy also begins to imagine things. She sees the ghostly nun that she has heard haunts the school and this further excites her nervous anxiety. Lucy becomes so worried and depressed that she seeks the help of a Catholic priest to whom she confesses her unhappy state,

> *I said, I was perishing for a word of advice or an accent of comfort. I had been living for some weeks quite alone; I had been ill; I had a pressure of affliction on my mind of which it would hardly any longer endure the weight.*
>
> (C. Brontë, *Villette*, 1984) p. 233.

Lucy is suffering from depression brought on over a long period of loneliness but exacerbated by her isolation during the school holidays. Dr John diagnoses hypochondria; a state of mind brought about by extreme and lasting unhappiness. It is very similar to that which the reader saw in Caroline Helstone in *Shirley*; the gradual wearing down of the mind and spirit from long years of loneliness and despair with limited release in employment or interesting activities.

Charlotte had suffered the same fate as Lucy and knew exactly how her character would act and react and this makes these passages especially realistic and poignant. Charlotte also visited a Catholic priest during her time in Belgium, which was a measure of how lonely and sad her life and mood had become. Charlotte writes out this episode in her life in great detail in *Villette* and it gives the tale extra authenticity both in its investigation of how and why she became ill, and also how mental health issues can be influenced by external events which are then internalised. This was ground-breaking medical analysis, different from the accepted version of mental breakdown, especially in women, as seen by the Victorians. The nineteenth-century diagnosis more often linked female mental breakdown to sin or sexual deviance.

Lucy recovers somewhat in the safety and care of her godmother and the ministrations of Dr John, at their house in Villette, but she must return to her employment. Dr John has promised to write to her so that she has a friend and communication with the world outside of the school, another acknowledgement that this need for social interaction and recognition is a cause of her illness. Lucy returns but is still plagued by doubts and is still haunted by the ghostly figure of the 'nun', which prevents her from gaining a full recovery.

Lucy is naturally drawn to her saviour Dr John but instructs the reader not to suppose that she has any 'warmer feelings' for him. She obviously has but she wisely notices that he has two personae. He can be the sensible, strong and manly Dr John, but he is also the representation of the average male who can only judge women by their class, their youth and their appearance. He is blind to the artful deviance of Ginevra Fanshawe because of her superficial beauty. He is therefore unimpressed at the theatre by the brilliance of the performer, Vashti, because she is ugly, violent and strong. Lucy is shocked that Dr John is unable to appreciate her brilliance as an actress: 'In a few terse phrases he told me his opinion of, and feeling towards, the actress: he judges her as a woman, not an artist: it was a branding judgement.' (C. Brontë, *Villette*, 1984) p. 342.

Like most of Charlotte's main characters, their views and opinions change, or are changed for them, over time and this happens also to Dr John when he is reunited with Polly Home. Love makes him more tolerant and more perceptive. He is then able to recognise and appreciate women in ways other than their surface qualities. It is Charlotte's keen attention to the maturation of her characters and how and why this occurs that makes her books so crafted. She brings to her novels the keen eye of the miniaturist which she displayed in her drawings. She uncovers layer after layer of detail and faithfully records it. This includes everything, the warts and the lines and the blemishes, as part of her determination to be realistic.

In *Villette*, the reader is shown a wide variety of characters, some of whom appear cruel and offensive to Lucy, and others who are kind, but the portrait of Lucy demonstrates that her interpretation of the people around her is not necessarily accurate or reliable. Lucy is losing her self-control and her inner thoughts are displayed in a way that highlights her growing neurosis. She speaks her emotions and her subjective experiences because her creator, Charlotte Brontë, is living in an isolated emotional hiatus; bereft of her siblings and with the memory of long weeks of isolation at Brussels brought to the fore by her current predicament. The novel is less of a tale of social and political events than an exploration of Charlotte's own disturbed mind and unhappy disposition.

The passages describing Lucy's empty summer holidays at the school are an echo of Charlotte's lived experience. She too had wandered the empty corridors of the Pensionnat Heger and fantasised about ghosts and apparitions. Charlotte had also been tortured by feelings that she was unable to verbalise and she too was driven to despair by her loneliness and lack of occupation. Lucy describes tortured, sleepless nights as her mind sinks further into depression and her fear for her sanity increases. She dreams of people she once knew and loved, now dead, who return in nightmare guise to torment her.

> *I lay in a strange fever of the nerves and blood. Sleep went quite away. I used to rise in the night, look round for her, beseech her earnestly to return. A rattle of the window, a cry of the blast only replied – Sleep never came! ...Some fearful hours went over me: indescribably was I torn, racked and oppressed in mind. Amidst the horrors of that dream I think the worst lay here. Methought the well-loved dead, who had loved me well in life, met me elsewhere, alienated: galled was my inmost spirit with an unutterable sense of despair about the future.'*
> (C. Brontë, *Villette*, 1984) p. 231.

Again, Charlotte's own experiences are verbalised in her narrative. Charlotte also dreamt one night that her dead sisters had come to visit her at school and when she rushed downstairs to see them they were so changed and awful that she was deeply affected by the feeling of utter joy suddenly changed to horror.

This unexpected and disturbing way that dreams can work to upset the mind is described by Lord Byron in *Childe Harold's Pilgrimage*, a poem known and read by the Brontës. Byron fixes that awful moment when the known and familiar turns strange and alien. He wrote,

> Which out of things familiar, undesign'd
> When least we deem of such, calls up to view

> The spectres whom no exorcism can bind,
> The cold – the changed – perchance the dead – anew
> The mourn'd, the loved, the lost – too many, yet how few!
>
> (Byron, 1982)

The whole tapestry of Charlotte's experiences at the Pensionnat Heger are woven into *Villette*, as well as many of her personal feelings from different times and areas of her life. That she was living alone and in mourning when she wrote the book adds to the content and theme of her work. The subjectivity of the work is apparent and yet it still describes and identifies with universal themes of women's lack of opportunities and occupation and with feelings of isolation that can increase anxiety and cause disturbance and depression.

In contrast, there is also a great deal of light and life in the novel. After her recovery, Lucy attends the theatre and the fetes and various galleries and exhibitions. The town of Villette is shown as prospering from the effects of the industrial revolution. The wealth of the middle classes was increasing along with their need and ability to express it. At Mme Beck's school, there was none of the harsh austerity of Lowood and none of the cold and disease that plagued Jane Eyre. Lucy describes the warm fires of the winter and the light and pure air of the summer. The students and staff have plenty of food and activities, amusement and entertainment. There is everything to enjoy along with a liberal education and yet Lucy remains unhappy and lonely for most of the book.

What Charlotte describes is an authentic interpretation of the female who has no control over her environment. Lucy expresses less enjoyment for some of this carnival and more of a bewildered and confused reaction to it. There is too much; objects, display, colour, noise, music, laughter and people, and Lucy is carried along with little or no ability to direct her own path. This over indulgence in spectacle and pageant further contrasts with her inner isolation. When the noise and the people disappear, she returns into her own vacuity. Lucy has no-one to share her experiences with; no close confidante who can understand her emotions or assist her to overcome her fears.

Dr John's letters help her at first but Lucy is aware that his heart lies elsewhere. In another representation of personal experience, Charlotte describes the long wait for letters that do not arrive,

Those who live in retirement, whose lives have fallen amid the seclusion of schools or of other walled-in and guarded dwellings, are liable to be suddenly and for a long while dropped out of the memory of their friends, the denizens of a freer world ... there falls a stilly pause, a wordless silence, a long blank of oblivion. Unbroken always is this blank; alike entire and unexplained. The letter, the message once frequent, are cut off; the visit, formerly periodical, ceases to occur; the book, paper, or other token that indicated remembrance, comes no more.

(C. Brontë, *Villette*, 1984) p. 348.

Lucy cherishes Dr John's letters as if they are food for her starved existence. She is heartbroken when one is stolen. It is a measure of her need for communication and friendship. Charlotte Brontë, living at a time when letters were the only form of intimate communication between separated people, treasured her letters as a lifeline. The writing and receiving of letters was an important part of daily life just as emails and texts are today. When Monsieur Heger stopped responding to Charlotte's letters she was deeply hurt. It is hard to imagine the effect that this withdrawal of friendship and communication would have on a woman who felt that her whole being depended on the trust and acknowledgement of her 'master'. When Charlotte expresses Lucy's obsession with Dr John's letters and her need to treasure and guard them, it is part of her own bitter experience.

A reader may interpret Lucy's behaviour as extreme and unrealistic, but one must realise the times in which *Villette* was written and the experiences of its author. Charlotte is struggling with her own mental stability and grief and this is transposed on to her heroine. Lucy interprets the world according to her own perceptions and her unstable mental state. It is part of the modern interpretation of people as being socially constructed and was not something widely acknowledged in the 1840s. We can now see how each person is the product of gender, genes, upbringing and environment, but this was not a Victorian concept. The Victorians interpreted self in terms of class, wealth and gender with strict guidelines based on a religious code.

Charlotte is advocating the idea of people developing as a process of their environment and experiences. Lucy develops according to her external surroundings and internal conflicts. This idea of the socially constructed self is also a new concept in the literature of the time. Charlotte goes beyond just describing events and showing why and how people succeed or fail. She is trying to deconstruct Lucy's experiences as the catalyst for her psychological state.

By introducing mystery and suspense into the book and creating illusions where nothing is as it seems and no-one is as they are presented, Charlotte has closely examined the shifting qualities and personalities of her characters. There are times when there is an alteration in the story that makes both the character and the reader doubt what they are seeing. There are times when Lucy literally does not know where she is. In a dizzying, hallucinatory episode that links to the physical and psychological effects of a high fever, where the rising temperature affects the mind, the reader sees Lucy waking up in the home of her godmother. To wake up from sleep or collapse and to see both the familiar and unfamiliar is linked again to the 'uncanny' and the work of Sigmund Freud. The uncanny is that strange feeling of knowing and not knowing; the familiar linked to the unfamiliar, and there is a wonderful description of it in *Villette* when Lucy wakes up expecting to be in the dormitory at school and is instead in a strange room but surrounded by familiar objects.

My eye, prepared to take in the range of a long, large and white-washed chamber, blinked baffled, on encountering the limited area of a small cabinet – a cabinet with sea green walls: also, instead of five wide and naked windows, there was a high lattice, shaded with muslin festoons: instead of two dozen little stands of painted wood…. These articles of furniture could not be real, solid arm-chairs, looking glasses, and wash stands – they must be the ghosts of such articles … there remained but to conclude that I had myself passed into an abnormal state of mind; in short, that I was very ill and delirious: and even then, mine was the strangest figment with which delirium has ever harassed a victim … I knew – I was obliged to know – the green chintz of that little chair; the little snug chair itself … the very stand too, with its top of grey marble, splintered at one corner; – all these I was compelled to recognize and to hail.

(C. Brontë, *Villette*, 1984) p. 241.

Lucy is experiencing that detachment from reality which can occur when what we perceive does not match our known experience. Like most people who encounter an uncanny or strange experience they tend to blame their own faculties for the anomaly before any other explanation. Therefore, when objects or people are different, or out of their normal place, the mind finds it difficult to locate itself and the person encountering the phenomenon starts to believe that they are suffering from some form of insanity, often before seeking any rational interpretation. The famous play, *Gaslight* by Patrick Hamilton, written in 1939 and made into various film versions, is a classic example of how easy it can be to make a person think that they are losing their mind.

In the case of the ghostly nun in *Villette*, there is no 'uncanniness' because the nun is not a genuine apparition but a man dressed in a nun's habit. Lucy's mind has been excited by tales of haunting so that when Alfred de Hamal dresses up and *appears* to Lucy, her mind is predisposed to believe in what she is seeing. These episodes in the book all help to show how fragile Lucy's hold on reality has become and how easy it is for the mind to be fooled and upset by the unexpected and the concept of an alternate reality. Charlotte is asking the reader to decipher what constitutes reality and whether reality is a social construction. Again, this is very modern philosophy and shows Charlotte's own doubts and fears, as well as her knowledge and understanding of sanity and insanity and its links to the concept of reality.

It is interesting to note that Patrick Brontë's medical journal to which he constantly referred had many annotations regarding mental illness. It shows that he had a particular interest in medicine and the mind. His children would have been aware of this tome, *Domestic Medicine* by Thomas John Graham. Notably one finds here two of the names by which Dr John/Graham Bretton, is known in *Villette*.

Alongside Lucy's nervous and unstable condition is another recurring theme of the book which is that of people being watched; that peculiar affliction of those suffering from paranoia. Ironically, Lucy is the person who mostly watches others from her invisible stance as an unimportant and isolated character but it is she who feels that she is being spied on. Kate Millet describes Lucy in the following terms,

Lucy Snowe ... [is] bitter and she is honest; a neurotic revolutionary full of conflict, backsliding, anger, terrible self-doubt, and an unconquerable determination to win through. She is a pair of eyes watching society; weighing, ridiculing, judging. A piece of furniture that no one notices. Lucy sees everything and reports, cynically, compassionately, truthfully, analytically. She is no-

one, because she lacks any trait that might render her visible: beauty, money, conformity.

(Millett, 1970) p. 201.

Lucy is occasionally spied on by Madame Beck, but she is also looked upon by people who overtly wish to examine her for her own sake. M. Paul openly assesses Lucy's facial features to assess her character. This demonstrates the growing Victorian belief in physiognomy, the study of a person's facial features, and phrenology, the study of the contours of their skull, as indicators of their strength of character and personality. It was a time when a 'weak chin' or 'eyes too close together' could affect a person's prospects. Lucy is sometimes unable to distinguish between the watching over and concern of M. Paul and Dr John and the spying or natural interest of Mme Beck and the hallucinatory appearance of the nun, all who 'watch' her in different ways. There is a watchfulness imbued in the novel; people watch each other and the heroine, the reader also watch events and people, and there is a mysterious seeing eye, which watches over everything. Charlotte is the metaphysical presence who observes her characters and allows them to see both the real and the unreal, and this disturbs the reader who finds difficulty in interpreting Lucy and her story. This is then further upset by the use of dreams and hallucinations.

The watchfulness in the novel adds to its very modern and ground-breaking idea of the novel as a window on the social construction of people and their identities. It highlights what happens when people have no self-control in a society where such control is highly valued and a sign of mental stability. Lucy tries to keep her self-control but people and events conspire against her. Loss of self-control, as previously explained, was viewed as a weakness, especially in women, bordering on sexual deviance or mental disturbance. Neither of which could be tolerated. Women were expected to be innocent and virginal before marriage and so needed to remain sexually ignorant and chaste. Lucy's sexuality is hidden and then deliberately buried along with Dr John's letters. Lucy is no more able to express her sexuality than she can any other aspect of her complicated sense of self. When Lucy has feelings for Dr John she must deny them, partly because she knows that she can never attract him as a lover, and partly because she is conditioned to keep her own counsel. Passion is aligned with mental illness and yet it is in its denial, not in its expression, that Lucy's mental turmoil is partially rooted.

It is no accident that Lucy's name is Snowe, a metaphor for cold, frosty, white and innocent. This sense of ice and winter is part of the barrenness of the book. When Lucy is alone at the school it is the height of summer and the holidays, but she remains hidden and silent and there is no celebration or warmth for her. When the external environment is warm and gay it often agitates Lucy rather than comforts her, which suggests an inner core of ice that will only melt when she has both someone to care for her and, more importantly, her own independence; a time when she can let go and be herself without the constraints and the expectations of the external environment.

Charlotte not only shows why each character behaves in the way that they do but she also invites the reader to judge actions and behaviour so that they become an integral part of the story. This is especially so when she offers an ambiguous ending to the book which allows the reader to choose the fate of its hero and heroine. This was a new and innovative way of letting the reader decide which reality they think most appropriate. It helps to lift the book from the conventional marriage conclusion to an alternative that may be more likely and possibly more satisfying.

Charlotte makes a very important point here. If M. Paul drowns, or never returns, Lucy is never disappointed or unhappy in marriage. She has her school and an income and so she is well looked after and independent with plenty to occupy her. This can actually be a more acceptable lifestyle for Lucy, and for Charlotte. They have the best of both worlds. One wonders if this was Charlotte's ideal. She felt throughout her life that love and marriage were, in some ways, an illusion; even that marriage would spoil love as it broke the spell of mystery. Unrequited love is hard to bear, but it is never spoilt by the mundane or the repetitive. The domesticity of marriage can be the entity that smothers and kills it. Charlotte wanted drama and longing and excitement, and she appears to be very aware that the attributes which may draw people together can be ruined and extinguished by the over familiarity of close and continual contact.

These were not the conventional expectations of the lower middle-class female. Charlotte and her sisters had three alternatives: to work in very limited professions, to marry, or to live the lives of old maids in uncertain spinsterhood. Charlotte felt very early in her life, quite wrongly as it turned out, that her poor looks and lack of charm would preclude her from marriage, and it was from this perspective that she created her plain heroines. She then worked through several scenarios where the plain, orphaned governess could achieve the safety and sanctity of marriage – but always on her terms. Those terms had to include independence both mentally and financially, and marriage to a man who would respect her as an equal. Finally, her heroines could experience the joy of love and passion but without the burden of marriage and become independent and occupied.

One finds it difficult to believe that the once volatile and independent Shirley will succumb to her role as wife and mother, or that William Crimsworth and his wife shall live happily ever after. In *Jane Eyre* one senses a happier outcome because Jane has met and married Rochester on her own terms, but even their happiness could be compromised. In *Villette*, Charlotte has left the decision to the reader; there is no prescribed answer or neat finale. The reader has the choice of whether marriage or total independence is the best and most personally satisfying outcome for Lucy.

Had Charlotte herself not succumbed to the long unrequited devotion of her father's curate, Arthur Bell Nicholls, whom she married in 1855, she may well have lived longer and enjoyed a comfortable and financially secure future for herself and her father. She would have had the independence she sought, but also the esteem and approbation of her friends and associates. She would have travelled and continued to write as a successful and admired author. Is this what she is advocating for Lucy? Is it better to have loved and lost, so long as you can then move forward independently and successfully? When she wrote *Villette* it is possible that this was Charlotte's view and it was as new and modern as the thoughts and beliefs of the suffragettes and the early feminists.

Charlotte made her views clear in a letter to her publisher,

With regard to the momentous point – M. Paul's fate – in case anyone in future should request to be enlightened thereon – they may be told that it was designed that every reader should settle the catastrophe for himself, according to the quality of his disposition, the tender or remorseful impulse of his nature. Drowning and Matrimony are the fearful alternatives. The merciful ... will of course choose the former and milder doom – drown him to put him out of pain. The cruel-hearted will on the contrary pitilessly impale him on the second horn

of the dilemma – marrying him without ruth or compunction to that person –
that – that individual – Lucy Snowe.

(*Selected Letters of Charlotte Brontë*, 2007) p. 217.

It may seem strange that after all her written concerns regarding love and marriage, Charlotte married her father's Irish curate in June 1854. The story of Arthur Bell Nicholls' long admiration and love for Charlotte is also a tale that could be taken from a book. His devotion to Charlotte and his determination to marry her is legendary. The opposition from her father stalled all his attempts to start a courtship and he eventually left Haworth after an emotional farewell that saw many of his congregation, including Charlotte, in tears. Months of secret correspondence followed until Patrick finally agreed to let this 'lowly' curate become 'better acquainted' with his 'famous' daughter.

Charlotte wrote of her feelings for Arthur Nicholls in words that demonstrate that she had grave misgivings even though she greatly admired his fortitude and understood his long heartache. Her father had not treated Arthur well and Charlotte had admired the way in which Arthur had never been rude or hostile in return. When Patrick finally gave consent for their marriage it was on the proviso that they would live at the Parsonage and that Arthur would look after his father-in-law to the end of Patrick's life. A promise which he kept. Charlotte wrote to Ellen in April 1854,

What I taste of happiness is of the soberest order … I trust to love my husband, I am grateful for his tender love to me. I believe him to be an affectionate, a conscientious, a high-principled man; and if, with all this, I should yield to regrets that fine talents, congenial tastes and thoughts are not added, it seems to me I should be most presumptuous and thankless.

(Palmer, 2002) p. 118.

She further wrote to Mrs Gaskell, the following month about her decision to marry saying,

I cannot deny that I had a battle to fight with myself; I am not sure that I have even yet conquered certain inward combatants….My destiny will not be

brilliant, certainly, but Mr Nicholls is conscientious, affectionate, pure in heart and life ... I mean to try and make him happy, and Papa too.

(Palmer, 2002) p. 118.

In these words, Charlotte demonstrates her uncertainties. She is still unsure whether she is doing the right thing. She admires Arthur enormously but this is not a love match, at least not on Charlotte's side. His commitment to her has swayed her, plus his agreement to stay at the Parsonage and this is a measure of his devotion. It is notable that Charlotte wants to please both men in her life but does not foresee any remarkable expectation of her own happiness. She does not know how this union will work out, nor if she will grow to love her husband. Unfortunately, they had only nine months together. Charlotte died in early pregnancy when excessive sickness exacerbated her dormant symptoms of consumption. Once again, an early death befell the Brontë family, especially poignant at a time when Charlotte was beginning to settle into her marriage, her domestic arrangements and the success of her writing. She had everything to live for but the ever-present tubercular disease chose this time to claim its final Brontë victim.

Charlotte's death was a terrible and tragic end to the story of the six Brontë children and left their father and Mr Nicholls together in the Parsonage until Patrick finally died in June of 1861 in his eighty-fifth year. Arthur Nicholls returned to Ireland and the next incumbent, the Reverend Wade, moved into the Parsonage. The continuity of life in Haworth and at the Parsonage carried on and no-one would have been any the wiser of the lives of its remarkable family if the writing and publication of their books had never occurred. They would, like so many others, have faded into history with their lives and stories unknown and untold.

Luckily, and mainly through Charlotte's continuing endeavours and belief in her own and her sisters' talents, we know an enormous amount about them and their writings. Of the four who survived into adulthood, Emily is the one whom biographers and critics know the least about and the one whom is the most difficult to understand. We know the basics of her life story and we have her one novel, a couple of essays and her poetry. She and her writings have kept biographers and readers confounded for over 150 years.

Chapter Twenty-Two

'Stronger than a man, simpler than a child'

The above quote is from Charlotte Brontë's biographical notice to the 1850 edition of *Wuthering Heights* and is her description of her sister Emily. Emily Jane Brontë is perhaps the most elusive and enigmatic of the Brontë sisters, partly because we have very little extant writing and often because her character and description comes from people who scarcely knew her or never knew her at all. The only people who truly knew and understood Emily were her family and even with them she could be distant and aloof. There is no doubt that she was a rather insular and independent person who did not appear to seek friendship or companionship outside of her home. She had strength and stoicism, characteristics more often linked to a man than to a woman. She had little time for the frippery of femininity and when criticised by anyone would only answer repeatedly that she was as God had made her. Emily was therefore different to most females of the time.

From childhood, Emily had displayed physical as well as psychological differences. She was tall in a group of children noted for their diminutive heights. She was plain but not ugly, and at 16 years old, had, according to Ellen Nussey,

> ... *hair which was naturally as beautiful as Charlotte's was in the same unbecoming tight curl and frizz, and there was the same want of complexion. She had very beautiful eyes, kindly, kindling, liquid eyes, sometimes they looked grey, sometimes dark blue but she did not often look at you, she was too reserved. She talked very little. She and Anne were like twins, inseparable companions and in the very closest sympathy which never had any interruption.*
>
> (J.R.V. Barker, 2010) p. 227.

As previously explained, children in large families often align into pairs, especially where there is an even number of siblings. As children Charlotte and

Branwell paired up following the deaths of their elder sisters, Emily and Anne also became closer with an affinity which lasted throughout their lives. This deep empathy between the two youngest sisters was noted by visitors to the Parsonage and was only interrupted when one of them was away from home. It is very likely that when this occurred they wrote copious letters to each other but, unfortunately, none have ever been found. Very little of Emily's written work in still in existence; two volumes of manuscript poetry, one written for Gondal characters and one for herself, a couple of diary papers and her French essays which were written whilst at the Pensionnat Heger. The manuscript of *Wuthering Heights* has never been found and was probably destroyed by her publisher not long after the book was published.

It can be difficult therefore to know and understand Emily. She was not an ordinary woman and she was not part of a social circle where she had to maintain any social niceties; in fact she refused to do so. One feels that she chose to stay and live at the Parsonage because she could be herself there and did not have to socialise with strangers. She had little interest in the outside world apart from the moors and the world did nothing to satisfy her needs. She appears to have preferred her animals to people and to find happiness in nature rather than in the townships. Even her family could irritate and depress her and it appears that, apart from Anne, who was hardly at home for over six years, she led a life slightly apart and aloof from even her siblings. Charlotte could especially annoy her and seemed unable to appreciate when Emily wished to be left alone. How much this bothered Emily we will never know. She could be stubborn and made no effort to go out of her way to be liked or even to be noticed. She, of the three sisters, was the one most horrified at the idea of their identity becoming known to the reading public and her local community.

Charlotte had said that her character Shirley Keeldar possessed characteristics of Emily; possibly in her fearlessness and her independent will. Unlike Shirley, Emily was not one to give out her opinions or to seek admiration or praise, was neither beautiful nor flamboyant and did not have the means to support herself financially. Surprisingly, this strong-willed but quiet and shy female was happiest when living a retired and domestic life at home. She appears to have hated being away from her family and the Parsonage; at Roe Head school she was physically ill to the point where Charlotte thought that she would actually die from homesickness.

It is wrong to assume that people do not change over time and important to remember that the characteristics seen by one observer are not necessarily the same as another's. Personalities, likes and dislikes change over time. The adult Emily was naturally different from the child but we do know that she had an inner strength and an incredible ability to express herself in words and music. The 17-year-old Emily, who failed to survive at Roe Head school, appears to have travelled to Brussels seven years later and stayed for nine months, without raising any objections or reporting any health issues. Furthermore, she was admired by M. Heger for her intelligence and her abilities even though she was not amenable to him or any of her fellow pupils.

Emily appears as an enigmatic woman whose behaviour was not always consistent and who was a puzzle to many who knew her. Paradoxically, the reserve she showed in public was replaced by a loving and loved daughter at home where her father became, at times, particularly dependent on her. Patrick admired his daughter and saw in her some of the traits that he wished for in his son. Patrick and Emily had long periods at home together and grew very close. Patrick taught his daughter to shoot his pistols, and she used her physical and mental strength to support him when he was ill or needed her assistance.

Despite her skills and her intelligence, Emily appears to have been more than happy performing domestic chores around the home. There may be many reasons for this. Emily had no recollection of her mother but lived in the house where her mother had lived and this may well have comforted her. Her sister Maria and her Aunt Branwell had both died whilst Emily was away at school and this may have helped her make a conscious decision not to leave again. Also, it was traditional for a daughter to stay at home and look after her parents as they aged, so this may have been an agreement made between Emily and her father. Furthermore, whilst living at home Emily had unrestricted freedom to indulge in the things she loved the most: music, writing, her animals and walking out on the moors.

Like her siblings, Emily had learnt from childhood to read and write and to use her education and knowledge to indulge in a fantasy world of play. For all four of them this worked as a parallel to their lives and the writing down of it was only reluctantly relinquished by Branwell and Charlotte at some time in their late teens, possibly later. For Emily and Anne, they seem to have spent most of their lives thinking and writing about their world of Gondal. Anne's enthusiasm for it may have dwindled in her last months at Thorpe Green as she had more pressing and realistic issues to contend with. In the diary paper written on Emily's twenty-seventh birthday, their joint enthusiasm for the saga is still evident,

> *The Gondals still flourish as bright as ever. I am at present writing a work on the First Wars – Anne has been writing some articles on this and a book by Henry Saphona – we intend sticking firm by the rascals as long as they delight us which I am glad to say they do at present ....*
>
> (J.R.V. Barker, 2010) p. 535.

Whist visiting York the previous month, they had acted out the lives of some of their imaginary characters. Although Emily records that they went away together, her paper tells us nothing of what she saw or what she thought of the many historic and magnificent buildings in the city. Instead, she describes the following,

> *...though the weather was broken, we enjoyed ourselves very much except during a few hours at Bradford and during our excursion we were Ronald Macelgin, Henry Angora, Juliet Augusteena, Rosobelle Esraldan, Ella and Julien Egramont, Catherine Navarre and Cordelia Firzaphnold escaping from the Palaces of Instruction to join the Royalists who are hard driven at present by the victorious Republicans...*
>
> (J.R.V. Barker, 2010) p. 531.

As she was living permanently at home, Emily had more time and opportunity to indulge in the fantasy whilst Anne was away for many months working. Gondal was between Emily and Anne; their elder brother and sister played no part in it. There was nothing to stop Emily living and inventing her characters at any time, day or night, and there was no-one to encroach on this lifetime activity.

One begins to build a portrait of a highly intelligent and imaginative young lady who has artistic talents, sensitivity to nature and a fierce love of her family and of animals. Emily kept two dogs in adulthood but she was not a sentimental dog lover. She gained their devotion from a mutual respect and firm handling. Although there is evidence of Emily's writing talents, there is little record of her musical abilities. Emily is thought to have been a highly proficient, possibly gifted, pianist. She was asked to teach piano lessons to the pupils at the Pensionnat in Brussels, and although she hated to do it, she must have been talented to have been asked. The piano in Patrick's study is thought to have been bought by him particularly for Emily and she showed such promise that Patrick paid for expensive music lessons for her and for Anne. Some of Emily and Anne's music and song books still exist and show a wide range of classical as well as popular sheet music. Like her brother and sisters, Emily could also draw and paint, and some of her art works are on display at the Parsonage Museum.

Being fiercely private, one feels that Emily never wanted to exhibit her talents to outsiders. When she contributed to the *Gondal Saga* and wrote the accompanying poetry, it was for her and Anne's eyes only. This state of affairs would have remained and the world would never have known of it if Charlotte had not, much to her sister's rage and horror, uncovered and exposed some of the Gondal poetry. Charlotte wrote,

> *One day, in the Autumn of 1845, I accidently lighted on a MS. Volume of verse in my sister Emily's handwriting. Of course, I was not surprised, knowing that she could and did write verse: I looked it over, and something more than surprise seized me. – a deep conviction that these were not common effusions, not at all like the poetry women generally write. I thought them condensed and terse, vigorous and genuine. To my ear, they had also a peculiar music – wild, melancholy and elevating.*
>
> (E. Brontë, *Wuthering Heights*, 1992) p. 16
> [C.B. Biographical Notice, 1850].

Emily's reaction to Charlotte's intrusion into her most private feelings was one of outrage. Charlotte wrote that,

> *My sister Emily was not a person of demonstrative character, nor one, on the recesses of whose mind and feelings, even those nearest and dearest to her could, with impunity, intrude unlicensed; it took hours to reconcile her to the discovery I had made, and days to persuade her that such poems merited publication.*
>
> (E. Brontë, *Wuthering Heights*, 1992) p. 16
> [C.B. Biographical Notice, 1850].

In the above sentence, we obtain a glimpse of Emily. She is reserved and she is private, even at times from her sisters. What Charlotte did was against Emily's principles. Emily believed in privacy and loyalty and must have felt doubly betrayed and exposed by a sister whom she loved and trusted. One can imagine the battle that ensued. Charlotte had transgressed Emily's private, inner world, something that no-one had ever done before without her permission. Emily had felt protected enough and closeted enough in her home to put her feelings down on paper in the knowledge that they were safe from prying eyes. For them to have been 'accidentally alighted on' can be interpreted in many ways and we have only Charlotte's word that this was what really happened.

It is, of course, to the benefit of everyone that this literary transgression sparked a trail of events that led to all the Brontë sisters' subsequent publications and brought their amazing talents and story to the attention of the world. It is hard to condemn Charlotte's actions but it is a measure of Emily's need for anonymity that she never sought or enjoyed any level of public exposure. One feels that without the use of pseudonyms, Emily would never have agreed to have her work published. Had she lived, it is interesting to speculate how, or even if, she could possibly have coped with the notoriety that Charlotte came to enjoy.

Emily's poetry is now recognised as amongst some of the finest lyric verse in the English language. The wording and lyricism veer between the simplest and the most powerful. She writes clear, modest verse about her love of home, amongst deeply philosophical and challenging stanzas that question the whole of the universe. Emily recognised the use of music as a language. Music is a form of communication that 'speaks' to many people and she uses cadences in her poetry that have the echo of musical notes. There follows two examples of the diversity of her range and power. The first contains four stanzas from Emily's poem entitled, *A little while, a little while,* written in December 1838, one verse of which has already been quoted,

> *There is a spot 'mid barren hills*
> *Where winter howls and driving rain,*
> *But if the dreary tempest chills*
> *There is a light that warms again.*

The house is old, the trees are bare
And moonless bends the misty dome
But what on earth is half so dear,
So longed for as the hearth of home?

A little and a lone green lane
That opened on a common wide:
A distant, dreamy, dim blue chain
Of mountains circling every side;

A heaven so clear, an earth so calm,
So sweet, so soft, so hushed an air
And, deepening still the dream-like charm,
Wild moor-sheep feeding everywhere-

(E. Brontë, *The Complete Poems of
Emily Jane Brontë*, 1941) p. 94.

The second group of verses is taken from a longer poem entitled *The Prisoner* and are lines spoken from Julian M and A. G. Rochelle, central characters in the *Gondal Saga*. It was written in October 1845. The ecstasy and the agony conveyed in these few simple lines is a measure of Emily's linguistic talents and musical influences.

But, first a hush of peace – a soundless calm descends:
The struggle of distress, and fierce impatience ends.
Mute music soothes my breast, unuttered harmony,
That I could never dream, till Earth was lost to me.

Then dawns the Invisible; the Unseen its truth reveals;
My outward sense is gone, my inward essence feels:
Its wings are almost free – its home, its harbour found,
Measuring the gulf, it stoops, and dares the final bound.

Oh, dreadful is the check – intense the agony-
When the ear begins to hear, and the eye begins to see;

When the pulse begins to throb, the brain to think again,
The soul to feel the flesh, and the flesh to feel the chain!

Yet I would lose no sting, would wish no torture less;
The more that anguish racks the earlier it will bless;
And robed in fires of Hell, or bright with heavenly shine,
If it but herald Death, the vision is divine.

(E. Brontë, *The Complete Poems of*
Emily Jane Brontë, 1941) p. 239.

It is apparent that a great deal of Emily's poetry deals with loss, and regret and longing. There is a preoccupation with imprisonment, dungeons and tombs, and a central theme of love that has been spoiled or thwarted, by absence or death. Nature and the weather feature strongly but they are often stormy and cold. Even when there is sunshine it usually turns to shadow. The editing of Emily's poetry has taken place over many years by various scholars and there is dispute over the wording and even which poems belong to which sister. Charlotte edited some of her sister's poetry and early critics wrongly assigned parts of the verse or deliberately misled future collectors and publishers. In 1941, C.W. Hatfield made a comprehensive effort to research Emily's poetry and present it in an authentic and logical manner. The similarity between some of the sisters' wording and subject matter has always made it difficult to be completely sure of authorship, although there are some that are definitely Emily's. These poems are written in her hand and attributed to her by her sisters. These are the most powerful and the most poignant and it is a great tragedy that so much of it has been lost. It is also thought that Emily was possibly in the process of writing her second novel when she died; there is mention of it by her publisher. It could be that after her death, and with such harsh reviews of *Wuthering Heights*, Charlotte may have destroyed it. She may also, after the death of Anne, removed all evidence of the Gondal epic.

What Emily's poetry does reveal is an author who has a huge knowledge of the Bible and of Hymns and Psalms. Her poetry uses this knowledge to question God and the universe and this is something she especially brings to fruition in her novel, *Wuthering Heights*. Emily knew of the Christian church and its codes and ethics as part of her life but there is a pessimism and darkness in some of her work where she, or her protagonist, is dissatisfied with life on earth and almost eager to die and to reach a special liberty. This is not necessarily a Christian ideal of heaven, but a freeing of the spirit from its earthly chains. In a poem entitled *The Old Stoic*, she describes this recurrent need for escape from earthly occupations and possessions.

> *Riches I hold in light esteem;*
> *And Love I laugh to scorn;*
> *And lust of fame was but a dream*
> *That vanished with the morn*
>
> *And if I pray, the only prayer*
> *That moves my lips for me*
> *Is, 'Leave the heart that now I bear,*
> *And give me liberty!'*
>
> *Yes, as my swift days near their goal,*
> *Tis all that I implore;*
> *In life and death, a chainless soul,*
> *With courage to endure.*
>
> (E. Brontë, *The Complete Poems of*
> *Emily Jane Brontë*, 1941) p. 163.

Emily's short life was hard and she lived it with a singular tenacity. She held her own council and could not be swayed once having made up her mind. Although her family were central to her life, she appears to have had a particular affinity with nature and, like Charlotte, an acute ability to dissect and analyse the world around her. I suggest that Emily went much further than this. Her poetry, her essays and her novel all examine reality in a way that suggests that the only reality is the earth itself and that all things come from it and return to it. Nature had the final say in all things human and divine. There is a fatalism here that all creatures are at war and that they ultimately destroy everything they create. Emily wrote in one of her French essays the following chilling words, as quoted and interpreted by Sue Lornoff and Stevie Davies,

The entire creation is equally meaningless. Behold those flies playing above the brook; the swallows and fish diminish their number every minute. These will become, in their turn, the prey of some tyrant of the air or water; and man for his amusement or his needs will kill their murderers. Nature is an inexplicable problem; it exists on a principle of destruction. Every being must be the tireless instrument of death to others, or itself must cease to live ... why was man created? He torments, he kills, he devours; he suffers, is devoured ... there you have his whole story.... At that moment the universe appeared to me a vast machine constructed only to produce evil.

(Davies, *Emily Brontë*, 1998) p. 57–58.

This treatise on the nature of nature and the meaning of existence is unique in women's writing of the time and amongst many of the questions being asked by scientists and philosophers over the centuries and to the current day. Why do we exist? Why does nature, the world and the universe appear as random chaos which is ultimately destructive? Man can only wonder at the reason, if there is one, for those millennia of earth and its living organisms. Emily seems to be saying that it will all ultimately end with no apparent purpose having been served.

Emily appears to have battled long and hard with these problems and did not necessarily see God or any divine intervention as a rational explanation. For Emily, all of nature was equally insane and equally random. Her writing reflects a belief that there is no divine heaven only a return to the ground for the body where it rots and mingles with the earth. It is amongst the moors and the heather that Emily finds answers to her questions and where the reality of life and death appear to exist in a continual and endless cycle. She wrote,

Often rebuked, yet always back returning
To those first feelings that were born with me,
And leaving busy chase of wealth and learning
For idle dreams of things which cannot be:

Today, I will seek not the shadowy region;
Its unsustaining vastness waxes drear;
And visions rising, legion after legion,
Bring the unreal world too strangely near.

I'll walk, but not in old heroic traces,
And not in paths of high morality,
And not among the half-distinguished faces,
The clouded forms of long-past history.

I'll walk where my own nature would be leading:
It vexes me to choose another guide:
Where the grey flocks in ferny glens are feeding;
Where the wild wind blows on the mountain side.

What have those lonely mountains worth revealing?
More glory and more grief than I can tell:
The earth that wakes one human heart to feeling
Can centre both the worlds of Heaven and Hell.

> (E. Brontë, *The Complete Poems of*
> *Emily Jane Brontë,* 1941) p. 255–256.

Emily's view of the world appears pantheistic with the notion of 'God' as a presence in nature, with its beauty equal to its violence and cruelty. Emily had witnessed the brutality of school, the untimely deaths of her two innocent sisters, spent years listening to the tolling of the church bell as hundreds of people were interred in the graveyard outside of her window. She saw William Weightman cut down in the prime of his life and she learnt how her mother and aunt had both died in agony. The arbitrary nature of life and death surrounded her and cannot have failed to make her question a religion that offered no clear and reliable answers.

As previously discussed, there was one escape and that was into the imagination; the only 'other world' available to the human mind. It was an escape that the four remaining Brontës took and thoroughly embraced after the deaths of their sisters, and one which upset their mental state in both positive and negative ways. Positively it led them to create and to write and to question and to seek for knowledge. Negatively, it became a torture that interfered with their reality and drove them, at times, to desperation. Charlotte and Branwell tore themselves free of it and possibly Anne did too. Emily most clearly did not and may not have ever wanted to. Speaking in one of her poems she casts reason aside and seems to be explaining her control over Gondal and her need for imaginative escape.

> *...Thee ever present, phantom thing-*
> *My slave, my comrade, and my king!*
>
> *A slave because I rule thee still;*
> *Incline thee to my changeful will*
> *And make thy influence good or ill-*
> *A comrade, for by day and night*
> *Thou art my intimate delight-*
>
> *My Darling Pain that wounds and sears*
> *And wrings a blessing out from tears*
> *By deadening me to earthly cares;*
> *And yet, a king – though prudence well*
> *Have taught thy subject to rebel.*
>
> *And am I wrong to worship where*
> *Faith cannot doubt nor Hope despair*
> *Since my own soul can grant my prayer?*
> *Speak, God of visions, plead for me*
> *And tell why I have chosen thee!*
>
> (E. Brontë, *The Complete Poems of*
> *Emily Jane Brontë*, 1941) p. 208–209.

All the Brontë siblings used and abused their gift of imagination and whilst it was a comfort for many years it appears to the modern observer as something rather weird and unnatural when it continues beyond childhood. How do we view the person who has an invented friend when they are in their twenties? There is a reason why some people 'see' and need an alternative reality, but it also suggests a lack of social skills and an inability to both put aside childish things and to cope with adulthood.

As mentioned earlier, biographers and some medics have long felt that these gifted children may all have suffered from some mental health problems. It is difficult for us to analyse their psychological states but we do know of Branwell's morbidity, his possible epilepsy and his later physical and mental deterioration. We know of Charlotte's nervous disabilities, breakdown and frequent illnesses and that Anne had a similar weak and delicate constitution with times of religious crisis and depression. Emily displays some of the symptoms of paranoid schizophrenia – hallucinations, paranoia, pathological self-control – which are difficult to ignore. The 'living in an unreal world' is also a symptom of mental disturbance and yet it can also be interpreted as a sign of prodigious mental faculty and extraordinary ability. All authors of fiction use their heightened imaginations to write about a world that is not real but can be re-invented and re-imagined in the mind of the reader. All the Brontës achieved this, but Emily perhaps stands out as the greatest in terms of her ability to merge her own inner thoughts and feelings with aspects of the harsh and chaotic actual world.

Chapter Twenty-Three

Wuthering Heights

W*uthering Heights* is a book that has defied any single interpretation and that is one of its greatest achievements. Over the years since it first appeared in print in 1847, every word and every line has been examined and analysed by hundreds of readers and critics who have sought to discover its 'meaning'. Every few years an academic will offer a new interpretation given against the prevailing literary and social attitudes of the times. It has been researched by, among others, feminists, marxists, deconstructionists, musicians, poets and religious groups, and also by readers who have just wanted to read a simple and romantic tale of love and loss in the setting of a Yorkshire moor. They have all been satisfied and they may each be correct in their interpretation. However, the genius of this novel is that its multiple interpretations, its duality, its philosophy and its Shakespearean canopy will continue to delight and frustrate for many years to come because there is no single definition.

When first published, *Wuthering Heights* was not well received by the critics, most of whom found it 'coarse and loathsome' with a savagery that they felt should never appear in a work of art. Together with Anne's, *The Tenant of Wildfell Hall*, the two books were deemed unfit for ladies and even too 'uncultivated' for men. Consequently, when re-issued in 1850 after the deaths of both authors, their most famous and outspoken critic took pen to paper to 'defend' them. That critic was none other than their sister, Charlotte.

Charlotte had been deeply affected by the on-going bad publicity of her sisters' novels and decided to write an introduction to the new editions in the form of a 'Biographical notice of Ellis and Acton Bell 1850'. in which she tried to mollify some of the worst reviews. She explained that her sisters were two quiet and retiring women who had led a secluded life and, by inference, could not be blamed if their muse caused them to write about people and places they had little knowledge or experience of. Describing Emily and Anne, Charlotte wrote,

In Emily's nature the extremes of vigour and simplicity seemed to meet. Under an unsophisticated culture, inartificial tastes, and an unpretending outside, lay a secret power and fire that might have informed the brain and kindled the veins of a hero; but she had no worldly wisdom; her powers were un-adapted to the practical business of life ... an interpreter ought always to have stood between her and the world. Her will was not very flexible, and it generally opposed her interest. Her temper was magnanimous, but warm and sudden; her spirit altogether unbending.... Neither Emily nor Anne was learned; they had no thought of filling their pitchers at the well-spring of other minds; they always wrote from the impulse of nature, the dictates of intuition, and from such stores of observation as their limited experience had enabled them to amass.

(E. Brontë, *Wuthering Heights*, 1992) p. 20.

It is difficult to imagine what her sisters would have thought of Charlotte's attempt to vindicate them as authors whilst condemning their works. Charlotte went further and added an 'Editor's Preface' to her biographical notice. In this she again attempted to champion Emily whilst criticising her choice of characters and lack of feminine taste and propriety. She does acknowledge the force of the book, but sees it as being overwhelmed by a brooding, 'horror of great darkness' (p. 23). Like many readers, Charlotte believed that the 'good' characters like Edgar Linton and Nelly Dean, brought some sunshine and benevolence to the story, without acknowledging the damage that they actually caused. Alternatively, she saw no human feeling in Heathcliff, saying that,

Heathcliff, indeed, stands unredeemed; never once swerving in his arrow-straight course to perdition, from the time when 'the little black-haired, swarthy thing, as dark as if it came from the Devil,' was first unrolled out of the bundle and set on its feet in the farmhouse kitchen, to the hour when Nelly Dean found the grim, stalwart corpse...

(E. Brontë, *Wuthering Heights*, 1992) p. 23.

Wuthering Heights is a conundrum where nothing and nobody is as it seems. Emily sets her story on a wild moor and the action takes place between two houses: Wuthering Heights, an exposed old farmhouse high on the hills, and Thrushcross Grange, a gentleman's residence four miles away in a sheltered valley. I alluded earlier to a Shakespearian influence in this novel and there are some similarities with *Romeo and Juliet* and *King Lear*. It echoes the rambling of the mad Lear and expands on the story of star-crossed lovers who are the subject of two warring families. In Emily's story, the difference is that the families are intermingled and their lives misinterpreted and interrupted by different narrators and different time-scales. All the action in *Wuthering Heights* takes place in and around the two houses with an intense and passionate but limited cast. These characters display almost all aspects of the human condition, many of which are violent and 'uncivilised'.

It is by exposing the 'civility' and revealing the veneer of respectability, that Emily masters her characters and her theme. She considers their background, upbringing and the environment, and demonstrates to the reader the basics of all human behaviour. She shows that the human being is an animal, like all other animals, and when it is threatened, abused or misunderstood, it will resort to defending itself in ways that are devoid of the construed and false manners of the 'civilised' world.

The philosopher R.D. Laing discussed this notion of self in his book, *Self and Others* (1976) and further in his celebrated work, *The Divided Self* (1976). He suggested that people live the life which is expected of them. They role-play in society because it gives an outward appearance of the sane and the normal. Whilst everyone is believing in, and behaving to, a certain code of conduct, a level of normality can be identified and maintained. It is what philosophy terms, 'Bad Faith', and it involves the conditioning of infants and children to the social norms and mores of the society. One can see the benefits of this and the alternative anarchy that would ensue if all citizens decided to behave exactly as they pleased. Yet for some people playing the social game is, or becomes, unacceptable and alien to their nature and they are then seen as 'different' and often as anti-social or deviant. The need to separate the normal from the abnormal can be viewed as the history of the diagnosis and treatment of mental health. Deviation from the norm upsets the social equilibrium and then needs to be dealt with. Notwithstanding, there are unquestionably, both now and historically, groups living 'antisocially' in which a sane person can be cast out by the same reasoning. An individual living in absurd and wholly alien environments can make a very sane decision to opt out, or refuse to participate, but they may be labelled by the majority as insane or abnormal.

Jean Paul Sartre also examined this idea of man as a social construction who needed the boundaries and constraints of the social structure to keep their sense of balance. People needed a referential framework to protect their sanity. Goethe also recognises the need for surroundings and habits which create order and 'normality'. He wrote that, 'All comfort in life is based upon a regular occurrence of external phenomena'. (C. Brontë, *Villette*, 1984) Introduction p. 7.

Without these signposts and reference points people can become too overwhelmed and fall into a state of anomie where there are no boundaries but neither are there goals or problems to overcome. In Emily's novel, there are various characters who do not follow the social rules and yet do not recognise that their behaviour is abnormal or unacceptable. They therefore see others as mad and only themselves as sane. At one point the deluded and interfering Nelly Dean states that she is the only sane person in the house!

One may immediately think of Heathcliff as bad and mad, but he is especially someone who has developed according to his upbringing and experiences and reacts accordingly. His reactions are extreme because his life has been extreme and he has suffered the worst of all childhood sorrows; rejection and abandonment by anyone who ever loved him. It is in characters like Lockwood, Hindley, Nelly and Joseph where one sees people who have little sense of right and wrong and who misjudge and miscalculate the damage they inflict on others because they lack the sensitivity and empathy with their fellow beings. This does not mean that one can dismiss or condone Heathcliff's behaviour after the death of Catherine and his revenge on the Linton and Earnshaw families, but one can understand some of his motives.

What Emily Brontë reveals in Heathcliff is a side of her own personality. She too was a motherless child and writes of motherless children. These children are 'lost' in the book and they look to other children to support them. Heathcliff and Catherine are two people but behave as one person, totally dependent on each other, like two halves of the same whole. Catherine says to Nelly, 'I am Heathcliff'. The pair behave like wild animals who roam the moors and escape all human efforts to domesticate and civilise them. Catherine's father despairs of her wild behaviour and Joseph rants and raves at the children because they will not observe the Sabbath or adhere to his twisted religious mania. Nelly is constantly chastising Catherine for her unfeminine conduct and telling Heathcliff to smarten himself up. Catherine's brother, Hindley, hates Heathcliff whom he sees as a usurper of his father's affections and his own inheritance and treats him with extreme brutality. Heathcliff's childhood is one of rejection until Mr Earnshaw plucks the orphan child out of poverty in Liverpool and brings him to the Heights. Here he finds his soulmate, Catherine, and for the first time has someone he can love. One of the central themes of the book focuses on Catherine's rejection of her former playmate and his animalistic charms for the civilised and well-mannered, Edgar Linton. This separation of Catherine from Heathcliff's world of nature into the drawing rooms of the middle classes, is what ultimately kills her and causes Heathcliff to spend the next eighteen years searching for her.

Wuthering Heights is a timeless tale of such power and violence that many critics condemned its lack of refinement and Christian morals. It is a harsh story set in difficult times amongst an unforgiving yet often beautiful environment where people are detached from the lives and manners of the more 'sophisticated' town dwellers. It is at times ungodly and anti-religious and for that it received much disapproval. Heathcliff is more devil than man and his revenge on the Earnshaw and Linton families is, for most of his life, his abiding goal. He marries only to torment and torture his affected wife, Isabella, and to make her an object of his loathing. His son is sickly and weak and forced by his father to marry his cousin, the young Cathy, in an attempt by Heathcliff to inherit both the houses of Thrushcross Grange and Wuthering Heights and finally triumph over all those who oppressed him in childhood.

Emily Brontë's novel is a wonderful and complicated jigsaw of human emotions, but she carefully shows how and why the characters behave as they do. Heathcliff is a foundling who is rejected at the Heights by all but Catherine and her father. Catherine is drawn to Heathcliff and they race over the moors together unheeding of any adult or any moral or religious code. Nature and the elements are far more real to them and they are happy in the total innocence of childhood. Emily shows how this utopian state inevitably changes and adulthood arrives and alters their relationship. The change from childhood to adulthood is inevitable and unstoppable and Emily explores the consequences when the child moves from the natural and instinctive world to that of social conformity and constriction.

Emily's work is unique in so far as she can weave together the realities of life, including the harsh actualities of growing up; the sense of loss, the grief of memory and remembrance of a time no longer present and which can never return, within a story which also questions many of the conventional beliefs of the times and hopes for the future. She shows life played out on a background of nature; of an un-changing moorland where rocks and heath stay the same no matter what type of man and his earthly concerns are played out against them. Heathcliff, by his very name and nature, is solid, indestructible and timeless; a product of nature rather than a human being. Catherine describes her love for him in the following words,

> *If all else perished, and he remained, I should still continue to be; and, if all else remained, and he were annihilated, the Universe would turn to a mighty stranger. I should not seem part of it. My love for Linton is like the foliage in the woods. Time will change it, I'm well aware, as winter changes the trees – my love for Heathcliff resembles the eternal rocks beneath – a source of little visible delight, but necessary, Nelly, I am Heathcliff.*
>
> (E. Brontë, *Wuthering Heights*, 1992) p. 87.

The idea of a loved and loving Christian God never enters this book. The religious doggerel spouted by Joseph, the manservant, is brutal and based on Hell rather than Heaven. In a scene where Heathcliff attempts to dig up Catherine's corpse so that he can see and touch her once again, one can appreciate the horror with which this would have been received by its readers. Catherine is not buried in the consecrated ground of the churchyard but out on the moorland slopes where she is 'free'. That freedom means that after Heathcliff's death, when he is buried beside her, their corpses can dissolve into one another. Emily tackles the issues of life after death by allowing Heathcliff and Catherine to wander the moors as ghosts. As their spirits are unreal they are untouchable. These scenes, written by a clergyman's daughter, are shocking even now and caused many critics to severely condemn its author and the language and nature of the story.

It wasn't only the critics of the novel who were shocked; even Charlotte felt that it needed some qualifying. In Charlotte's 1850 preface to the second edition of the book she tries to defend Emily and explain how the book came about. She argues that Emily created a being over whom she had little control, that her sheltered upbringing did her no favours and that she knew little of the people who passed by the door. Very little of this was true or accurate, but Charlotte's intention was to silence the critics and promote Emily's unique, but as Charlotte viewed them, limited or naive abilities.

Whether Charlotte believed her own rhetoric is unclear. Her own abilities would suggest that she was aware of Emily's creative genius but found her language and subject too extreme. For many readers, there is a beauty and poetry in Emily's novel and at times a musicality in its language and rhythm. Heathcliff cries out for Catherine after her death, in words that are an echo of those spoken by mankind for centuries: 'The entire world is a dreadful collection of memoranda that she did exist, and that I have lost her.' (E. Brontë, *Wuthering Heights*, 1992) p. 274. Earlier he had called out to her to, 'Be with me always – take any form – drive me mad! Only do not leave me in this abyss where I cannot find you.' (E. Brontë, *Wuthering Heights*, 1992) p. 154.

This is not the parlour talk of young ladies in middle-class nineteenth-century drawing rooms. It is not the civilised and controlled language of the well-educated and the conventional. It is instead the raw emotions of a person in agony, a person who is bereft of the one thing that can restore his mind and his life and the one thing that he can never attain.

Loss is central to *Wuthering Heights* and it is cleverly displayed and articulated by a woman who had experienced and lived the utter misery of it. Whilst Emily was writing *Wuthering Heights*, Branwell was slowly collapsing in a similar way to Heathcliff, but whereas Heathcliff's decline took twenty years and was based on the loss of a woman who was already dead, Branwell was still living in hope. Both Heathcliff and Branwell are pining for a woman who is unattainable and a love that existed only in the memory and could never be satisfied. Emily touched on the nerve of human emotions with a universality that appeals to anyone who cannot have the person they love for any reason, including death.

Whilst examining these extreme emotions, Emily goes even further and questions the whole notion of death and an afterlife. She questions the existence and location of 'heaven', and asks whether it is the right and best place to be. Her novel offers a possible alternative for Heathcliff and Catherine which is very anti-Christian in its presentation. Catherine relates a dream she had to Nelly and tells her how alien heaven would be to her. She says,

'If I were in heaven, Nelly, I should be extremely miserable.'

'Because you are not fit to go there,' I answered. 'All sinners would be miserable in heaven.'

'But it is not for that, I dreamt once that I was there ... heaven did not seem to be my home; and I broke my heart with weeping to come back to earth; and the angels were so angry that they flung me out into the middle of the heath on the top of Wuthering Heights; where I woke sobbing for joy...'

(E. Brontë, *Wuthering Heights*, 1992) p. 85–86.

Although Emily links nature and the natural world as part of her picture of the divine presence of 'God' on earth, she cannot reconcile the likes of Catherine and Heathcliff in a divine heaven. Their afterlife is spent haunting the moors. As noted earlier, in an introduction to a 1965 edition of *Wuthering Heights*, the scholar, David Daiches, stated that: 'One of Emily Brontë's most extraordinary achievements in this novel is the domiciling of the monstrous in the ordinary rhythms of life and work, thereby making it at the same time less monstrous and more disturbing' (Daiches, 1965).

To help to achieve this, Emily chose to tell the story through several seemingly harmless and 'normal' narrators; mainly the foppish, town-bred, Mr Lockwood, and the pillar of common sense and country ways, Nelly Dean. At first the reader is lulled into a false sense of security as they listen to Lockwood's story of a visit to his landlord, Heathcliff, the current owner of the Heights and the Grange. Lockwood has rented Thrushcross Grange from him and has walked over to introduce himself to his new landlord. This first paragraph takes place eighteen years into the story, when the passion and violence of the first Catherine are seemingly over. Lockwood does not know or recognise the 'uncanny' or the 'extraordinary' and sees all things in the conventional way as he has been taught to do. He has never set foot in a northern farmhouse before and coming from a world of routine and social order he totally misreads and misjudges everything and everybody in the building. He visits twice in two days because he is so determined to strike up a gentlemanly acquaintance with Heathcliff. On his second visit, a snow storm and an attack by the farm dogs forces him to stay the night in a house where he finally realises that he is decidedly unwelcome.

The established domestic patterns that Lockwood expected to find at the Heights and which would have provided him with all the necessary signs of time, place and relationships are not present and he goes to bed upset and perplexed. Whilst trying to sleep, the agitated Lockwood finds some mildewed books on a shelf where the names, 'Catherine Earnshaw', 'Catherine Heathcliff' and 'Catherine Linton', have been carved into the wood. Lockwood examines one of the books and it is Catherine's diary, written a quarter of a century earlier. The writing disturbs him further and when he finally goes to sleep he has a dream that turns into a nightmare. He is woken suddenly by what he thinks is a branch banging in the storm against the window. The clasp is soldered shut but in desperation to stop the incessant noise, Lockwood thrusts his arm through the glass and his hand closes round the small, icy hand of a child.

Lockwood is, understandably, terrified and tries to disentangle himself, but the child begs to be let in. Lockwood is by now frantic with fear and states that: 'Terror made me cruel; and finding it useless to attempt shaking the creature off, I pulled its wrist on to the broken pane, and rubbed it to and fro till the blood ran down.' (E. Brontë, *Wuthering Heights*, 1992) p. 42.

This gothic scene is vital to an understanding of the book. For Emily Brontë, ghosts and spirits are a natural phenomenon. At a time when there was no scientific explanation for the extraordinary, many people experienced phenomena they could not explain. These occurrences were far more prevalent in areas and houses where there was upset, agitation, death and darkness; places where the imagination could conjure up sights or experience strangeness. Emily's dilemma here is that having been brought up in a Protestant household, and attended church and prayers on an almost daily basis, she had to reconcile her appreciation and experience of unexplained phenomena with a faith in the Christian God. This was something she seemed to struggle with and her novel examines this problem.

Whilst Lockwood is horrified and traumatised by his ordeal, Heathcliff rushes to the casement, flings open the windows and begs Catherine to return. As one man is appalled, and needs to rid himself of the 'apparition' the other man is desperate for it to return. Lockwood puts his nightmare down to 'bad tea' and 'bad temper', but his reaction to Catherine's ghost is cruel beyond extreme. He physically rubs her wrist against the glass in a frenzied effort to 'kill' her. He is experiencing something so far beyond his understanding of the world; an 'otherness' that is too far from the normal. His reaction is an animal instinct to rid himself of this 'thing' that he cannot comprehend. It is the only time he breaks out of his conditioned behaviour and does something instinctively and it is barbaric.

Many critics have highlighted the 'window' metaphor in the book, as representing the exchange between inside and outside, domestic and wild, warmth and cold, light and dark, culture and anarchy, and life and death. One could add religion and atheism. In this book, the threat is always from the inside. It causes Catherine to literally wish to spring from the window out on to the moors where she can live and breathe. The use of metaphor was noticeable in nineteenth-century writing by women. Rarely able to express themselves openly, the use of metaphor and symbol was used to overcome barriers, especially regarding physical and emotional issues that were unmentionable or objectionable. The definition of the word 'metaphor' means 'to carry over' and this includes crossing barriers. Emily uses it to carry unfamiliar and unresolved puzzles in her own life, into her fiction. Her book is a treatise on life and death and questions whether life is annihilated by death or whether it continues in some shape or form.

The name Heathcliff is itself a metaphor for the moors and the name Catherine derives from the Greek for 'pure'. These are not names chosen at random but as part of their creator's need to carry across the idea of two people occupying a place of eternal purity; the heath and the rocks beneath. This is, for them, and possibly for Emily, a more desirable abode than any religious notion of Heaven. This portrayal is partly what horrified its readers and critics who found the book 'blasphemous'. The violence displayed by some of the characters appalled many readers and the use of offensive words such as 'Hell' typed out in full, did little to endear it to the reading public. Emily, of course, cared little or nothing about convention or what people thought. She was also writing under a pseudonym and she never expected to be exposed.

The reader of *Wuthering Heights* may begin to accept the story as portrayed by the narrators until they realise how unreliable they are. The narrators understand very little of the action and tend to assume rather than know what is happening. The reader is often confused at the many displacements and dualities as Emily plays around with names, symbols and shifting timescales. The book provides no map or guide for the reader or for the characters to follow. Lockwood begs to be shown the way home from the Heights and asks for landmarks. There are no landmarks on the moors except for one signpost at a crossroads. It bears no names, just initials which would only be recognised by people local to the area. Again, there is the symbolism of a crossroads as the traditional ancient place of fear associated with gibbets and the crossing over from life to death. It is here that Nelly 'sees' her old playmate Hindley and is doubly confused when she arrives at the Heights and finds that: 'The apparition had outstripped me; it stood looking through the gate. This was my first idea on observing an elf-locked, brown-eyed boy setting his ruddy countenance against the bars.' (E. Brontë, *Wuthering Heights*, 1992) p. 108.

When asked to fetch his father, the boy brings Heathcliff instead of Hindley, but the boy is Hareton, Hindley's son. Heathcliff is now his guardian as Hindley is dead. The reader needs to learn, along with the characters, what has happened in the past and how each character is related and descended from the earlier families. Even Nelly is confused by the genetics and the time shifts. Furthermore, Hareton has a remarkable likeness to the first Catherine, his aunt, and it unsettles and disarms Heathcliff.

One of the most notable examples of genetic repetition in the novel are the young Cathy's eyes which are 'those of Catherine Earnshaw', her mother. These metaphoric windows remind Heathcliff of Catherine and help to haunt him so that when he cries out that the whole world is 'a dreadful recollection of memoranda that she did exist, and that I have lost her', it is because he is haunted every day by the genetic links which give him glimpses of Catherine but are not Catherine. This constant 'memento mori' helps to drive Heathcliff to the edge of madness when he sees Catherine's likeness everywhere, in everything and implores her not to leave him in 'the terrible abyss', where he cannot find her.

These passages could be describing the Brontë household following the deaths of Mrs Brontë, Maria and Elizabeth. Everywhere their clothes and belongings would be seen and their memories evoked. Like all parents and siblings, they will have had strong genetic likenesses in personality, speech and looks. Charlotte wept when she saw George Richmond's finished portrait of herself, saying that it was 'so like my sister, Emily.' Patrick Brontë must have watched and noticed the traits and looks of his wife in his children and it must have both comforted and distressed him. Similarly, his children probably wore hand-me-downs from their dead sisters and uncannily resembled them. Genetic repetition is fascinating but can also be disturbing; in *Wuthering Heights*, Emily uses it to haunt and unnerve various characters in a way that suggests the dead are still uncannily alive. George Eliot described this phenomena in her novel, *Adam Bede* saying,

> *Family likeness has often a deep sadness in it. Nature, that great tragic dramatist, knits us together by bone and muscle, and divides us by the subtler web of our brains; blends yearning and repulsion; and ties us by our heart-strings to the beings that jar us at every movement. We hear a voice with the very cadence of our own ... we see eyes – Ah! So like our mother's ... and our last darling child startles us with the air and gesture of the sister we parted from in bitterness long years ago ... the long-lost mother, whose face we begin to see in the glass as our own wrinkles come, once fretted our young souls with her anxious humours and irrational persistence.*

(Eliot, *Adam Bede*, 1952) p. 41–42.

Wuthering Heights is a dual story in two volumes where the second story mirrors and repeats aspects of the first, but with some new children who are the offspring of the dead. Hareton is Hindley's son and Cathy is Catherine and Edgar Linton's daughter. Heathcliff's calculated and hateful marriage to Isabella produced the sickly boy, Linton. They are all motherless and they are all controlled by Heathcliff as part of his revenge for his maltreatment by Hindley and the Lintons. His revenge is further complicated because as much as he loved Catherine, he hated the fact that she married Edgar Linton and in many ways, he seeks revenge on her too by taking her daughter, Cathy, and mistreating her.

The first half of the book deals with Catherine and Heathcliff's story and how they were forced apart by Catherine's decision to court and marry Edgar Linton. The Linton's had charm, money and property and Catherine was attracted to these trappings. Having been lulled into the world of Thrushcross Grange, Catherine tells Nelly that: 'It would degrade me to marry Heathcliff now; so he shall never know how I love him: and that, not because he is handsome, Nelly, but because he's more myself that I am.' (E. Brontë, *Wuthering Heights*, 1992) p. 86.

Catherine qualifies this statement by explaining that if she and Heathcliff married they would have nothing, they 'would be beggars'. It is sometimes forgotten that her explanation for marrying Edgar included the fact that she hoped that his wealth and her new position may be used to help Heathcliff out of both poverty and the clutches of her brother Hindley. As in any good plot, Heathcliff leaves the room, where he has been listening unobserved, before he hears Catherine's explanation. He only hears her say that it would degrade her to marry him. He disappears for some years and returns a gentleman with a fortune and systematically sets about to persecute and destroy his former tormentors. Catherine is confused and distressed by his return and is so torn between Edgar and Heathcliff, and the realisation that she has chosen the wrong man, that she breaks down physically and mentally and dies giving birth prematurely to her daughter Cathy a few days later.

In the second part of the book, Heathcliff has become the monster who buys the Heights and forces his son, Linton, to marry Cathy so that he (Heathcliff) will also inherit Thrushcross Grange. He systematically neglects and controls the three children with a sadism which matches that of the despised and dead Hindley. Heathcliff is the abused child who becomes the adult abuser, either unwilling or unable to forgive or forget his past and only interested in revenge at any cost. He manipulates everyone so that he can reach his goals, but of course there is one goal which continually eludes him and that is his reunion with Catherine.

Eventually, Heathcliff loses his drive and his fight. His love for Catherine has twisted him and brought him no happiness. His constant search for her has been fruitless; his imploring to be haunted by her ghost has instead been cruelly experienced by the unsuspecting Lockwood. Heathcliff even digs up Catherine's corpse to check that she is still there and he feels she is unaltered and waiting for him. By now he is moving away from reality and willing himself to die. He has failed to find Catherine in life and will search for her in death. This he achieves by starving himself and he dies at the casement window where Catherine's ghost appeared to Lockwood in the room where she and Heathcliff had slept as children.

The ending of *Wuthering Heights* is in some ways left, like *Villette*, open for the reader to interpret and it is Emily's questioning between Christianity and nature, and between a religious God and a spiritual freedom beyond the grave. Lockwood has heard the full tale from Nelly of the demise of Heathcliff and the destiny of Cathy and Hareton, who are to move out of the Heights into Thrushcross Grange. Nelly tells Lockwood that some of the country folk swear to have seen Heathcliff's ghost and that one night she met a shepherd boy who claimed to have seen Heathcliff and a woman on the moors and he was afraid to go near them. Lockwood sets off back across the moor and diverts his walk to the old kirk, which is now in total disrepair with its ruin fast becoming claimed by the surrounding moorland. Lockwood finds the three headstones, Catherine's half buried, Edgar Linton's with moss creeping over it, and Heathcliff's still bare of grass or heather. Lockwood informs the reader,

> ... I lingered round them, under that benign sky: watched the moths fluttering among the heath and hare-bells; listened to the soft wind breathing through the grass; and wondered how anyone could ever imagine unquiet slumbers for the sleepers in that quiet earth.
>
> (E. Brontë, *Wuthering Heights*, 1992) p. 285.

The reader is left with their own conclusions. They can believe the country folk with their insistence on the ghosts or the gentleman Lockwood and his belief that 'all's well that ends well', and Heathcliff and Catherine are safely dead and buried.

One can understand why the critics of the 1840s found this book so offensive and why Charlotte chose to defend her sister's name. However, in a beautiful piece of prose written at the end of her 1850 Editors preface to *Wuthering Heights*, Charlotte described her sister's book in the following way:

> *Wuthering Heights* was hewn in a wild workshop, with simple tools, out of homely materials. The statuary found a granite block on a solitary moor: gazing thereon, he saw how from the crag might be elicited a head, savage, swart, sinister; a form moulded with at least one element of grandeur – power. He wrought with a rude chisel, and from no model but the vision of his meditations. With time and labour, the crag took human shape; and there it stands colossal, dark, and frowning, half statue, half rock: in the former sense, terrible and goblin-like; in the latter, almost beautiful, for its colouring is of mellow grey, and moorland moss clothes it; and heath, with its blooming bells and balmy fragrance, grows faithfully close to the giant's foot.
>
> (E. Brontë, *Wuthering Heights*, 1992) p. 24.

To write a book of the scope and calibre of *Wuthering Heights* shows a mind of great intelligence and deep philosophical reasoning. Emily tackled many offensive and taboo subjects in her book and it is to her credit that she was willing to question and challenge some of the beliefs of the society in which she had been born and raised. She spares no detail and offers no parameters. Emily knew Haworth Moor intimately, and some of the people who lived there, and these moors were as alive and important to her book as the characters she created. The moors were 'uncivilised' in the truest sense of the word. They were raw and untamed and so were Heathcliff and Catherine. Emily fuses nature with emotion, and people with nature in a combination that brings the wind and the snow into the reader's imagination and allows them to 'see, hear and feel' the events as in a gigantic musical extravaganza. As a trailblazer of women's literature, she stands unique.

Chapter Twenty-Four

Themes and Perspectives

Having examined some of the extensive writings of the Brontë sisters, it is clear to see that they had an enormous subject range and did not limit themselves necessarily to Victorian conventions or standards of female propriety. The sisters wrote from their experience, their knowledge and their perspective. This meant that they were not bound as storytellers to offer standard fictional tales but were each able to investigate the human condition and the many influences on behaviour. These authors were not prim maidens in the depths of isolation, they were intelligent, well-educated, travellers and workers who had a wealth of material from which to choose their locations, characters and events.

The Brontës' juvenilia had been their writing apprenticeship in ways that echoed stories and newspaper articles about many major subjects affecting the country in the first twenty-five years of the nineteenth century. These included the Napoleonic wars and the leadership of the Duke of Wellington, colonialism and rising industrialisation. Their Glasstown saga reflected the newspaper reports and the lives of individual heroes, politicians, statesmen and royalty. Under the influence of Branwell and his twelve soldiers, the emphasis on war was particularly noticeable, but, even in these early years they also built on stories of love and tragedy with all the enthusiasm and excitement of children suddenly in control of major events, no matter how fantastic.

Gradually separating into Charlotte and Branwell's 'Angria' and Emily and Anne's 'Gondal', they moved apart in their stories and worked on different fantasy lands where war continued but the focus was more on the individuals and their behaviours, which were often amoral and violent. There is in these stories a sexual undercurrent as the children grew and developed their own sexuality. No matter what the time in history, all children will necessarily experience puberty and the emotional changes that accompany it. The Brontës were not sexually unaware and there are many references and metaphors in their juvenilia dealing with passionate love, rejection and heartache which is often associated with loss and the need for union and reunion, with husbands, wives and lovers. Their later poetry, much of it written to accompany their sagas, is invariably love poetry or poetry about loss. This applies especially to those of Emily and Anne in their Gondal verses.

By the time of writing their novels, they had the maturity to write semi-biographical works alongside fiction which incorporated many of their own experiences and their own perspectives. They could tell stories which had elements of truth and realism as they saw and experienced it. This was different to other novels of the time. When Mrs Gaskell was writing *Ruth* and *Mary Barton*, she was not suffering the life of a fallen woman or the poverty of the mill worker, although she was obviously aware of these issues. The Brontës did not write about people or events that were alien to them. Each of their novels describes people and places that were familiar but reworked into a fictional story. There is obvious personal experience and incident but it is incorporated into the tale in a way that adds authenticity rather than as pure self-indulgence. When Charlotte writes about Lowood school, one knows that she is reliving sights and sounds and people from the time but it is with the distance and maturity of an adult. She can describe her experience with the right amount of emotion to engage the reader rather than to repel them.

There are several themes that run through the Brontë novels that had not been fully addressed by writers, male or female, before and certainly not in fiction. These included the role of women and especially the single, middle-class woman who had no personal wealth or marriage prospects. All three of the Brontë sisters had experience as teachers or governesses, or both, which involved working in other people's houses and schools, and they all disliked, even hated it. These experiences are reworked into their stories and offer an important realism. Anne's six years as a governess, and what she saw and suffered, compelled her to write her two vastly different, but topically linked, novels. Each sister had experienced the long hours, the loneliness, the displaced status which meant a lack of adult companionship in households where they were neither servant nor family. They had felt the hardship of the poor wages, the constant stress of trying to control and teach other people's children and the pressure to show results. These experiences were embedded in their psyche and it is little wonder that Anne and Charlotte chose these themes in their works.

Emily, noticeably, offers no tutor or governess for any of the children in her story.

Their own education in childhood had, for Emily and Charlotte, included the disaster of the school at Cowan Bridge, but it was surrounded by the fruitful and enjoyable years spent at home. In that liberal environment, they had the time and space for free thought along with a mass of knowledge in a wide variety of subjects and the opportunity to practice various skills. Unfortunately, their home schooling did not prepare them for an appreciation of how different other children and childhoods were to their own. They seem to have expected all children to share their interest and thirst for knowledge. They were upset and disappointed to find that many children were far more interested in their clothes and toys and various pleasures of which the Brontë sisters had little or no interest.

Roe Head and Brussels taught the sisters some of the refinements necessary for their work roles but it also highlighted, in Charlotte and Emily, their lack of empathy with children and their inability to forge working relationships with their employers. Only Anne succeeded in gradually gaining the confidence and friendship of her pupils, at Thorpe Green, but it took her years to gain their respect. Emily and Charlotte lacked the patience and temperament to devote their time and energy to children who did not wish to learn. Emily is almost spiteful in making her pupils at the Pensionnat take their music lessons during their break times and there is little wonder that they disliked her and her methods.

Their novels demonstrate that for women of their class and status they had very limited options as adults, and that even marriage was not necessarily a fulfilling option. Anne, in *The Tenant of Wildfell Hall*, highlights what can happen when a marriage goes wrong and the trauma it involves. Charlotte also sees beyond the romance of marriage into the obverse side of a union which the law requires to be unequal. Careful attention to the ending of all her novels show that they can be interpreted as ambiguous, and the marriages, where they occur, are not necessarily happy or fulfilling to either party. The observations of marriage in their books displays an imbalance of power and decision-making, a lack of unity and, in some, a slavish adherence to convention. Marriage to a person of means and standing is shown as the best and correct goal for any young girl, but if she achieves it she will have status but not necessarily happiness. If she fails to attract a man she has only her education to fall back on, and the isolation of the old maid. Of course, the main influence on all of this was wealth and physical attraction. A woman who lacked either had very little chance of attracting a man who could keep her in a comfortable, even though dependent, situation.

It is interesting to deduce a reflection of the Brontë sisters' personalities from the novels. Anne appears to wish for a handsome young man to marry and live happily ever after in a mutual partnership. Charlotte also seems to want this but her need for independence is stronger and she describes a union where being herself and earning her own wages is as important as marriage. She is one of the first to offer an alternative to marriage which is, for her, equally satisfying. If M. Paul Emanuel returns at the end of *Villette*, that is good; but if he does not, that is also alright because Lucy has her independence. One sees them as future independent companions as much as man and wife. Emily shows contempt for marriage and sees emotions far more in terms of storm and calm which do not adhere to any conventional or religious dictates. Her characters have a spiritual union that is everlasting as opposed to a temporary, earthbound domestic arrangement.

The Brontës also experienced and understood the roles of various women in Victorian society. They knew the role of the servant, the maid, the nurse, the spinster, the middle-class single girl in search of a good marriage, the teacher, the governess, the wife and mother, the single parent, the abused spouse and the heartless mistress. Their keen powers of observation meant that they could write with confidence about these women and expound their virtues and vices with a degree of authenticity. It was not done specifically as a treatise on women's subjugation, in the vein of Mary Wollstonecraft, but as part of carefully crafted fiction that highlighted problems and issues faced by women and their children who had little or no control over their own destinies.

It does beg the question of whether one must suffer something to truly understand and write about it. One can argue that in the case of the Brontë sisters, they did suffer many negative aspects of the female condition, both as children and adults. Their thirst for knowledge and keen observation of the women they knew and lived amongst in various places and households, including their own, allowed them to appreciate the issues involved and record their findings. One of the female roles they saw every day was that of their aunt Branwell. This woman felt it her duty to raise her sister's children and she did so at great sacrifice to her own life and future. The law prevented her from ever having a relationship with Patrick and yet they shared the same house for over twenty years. She never returned to Cornwall and she never married or had children of her own. One wonders how much of her devotion was based on conventional duty and how much, if any, was of her own free will. As a single and available relative, she was able and probably expected to step into the breach. She cannot have known at the time that it would take up the whole of the rest of her life. She may well have grown to love her nephew and nieces or she may have resented them, we do not know. We do know that Patrick's failure to find another wife left her in a position where she had to stay at the Parsonage whether she wanted to or not. There is no doubt that the Brontë sisters appreciated their aunt and all she did for them, but her life was also a warning of how easily control could be taken away from women when duty called.

This devotion to duty was very strong in Anne and Charlotte, both in their lives and, as demonstrated, in their writing. Their female characters often display strength and fortitude which carries them forward as they fulfil their roles and their duties to all around them. There is a selfless characteristic which is part of a woman's duty and attraction and it is often linked to a religious benevolence. In *Agnes Grey*, Agnes is kind, thoughtful, patient, tireless and duty-bound, in many ways like her creator. Anne's devotion to duty and her willingness to help to offset the family income by suffering years of work in a situation she strongly disliked, not only shows the influence of her aunt, but also the female traits expected in women of her class. It bordered on subservient, passive and void of independence, but was praised for being noble and self-sacrificing.

The sisters were also close to the other females in their household. As children, they had their two nurses, the Garrs sisters, and later the servants Martha Brown and Tabby Aykroyd. The Brontë family appreciated these women and grew fond of them whilst observing their speech, manners and habits. They understood Martha and Tabby's situations and their need to earn a living, and they also learnt something of the rough and ready ways of the two Yorkshire working class women. Nursemaids and servants were part of the Brontës' lives in a way that we no longer see. Their relationships with these women were long and close and they appear in many guises throughout their writing, in characters like Zillah and Nelly in *Wuthering Heights*, Mrs Pryor in *Shirley* or

Mrs Bretton in *Villette*. They are caring and capable mother figures who do not always get things right but are a very necessary part of the background. Other strong women in their lives included Margaret Wooler and her sisters, Madame Heger and Mary Taylor. Each appears in their novels in various guises and show that the sisters watched and recorded the strengths and weaknesses of the women they knew.

Added to the Brontës' observation of women and women's roles was their knowledge of the law, especially regarding women's rights and property. All three sisters use aspects of the law in their novels which are sometimes quite complicated and obscure and not usually known or understood by the average woman, even when she was affected by them. In *Wuthering Heights*, Emily can successfully include the law of chancery, inheritance, entails and mortgages in Heathcliff's fight to attain both the Heights and Thrushcross Grange. Anne explores the Married Women's Property Act in *The Tenant of Wildfell Hall* with great effect. Helen Huntingdon is put in a position where she must leave her husband and live in secret if she is to escape his violence and keep her own child. The law on male inheritance and property, and how this gave men absolute power over their wives and children, is a major theme of the work. Charlotte tackles this again in *Jane Eyre* with the complications of Rochester's marriage to Bertha, where he gains her £30,000 dowry. Charlotte uses the law to manipulate some of the plot, including the law on bigamy and the laws surrounding the treatment of mental health. Jane is only allowed to inherit from her uncle because of an entail in his will that 'is contrary to all custom' and bypasses primogeniture. All three Brontë sisters investigate current laws and use them to support their arguments for female equality in property, wealth and marriage. They do this not only by showing the poor situation of women, but also the power and dictatorship of some of the men.

Linked to their knowledge of the law is their appreciation of the growing interest in and legislation for mental health. There had been various Acts of Parliament intended to control and confine people who were mentally ill or deviant. In the eighteenth and nineteenth centuries many extra workhouses and lunatic asylums sprang up throughout the British Isles, in both the public and private sectors. The idea of separation of both the poor and the mentally ill from the general population, and an unwarranted link between them, was further addressed in the Poor Act of 1832 and its 1834 amendment. These Acts attempted to curb the relief handed out to the poor and created workhouses so awful that only the truly destitute would go there. The idea of confining and controlling people who were a burden or an embarrassment to society was not new, but it was now organised on a much bigger scale and included the mentally ill. Everyone had an opinion on what constituted mental illness. Various Lunacy Acts were passed by Parliament throughout the nineteenth century in an attempt to diagnose and control the problem. Unfortunately, the laws were not based on research and they helped to ensure that not only those who were ill, but also many innocent or destitute people, including some unmarried mothers, were confined for life, sometimes in appalling and violent conditions.

The problem was based on a real fear of insanity which had no medical explanation until science and accurate psychological research could produce hard evidence of cause and effect. This helped to eventually dispel popular misguided beliefs, although some of the fear and misunderstanding still endures today. The Victorian obsession with phrenology and amateur psychology did little to help those suffering from mental illness, and especially women with the condition which is recognised now as post-natal depression. Suicide was a crime rather than a cry for help and was a disgrace to any family. In *Jane Eyre*, Charlotte describes the popular concept and actual practice of the 'madwoman in the attic' in her description of Bertha Mason/Rochester,

> ... *it snatched and growled like some strange wild animal: but it was covered in clothing: and a quantity of dark, grizzled hair, wild as a mane, hid its head and face ... the clothed hyena rose up, and stood tall on its hind feet.... The maniac bellowed: she parted her shaggy locks from her visage, and gazed wildly at her visitors. I recognised well that purple face – those bloated features ... the lunatic sprang and grappled his throat viciously, and laid her teeth to his cheek ... she showed virile force in the contest – more than once she almost throttled him, athletic as she was.... At last he mastered her arms; Grace Poole gave him a cord, and he pinioned them behind her: with more rope, which was at hand, he bound her to a chair.*

(C. Brontë, *Jane Eyre*, 1980) p. 257–258.

This is the stereotypical Victorian description of madness with all its animalistic symbolism and terminology. It further highlights the Victorian answer to the problem: the hiding away in a separate part of the house and the vicious binding of the demented woman to a chair. Charlotte shows this scene to justify Rochester's decision to enter a bigamous marriage with Jane. It is violent and shows no mercy or sympathy for Bertha. The raving woman is seen in stark contrast with the small, quiet and fair Jane watching in the background. However, one suspects that Charlotte may have over protested! Our current understanding of mental illness is rarely represented by people turned into wild animals, screaming and attacking in violent and uncontrolled frenzy. One could argue that any person locked in an attic room with no stimulation or company, in a foreign country, may well develop mental trauma. If a serious illness like schizophrenia is added to the mix, one can appreciate the result. Charlotte is presenting the two sides of the female persona, the devil and the angel, in as violent and obvious disparity as possible. She was, however, far more aware than this and in *Villette* she shows all the subtlety of a woman who has experienced and dealt with her own mental stresses.

There is none of the ravings of Bertha Mason, but just as sad and awful is Lucy's breakdown and depression and her inability to connect with people or to enjoy her life. Caroline suffers mental breakdown in *Shirley* and it is in Charlotte's ability to take her reader into the darkness of the mind in quiet torment that is the more genuine and, at that time, unexplored area of psychiatric illness.

In *Wuthering Heights*, Emily demonstrates Heathcliff's insanity of the emotions, where his lifelong rejection centres his mind on revenge in a manner that can be likened to the criminally insane. Heathcliff will gladly kill or destroy anyone who gets in his way. His mind is twisted by torment in a type of madness that is especially violent and long-standing but includes some deliberation and cunning. Catherine is similarly haunted and distressed by the past and by her own folly and she dies in circumstances brought on by her delusions and her deliberate self-destruction. They are mad, however, only as seen by those who have not suffered the same lives and circumstances. The whole question of mental illness runs through these novels and the definition of insanity is always a problem with no clear answer. It was the false sense of normality demanded by society which appears to upset the various characters and cause them to question their own sanity and the madness they see around them. For those characters in the novels who are unable to appreciate when and what is 'normal', their authors let the readers do it for them. This explains some of the enduring quality and longevity of the Brontë novels for the way in which each generation can discover and re-interpret aspects of the themes and characters in the light of on-going scientific and social research.

The Brontë family suffered a wide variety of physical disabilities as well as bouts of mental and emotional distress. The death of their elder sisters from pulmonary tuberculosis, or consumption as it was often described, was a disease which could lie dormant in people and symptoms could flare up and die down before the final fatal attack. The disease was well established in Haworth and in the Parsonage, eventually claiming the lives of the remaining siblings, sometimes with added complications. The novels reflect the authors' on-going ill-health and there are many references to illness in their books. It is part of the realism and the biographical nature of the writing that the authors include psychological incapacity, both as part of the plot and as a demonstration of the effects of living conditions and lifestyles on the body.

Knowing of Branwell's addictions and the suffering that this caused to his sisters, it is little wonder that drink and excess is a feature, especially in Anne's writing. In *The Tenant of Wildfell Hall*, Arthur Huntingdon's drunkenness is an important influence on his behaviour and his later breakdown in health and his subsequent death. The fact that Helen is so desperate to remove her son from alcohol also includes the worry that there may be some hereditary link causing alcoholism and this, even today, is still being researched. Historically, and in the Victorian age, there was an enduring belief that the body needed to be 'balanced' to keep both the mind and the body healthy. This is a balancing of all aspects of health including the quantity and type of food and drink, exercise, work and relaxation and is still part of modern thinking surrounding good health. The drunkenness of Arthur Huntingdon in *The Tenant of Wildfell Hall* and Hindley Earnshaw in *Wuthering Heights*, demonstrates the links between excess and physical and mental breakdown. Both men are portrayed as violent and vicious and it is especially due to their alcoholism which further affects and alters their personalities. There is little or no sympathy for these characters. Alcohol was self-inflicted so did not warrant understanding or excuse. There is no explanation of the nature of addiction but more a condemnation for over indulgence.

By portraying alcoholism, the stories also demonstrate the effects that drink had not only on the alcoholic but also those around them. Helen suffers mentally and physically from her husband's alcoholism and his abuse of their son. Hindley is portrayed in his extreme state of drunken violence when he is completely out of control. This lack of self–control, whether caused by drink or any other influence, was especially abhorred in a society where the ability to control one's feelings and behaviour was admired. Although drunkenness in the lower classes was condemned, it was tolerated in the upper classes, only becoming unacceptable if a man let it destroy his health and affect his livelihood. Women were not expected to drink and certainly not to excess, and this was due, in part, to the danger of alcohol breaking down the inhibitions which kept her feminine and chaste. To be respectable she had to be sober and restrained.

There is evidence in the novels of characters who waste away both through lack of physical as well as psychological or spiritual sustenance. There are many scenes involving illness and it is whilst they are ill that some of the characters reach a crisis in their lives. Some survive and others do not. Catherine Linton starves herself to death and Caroline Helstone nearly dies through mental trauma that undermines her physical health. Lucy Snowe is worn down by her isolation and she suffers the physical effects of fatigue in the form of fainting, headaches and sickness before her mental health also collapses. Heathcliff also starves himself to death and as his energy drains, his fever and hallucinations increase. Jane Eyre collapses following days of wandering lost on the moors at a time when her mind is in turmoil and her physical strength is wasted.

There is however, a greater message in the amount of illness in the novels. Illness and suffering is a part of the Christian creed that maintains that people must suffer as part of the development of spiritual strength. The saintly Helen Burns, at Lowood school, suffers and dies but her death opens the door to heaven. Physical and mental distress is shown as part of the doctrine of preparing oneself for a better afterlife. Pain and suffering can be the prerequisites which allow people to develop and test their faith in God. Christians believed that the greater the suffering the greater the ultimate reunion with God. This was a strong belief in Victorian times and part of the Brontë sisters' religious upbringing. Without the trials of life there would be nothing to test a person's moral and spiritual development and without that, for the Brontës, there would be no reason and no comfort for the deaths of their mother and sisters. Their suffering and deaths would have had no purpose.

For people with strong faith, the evil and sadness in the world is the will of God moving in His mysterious ways. If one is ill, or suffers more than another person, then there is a reason for it beyond human understanding. This was the Brontës' belief and it could not be otherwise, they were indoctrinated with the prevailing Christian creed. There is no doubt, however, that each one of them questioned this doctrine and, at times, sought alternative explanations. Emily was probably the most radical in her thinking and the one strong enough to suggest an alternative but there is little doubt that they each had confidence in the Christian God and the hope of an afterlife in the paradise promised in the Bible.

The Brontës' education and their love of reading and learning made them very aware of the times in which they lived. It was a time of enormous upheaval and change in all areas of life. Industrialisation was building momentum and the agricultural way of life was changing, though at a much slower rate. The division between the classes was widening and there was a huge gulf between the rich and the poor. Whilst the Brontës do not attempt to delve too deeply into poverty or the working classes, they do know and write about many other aspects of their times. They followed political argument and kept up to date with Parliament and its reforms. Their Irish background and English upbringing kept them interested in British politics, especially Catholic emancipation, the Reform Bills and the Poor Law amendments. They knew about immigration and the great Irish potato famine of 1848. Charlotte describes the activities of the Luddites and was very aware of the Chartist movement and had some sympathy towards its cause. The Brontës studied the political and social unrest sparked by revolution in France and industrialisation in Britain and lived through a time of enormous social change and disruption. From early childhood, they had read the newspapers with all their parliamentary recordings and the lives of the statesmen and leaders of the time. This interest and knowledge is incorporated into their works and argued through. One sees the journalist in Charlotte and the reformer in Anne, both trying to record the times with all their issues and problems, as faithfully and truthfully as they saw it.

For daughters of a clergyman, reared from babyhood on the Bible, it would be difficult for the sisters not to include this major influence in their writings.

The other important literary influences were Shakespeare and John Bunyan's *Pilgrims Progress*, a tract which emphasises the journey of man from evil and despair to deliverance and the Celestial City. Charlotte especially sprinkles Biblical tracts and references throughout her novels in a way that makes some of the language and symbolism difficult for the modern reader to appreciate or understand. The Brontës attended church, taught in the Sunday school, read their Bibles and knew their prayer books and hymns. They were instilled with religious text which would have been familiar to many of their readers. The moral theme of many of their works expresses a natural tendency to good as opposed to evil. Most of the heroes and heroines must embark on a moral journey of discovery before they are fit to achieve their goals, whether they are wealth, marriage or independence.

However, there is also representation of religion used as a tool to persecute and threaten the characters. In both *Wuthering Heights* and *Jane Eyre* one sees religion being corrupted and used to cause harm. In the hands of Joseph and in Mr Brocklehurst one witnesses all the cant and Calvinistic rantings of the hypocrite who sees only himself as God's chosen favourite. These men do not conform to the Brontës understanding of Christianity. Both are hard and ruthless men and have no love or care for the children they encounter, or anyone else. Joseph is, in effect, one of the narrators in *Wuthering Heights* who is often present and always willing to denounce or degrade the people around him. He actively condones Heathcliff's bad behaviour, as much as he formerly encouraged Hindley to abuse him. He is a man with no morals and no guilt and can be seen at times as more wicked than Heathcliff. Mr Brocklehurst betrays the children at Lowood School whom he is meant to protect and cherish. He is one of the most detestable characters in *Jane Eyre*, using religion as a weapon to terrify the sad and deprived children.

Charlotte and Emily's own religious crises are evident in their books. Emily is unable to reconcile the Christian heaven with man's inhumanity to man. Can, or even should, the likes of Heathcliff and Catherine enter an afterlife in paradise? They both, in effect, killed themselves and neither was buried in 'hallowed ground'. Like many people who tackle philosophical problems and question areas of mortality one needs to have tremendous knowledge of them, and Emily had. She did not flaunt her religious knowledge in the same way as Anne and Charlotte but she used it to expose the problems within it, rather than propose solutions. Charlotte highlights characters like St John Rivers, in *Jane Eyre*, The Rev. Helstone in *Shirley* and Lucy Snowe in *Villette* as they each portray a version of religious faith that is a corruption or a misunderstanding of its message. Charlotte is demonstrating that faith can be interpreted by different people in different ways and this was not usually vocalised in the novel. It heralded secularisation which was a growing force in the country. Charlotte adhered to her father's faith and his church but she was also aware of the changes in beliefs and the growing effect of scientific discovery. Although, like her father, she abhorred the dogma and ceremony of Roman Catholicism, she describes Monsieur Paul at the end of *Villette* as honest and genuine and not a bigot. She is beginning to understand and demonstrate that religion is unique to the individual as well as universal in its teaching.

In *Agnes Grey*, one sees Anne's idealistic views in her Christian cleric, Mr Weston, who is kind and good and genuine as he prays and preaches with love and happiness to all who meet him. His religious life contrasts with 'the shower of curates' at the beginning of *Shirley*, who demonstrate no genuine faith. They argue and jest over 'minute points of ecclesiastical discipline' which are frivolous and meaningless. They have no feel for, or belief in, what they are preaching. Similarly, Mr Weston's rector, Reverend Hatfield, in *Agnes Grey*, is another uncaring and self-absorbed character who enjoys discipline and ceremony as opposed to pastoral care and genuine empathy. These men will preach at their flock but not with them, and will rail against them rather than gather them into the church.

The Brontë sisters each express their own religious perspectives in their novels. Emily is mysterious with Gothic undertones that suggest a spiritual world within that is beyond religion and away from dogma. She displays doubt, and questions heaven and earth and its symbiotic attachment. Anne shows various religious perspectives but settles firmly on God as good and all enveloping. Charlotte appears strong and argumentative and quick to ridicule, but also to seriously question and address religious views and beliefs. Their approaches are unconventional and once it was known that they were the daughters of a clergyman in the church of England, their critics became more vindictive.

Along with the religious themes in the novels, some of which caused offence, there was the covert and overt sexuality that runs as an undercurrent in all the books, often by the use of metaphor and symbolism. It is a very present theme and in a way that is possibly more obvious to the modern reader with our knowledge of Freud and child development. It is difficult to talk about human relationships without referring to sexuality but the Victorians found it very problematic to discuss or even mention it. Women, and women writers, were not expected, or invited, to use it as a topic of conversation or as a subject in their reading material. The label of 'coarseness' which was applied to some of the Brontës works, was especially due to the religious and sexual references as well as the violence and the savagery of the characters. However, there are many critics who argue that Victorian permissiveness abounded and that the Victorians had no better or higher morals than any other society. Henry Mayhew's research on the London poor estimated that 80,000 prostitutes lived and worked in the city in the 1860s, an indication that sexual behaviour was prevalent on the streets, but sacrosanct in the home.

Three sisters and a brother reared in such close proximity and with such a wide range of reading materials could not fail to be sexually aware, no matter what the conventions and manners of the day. A reading of any of the Brontës' juvenilia shows many sexual references. It is littered with love and longing and affairs and dalliances, which suggest that the children knew of, and fantasised about, sex even if they were not fully informed of the mechanics. As they grew older, Branwell was reported to have had some sexual encounters, and may have had a child. Many women fantasise about love and marriage and certainly the three sisters appear to have used this theme in their juvenilia and later in their poetry and novels. Whilst convention denied the writing of explicit sexual acts, they used passion and devotion as substitutes. Heathcliff and Catherine sleep together as children but are physically and metaphorically separated as adults before they can become sexually aware and active. Their love can be interpreted as pure and passionate because it is unconsummated and almost, therefore, untarnished. It is Adam and Eve before the fall, it is Romeo and Juliet and all the innocent lovers who do not consummate their relationships. This can be viewed as sexual in itself as it has all the sexual and emotional attraction without the physical release.

Charlotte certainly suffered for her love of a man she could not have and writes with all the longing and passion and the frustration that it involved. Many of the men in her books are handsome and passionate but unobtainable to the heroine unless she rises or they fall, socially and metaphorically. We know that Rochester has been married and was a womaniser and that Adele may be his illegitimate child. Men in the novels need to have a certain level of sexual awareness to make them attractive to the innocent and virginal women they wish to impress. For Charlotte, it must also include intelligence. For Anne, it needs to contain sensitivity and kindness. For Emily, it is difficult to know. Her poetry is beautiful and passionate and often recalls lost love. Her novel examines love but also evil and hate and jealousy and sexual competition with a realism that is perhaps more authentic and more disturbing.

There is a modern trend to see the Brontë novels as early forms of women's literature that was meant to tease and excite; Victorian versions of 'Fifty Shades of Grey'. They can be interpreted as 'bad' or 'secret' books that contain implicit sexual themes. That may be the case, although there is also a great deal more to them. It is doubtful that that was their authors' intention, but it is one interpretation that cannot be overlooked. The sisters were avid readers of Byron and knew of his lifestyle and sexual exploits. Heathcliff is described as a Byronic hero with his dark and brooding good looks and his demonic sexuality. There is a deep attraction for the male who has secrecy and power and Emily Brontë uses these aspects of sexuality to full effect.

Anne, in a remarkably intense chapter of *The Tenant of Wildfell Hall*, shows the viciousness engendered by Gilbert Markham when he attacks Helen's brother in a fit of sexual jealousy. It is unprovoked and one of the most violent scenes in the book. Anne has shown the reader the sexual and violent deviance of Arthur Huntingdon with his extra marital affairs, his gambling and his abuse of his wife, but Markham's attack is something even more shocking. Anne shows to the reader a man who loses control in an instant when his passionate emotions overrule his civilised conditioning. This is sexuality shown for what it is; an emotionally charged reaction which is not necessarily under one's control. It was this lack of sexual control in women that many men feared and was sometimes used as an explanation of female mental illness. It was her initial overt sexuality that precipitated Bertha Mason's downfall in *Jane Eyre*; she was too forward and too explicit. This is what was used to entrap Edward Rochester and which, afterwards, is shown as part of her disturbed mind.

Charlotte also introduces women of strong character and outspoken views who need to be 'tamed' to some extent before they can enter society as proper and reformed married women. Shirley Keeldar is one such lady, whose masculine traits cannot be allowed to continue if she is to be safely brought into a conventional relationship where she takes the subservient role. She must be ruled and mastered. By the time she comes to write *Villette*, Charlotte is able to allow Lucy to be independent. She can be single and strong in a move against the usual heterosexual arrangement. This is a very early acknowledgement towards the female as the person with power. In *Jane Eyre*, Charlotte shows another type of marriage where Jane takes the upper hand, sometimes from necessity because her husband is disabled, but she has already proved herself as a strong and capable woman, who is more than Rochester's equal in many ways. This does suggest some degree of female emancipation and if it is to spread and to succeed it must be in all aspects of life including the sexual.

The alterations and modifications that have occurred since the 1840s in attitudes and acceptance of sex and sexuality are enormous and continue to develop. The laws regarding sexual permission and permissiveness are still evolving. Modern technology, including television, film, and the internet has altered our perception of sexual activity and access to it, both as a social medium and as pornography. By bringing sex into the public domain it has demystified it and possibly debased it in a way that the Victorians could not have imagined. One can see the beginning of these changes in the Brontës' works where women began to address their sexuality and emotions from their own perspectives. Many of the women in their books question their roles as daughters, wives, mothers and workers, and there are female characters who lead rather than follow and who want more from life than to be in an unequal relationship with the men around them.

Another dominating theme in the novels is children and childhood. The books describe children who are mostly orphaned or separated from their parents. The Brontës own losses are traceable in all of their writings. There is a repeated rejection of the child and its search for fulfilment that is not satisfied until adulthood. We witness the torment of the young Jane Eyre, bullied and lonely, whose rejection leads to her appalling treatment at Lowood School. We read of Heathcliff's lonely childhood where he is rescued off the streets of Liverpool by Mr Earnshaw, only to be bullied and persecuted by Hindley. Catherine has no mother and turns to Heathcliff, especially after her father's death, as her only companion. The young Cathy is motherless and Heathcliff cruelly separates her from her father. Hareton is similarly rejected and bullied by everyone and treated as a lackey in a house that he should have inherited. Lucy Snowe is a lonely and isolated orphan. Carolyn Helstone has no parents and is reared by her chauvinistic uncle who does not understand her need for love and affection. Love only comes to her when her nurse finally reveals that she is her mother. Mother love, or the lack or loss of it, dominates the lives of many of the young characters.

However, the novels go further in their depiction of children. Edgar and Isabella Linton in *Wuthering Heights*, are shown in many ways as children whose lives and behaviours are thwarted by over indulgence. This is especially important and is new in the early novel genre. Like John Reed in *Jane Eyre* and the Bloomfield and Murray children in *Agnes Grey*, these characters represent the child who has too much, especially with regard to possessions. They are spoilt by their parents but not loved in a way that helps them to develop as caring and responsible adults. They are shown as lacking in morals and being totally selfish. Heathcliff and Catherine watch through the window of Thrushcross Grange whilst Edgar and Isabella Linton fight over their dog, to the point where they nearly pull it apart. This is a very telling picture of children who have access to every pleasure and object but have no knowledge of their proper value. Heathcliff is genuinely amazed at their behaviour. He describes the scene to Nelly,

Isabella ... lay screaming at the farther end of the room, shrieking as if witches were running red-hot needles into her. Edgar stood on the hearth weeping silently, and in the middle of the table sat a little dog, shaking its paw and yelping....The idiots! That was their pleasure! To quarrel who should hold a heap of warm hair, and each began to cry because both, after struggling to get it, refused to take it. We laughed outright at the petted things; we did despise them! When would you catch me wishing to have what Catherine wanted? Or find us by ourselves, seeking entertainment in yelling, and sobbing, and rolling on the ground, divided by the whole room? I'd not exchange, for a thousand lives, my condition here for Edgar Linton's at Thrushcross Grange – not if I had the privilege of flinging Joseph off the highest gable, and painting the house-front with Hindley's blood.

(E. Brontë, *Wuthering Heights*, 1992) p. 60.

The contrast between the lives of the two sets of children is extreme but it is a major scene in the novel, as Heathcliff and Catherine are introduced to the social world of the wealthy and the accessories that it involves. They are looking through a window; a transparent barrier between the two worlds of nature and civilisation. Catherine is attacked by the house dogs as she and Heathcliff try to leave and she is taken into the house, never to return to her wild ways on the moors with Heathcliff.

This scene demonstrates Catherine's baptism into adulthood and her leaving behind of childish ways and natural emotions. Emily successfully demonstrates the change from childhood to adulthood but not in the ways that her sisters chose. For Emily, childhood is free and wild and the trappings of society inhibit the natural and create a false persona. Where Jane Eyre, Caroline Helstone, Lucy Snowe, Agnes Grey and Helen Huntingdon suffer and overcome obstacles on a journey that finally has its rewards, Catherine throws away her natural beliefs and behaviours and is instantly charmed and overcome by the lure of wealth and status. For Emily, that is an unforgiveable betrayal and Catherine dies when she realises her terrible mistake.

Longing for a pre-industrial world is another theme that is evident in some of the books. *Wuthering Heights* is especially bound up in nature and the moors at a time before the growth of towns and the encroachment of enclosure and buildings.

Whilst in *Shirley*, a horrified Caroline listens to her husbands plans to desecrate the moors and valleys of Briarfield with his mill, workers' houses and outbuildings and roads. The old housekeeper describes the loss of the countryside in the book's final passages,

> *I can tell of it clean different again, when there was neither mill, nor cot, nor hall,*
> *except Fieldhead, within two miles of it. I can tell, one summer evening, fifty*
> *years syne, my mother coming running in just at the edge of dark, almost fleyed*
> *out of her wits, saying she had seen a fairish (fairy) in Fieldhead Hollow; and*
> *that was the last fairish that ever was seen on this countryside…. A lonesome*
> *spot it was, and a bonnie spot, full of oak-trees and nut trees. It is altered now.*
>
> (C. Brontë, *Shirley*, 1982) p. 599.

There is a longing to return to the old ways and the old times, before the noise and smoke and dirt of industrialisation. The Brontës spent their childhood roaming amongst the hills, valleys, dips and hollows of Haworth moor and examining the flora and fauna beside the becks, streams, pools and waterfalls. They saw it in all weathers and all seasons and it was part of the happiest times of their lives. It is understandable that they portray it in their books as another loss; another longing for something and somewhere that has changed and can never be recalled, except in memory. There is little welcoming or celebration of the new and the modern and more of a bringing down of a curtain on the past, especially in *Shirley* and *Wuthering Heights.*

The Brontës own experience of education and their involvement with teaching meant that it was a major theme in all their books. Their father was a living example of how education could lead to success and independence. His rise from Irish peasant farming stock to becoming a graduate of Cambridge University and then a respectable Church of England minister was quite extraordinary. Education was the key to achieving ambitions. The Brontë children were given, and gladly received, a broad education in which the girls studied and learnt as much as their brother, even if not always the same subjects. The sisters' schooling at various establishments did much to widen their horizons, increase their subject matter and, most importantly, allowed them to experience the negative sides of life and the harsh realities of growing up. This was something that their brother missed out on and his home education set up a cloistered existence that deprived him of the social interaction necessary for him to develop as a young man.

Whilst the Clergy Daughters' School at Cowan Bridge had a terrible and lasting effect on Charlotte, it was the source of some of her best fiction and this expands the idea of education beyond actual schooling or book-learning into the role of education as life experience. The sisters gained a great deal of life experience outside of their home as well as their formal lessons. They travelled and they met interesting people of different religions, cultures and classes. Without Roe Head, Charlotte would never have met Ellen Nussey and Mary Taylor, and would not have known their families, nor been familiar with their interesting lives set against the background of West Yorkshire manufacturing. Without Brussels, Charlotte and Emily's writing and language skills would not have developed to such an extent, Charlotte would not have felt the pain of unrequited love and Emily may not have settled back so well into a life at the Parsonage. They needed examples to set themselves against which allowed them to grow and develop as women and as writers. Anne disliked Roe Head but it gave her the experience of living away from home and her ability as a governess was the result of this further education.

The negative aspects of their education in some ways worked in their favour because it caused them to question the whole idea and methods of education at that time. Anne wonders at the differing education for boys from girls and the lack of subjects that would fit girls and young women for a more useful and satisfying life. Charlotte is acutely aware of teaching and education where it isolates and separates pupils and teachers, and where the individual is lost amongst the masses. One sees repeatedly in Charlotte's work the teacher who becomes far more: the master, the inspiration, the friend and even the lover. This is not strictly the classroom teacher as much as the mentor who shares and encourages knowledge in others. Caroline 'teaches' Shirley and Jane 'teaches' Rochester. It is a relationship which develops into mutual respect, the basis on which Charlotte felt all marriages and all friendships should depend. For Emily, education is learning about nature, and about good and evil and studying the philosophical questions about mankind and about religion. Education and learning in the novels included learning about life, making mistakes and trying again, and understanding how and why people acted and reacted. All the characters, as in life, are on a journey of discovery and some succeed and reach their goals and some do not.

Until the Brontë works, most novels centred on the home as a domestic refuge where men, women and children could be safe and protected from the trials of social and cultural adversity. The Brontës tend to destroy this haven and portray it more as a sinister and dangerous place, especially for women. Helen Huntingdon is the victim of domestic abuse. She moves forward as a single parent harbouring her son whom she has in effect 'kidnapped' from her husband. The law will not do anything to help her.

Anne Brontë graphically presents Helen's dilemma. She is married to a man who has little or no love for her and who takes every opportunity to humiliate her. He flaunts his mistresses; he drinks to excess and spends more time with his equally obnoxious friends than with his wife. He is determined that his son will be raised in the same vices as himself to make him 'a man'. Anne spares no details when she describes Arthur Huntingdon's behaviour. She takes the reader into the drawing room as a witness to drunkenness, debauchery and cruelty.

Whilst Helen endures her husband's violence because she is married to him and has vain hopes that she will, one day, be able to help him to reform, she cannot stand by and watch him drag her young son into the same habits and mindset.

There are many things being shown here. It is not just Arthur's mistreatment of Helen and his son but also the contrast between the rearing of sons and of daughters. There is a cultural belief in many societies that the male is stronger, both physically and mentally, than the female. This applied in Victorian England as much as it had ever done. It was accepted that boys should be reared to be tough, unsentimental and brave. To achieve these attributes, the middle and upper classes often sent young boys away to boarding schools where they could learn to survive away from female influences and could indulge in the fighting and bullying often prevalent in such institutions. They could be educated in more than just formal lessons and could witness and receive harsh punishments, play rough games and learn to be in control of their feelings. These schools accepted this as part of turning young boys into men. Boys of higher social classes were often tutored at home but were exposed to all manner of country pursuits and adult pleasures as part of their 'coming of age'.

One can see the logic in this. This was a time when Britain was fighting to acquire its empire and needed soldiers and leaders who could have no relapse into sentimentality or cowardice. The armed forces throughout most of history were male and needed to be strong and brave. Not until the cultural revolution of the 1960s could men begin to express their sensitivity openly, and not until the twenty-first century could men be openly gay or show 'feminine' emotions without penalty or ridicule in many societies. In the 1840s there was no question of boys being encouraged to flaunt any female or emotional characteristics. What Arthur Huntingdon does is beyond the natural wish of the father to make his son strong and independent. He tries to take away his son's natural affection for his mother and forces the child, who is barely 5 years old, to drink alcohol and to swear. He tries to teach his child to despise his mother's care and affection by ridiculing her in front of him. There is a duality here because Arthur is aware that the most successful way to hurt the mother is through her child, so he gains on both counts. Helen is determined to remove her son before his emotions are permanently damaged and her own life is ruined.

The novel shows how and why this situation has occurred. Anne demonstrates that Helen, like all others of her class, has been brought up to marry. She is given no help in choosing a man who is compatible to her and has no knowledge or experience of what to recognise as deviant or manipulative. When she first meets Arthur, she falls in love with his looks and his flattery, but by the time they marry she realises that there is falseness about him, and his lifestyle and brutality become apparent. In law, the marriage is absolute and no matter how badly her husband behaves, she is tied to him for life. Anne's warning is that whilst women remain uneducated in all matters of love and sexuality, they will go blindly into loveless and violent marriages from which they cannot escape. In Victorian times, men and women were still marrying to gain titles, property and wealth, often without any genuine affection.

As the children of the marriage were also the possessions of their father, the mothers had little or no say in their upbringing. The father ruled the household and everyone in it. He held the money and had the law on his side. It was an impossible situation for any woman who found herself married to a man who chose to abuse her. She was dependent on her husband for everything. This is shown in all the Brontë novels where the married women, even if they married for love, must give all their possessions to their husbands. This could also include their free time, their opinions and their beliefs.

It is interesting to note that by the time Charlotte finally married her father's curate, Arthur Nicholls, she was a successful and relatively wealthy woman. A codicil in her will stated that her father, not her husband, should inherit her money in the event of her death. Luckily, she had married a man who loved her and who faithfully cared for her father after her death and did not dispute this financial arrangement. It was an act of faith in her husband and a sign of her concern for her father's welfare that Charlotte organised this, and it is also a sign of a woman who has taken her affairs into her own hands. There were, of course, areas were Arthur made demands on her time and her activities. He specifically forbade her to continue writing to Ellen in the open and uncensored way she had always done. He instructed Charlotte to tell Ellen that she must burn all the letters which Charlotte had previously sent to her over the last twenty-five years. Charlotte carried out her husband's wishes but, luckily for posterity, Ellen did not!

Chapter Twenty-Five

The Brontës Today

Anyone walking up the steep Main Street in Haworth today will find themselves surrounded by the name Brontë. It is displayed on shop fronts, emblazons souvenirs and even advertises a removal firm! Above the Church of St Michael and All Angels, stands the Parsonage, as it has since 1778. It has been extended but is still recognizable as the home of the famous family. It is now The Brontë Parsonage Museum and contains a priceless collection of Brontë possessions and memorabilia. Thousands of people visit this place every year and marvel at all the furniture they used, the table they wrote their famous novels on and even some of the tiny handmade books they created for their first stories. One can browse their original drawings and paintings, see the piano on which Emily played and the songbook with which Anne accompanied her. There are cabinets containing their clothing, their letters and their personal possessions; writing desks, bonnets and even locks of their hair. It is a fascinating memorial to a remarkable family and has been a pilgrimage for Brontë enthusiasts since the identity of these Yorkshire authors was first revealed.

One of the oldest literary societies in the world, the Brontë Society preserves and protects this valuable collection and seeks to inform the world of the lives and achievements of its namesakes. Members of the Society and its scholars come from every part of the globe, most recently from Brazil and Eastern Asia. The Brontës' books have been translated into over a hundred languages and are taught in schools on every continent. *Jane Eyre* and *Wuthering Heights* have been on the British school and University curricula for over 100 years. The novels have been performed in numerous plays, adapted for television and made into major films, and continue to be reproduced in Hollywood blockbusters as much as in local village halls.

Beside the Parsonage is the fascinating graveyard and church tower that dominated the family's view from the windows and imbued their senses, with the tolling church bell and the stonemason's hammer. Thousands of people were buried here, many of them children and many from the repeated epidemics of cholera and typhus which regularly decimated the population. At a time when nothing was known of the effects of rotting bodies on the drainage system which fed the springs in Haworth, this most unhealthy of places continued to contaminate the water supply for many years. Walking amongst the graves today beneath the many trees and through the leaves, it is a place of calm and sadness. The rambler can, however, imagine it on cold and stormy nights when small, frightened children watched it from their bedroom windows in the darkness and made up thrilling stories of ghosts and ghouls.

Visitors to Haworth do not come only to see the home of the Brontës, but also to experience the landscape that so inspired them. There is nothing to the west of Haworth parsonage, even today, but miles of, mostly uninhabited, moorland. Walkers and ramblers, day visitors and holidaymakers, follow in the footsteps of the Brontës and visit the many ancient farm buildings, becks and rocky outcrops that they knew. The ruins of Top Withins Farm still stand on one of the highest points, open to the elements but looking down majestically on acres of rolling moorland. It is the supposed location for Emily's Wuthering Heights Farm and there is a corresponding Thrushcross Grange in the former house of the ancient Heaton family, Ponden Hall, a few miles further down in the valley. Any reader of Emily's novel can imagine the people and events of the book when visiting Top Withins, especially when the weather is wild and wet, as it so often is.

The interest in the Brontës lives and works has not abated since their novels made them famous and there are several reasons why. Apart from their works, the lives of the Brontës are as fascinating and as tragic as any of their books. The life of Patrick Brontë is as remarkable as any gentleman of his time and his unique and talented family capture the imagination of generations of people who wonder at how and why they had such remarkable talents. Their lives had all the drama and intensity of nineteenth century families who lived in the constant fear of illness and death. They had little money but learned to love knowledge and fed their enquiring minds on books and study, and created a magical world of the imagination which occupied and sustained them into adulthood.

Their losses and the sadness that surrounded their short lives attract people, as does any sad and dramatic story. People wonder at their rare talents, their capacity to work and suffer, and their remarkable launch into the world of foreign travel and publication. These three shy but determined women broke barriers in many areas that were normally forbidden to their gender and class. The tale of Charlotte and Anne's appearance at the offices of Smith and Elder, Charlotte's publisher in London, reads like the script from a film. The decline and death of Branwell is fascinating and troubling for his waste of talent. The death of Emily is that of the Victorian heroine who fights to the bitter end but dies in the prime of her life just when her talents are beginning to be recognised. Anne's death leaves the shattered and lonely Charlotte grieving for months, alone in the Parsonage with her aging and ailing father. Just when all is lost, the handsome and devoted Arthur Nicholls declares his love and is eventually allowed to marry Charlotte. Unfortunately, as with any Brontë story, their happiness is short-lived and Charlotte tragically dies and her unborn child with her. The Brontës' lives are a Victorian novel!

Whilst we know so much about the Brontë family, it is in their poetry, letters and novels that we observe their rare accomplishments. With remarkable honesty and accuracy, they turned aspects of their own lives into literature and in so doing could show their readers what was happening locally and nationally to the men and women of the time. They demonstrate many of the ills of the society but they also examine the everyday lives of ordinary people and what makes them sad or happy. Much of the dialogue explores the role and experiences of women and the battles they had to fight for any recognition in a patriarchal society.

The biographical nature of the books lends them to historical interpretation. We know that some of the events were directly experienced by the authors. Charlotte is explicit and vehement in her depiction of Lowood school and her vivid portrayal identifies the reader with the four Brontë sisters' suffering in a school where they are at the mercy of unsympathetic adults and a harsh system and environment. It is a feeling experienced by many children at some time in their schooling. When one can identify with characters, places or events, they become more interesting and more authentic. The Brontës watched and mimicked people they met. They recognised accents, dress, behaviour and idiosyncrasies which they could then transfer into their fiction. It is often in the minutia of the everyday that the reader can see and feel the emotions involved as well as appreciating the dramatic.

This ability to engage the reader is part of the appeal of the novels but the stories themselves have a draw that is universal. These stories are especially vivid and they each deal with an aspect of the human condition concerning the emotions. They are about love, life and loss in a wide variety of appearances.

Most people experience love in some shape or form in their lives and can recognise it and feel it. In the Brontë novels, love is shown as both a good and a bad emotion. It can destroy as well as heal and it can be as much a burden as a relief. Childhood love is often missing in the novels and this helps to engage the reader who can empathise with characters like Agnes, Helen, Jane, Heathcliff, Caroline and Lucy in their search for it. Love is central to the works yet it is often viewed from an almost cynical perspective. It is never simple or straightforward and it must be earned through long and laboured suffering before the heroes and heroines can achieve their union. Even then, the result can be unsatisfying and even deadly.

Because the novels deal so much with the emotions they are open to continual interpretation and reinterpretation and this is one of their fascinations. There is no real answer to any of them they all have ambiguous endings; even when they appear to end happily, the reader is left to ponder just how these lives will continue. It is not just *Villette* that leaves the reader with alternatives. Will Jane's marriage last? Will Caroline and Shirley be happy in the roles they have chosen with the men they have fallen in love with? Is William Crimsworth capable of fulfilling the role of husband? Will Gilbert Markham be a better husband than Arthur Huntingdon? Can Cathy and Hareton live happily ever after in the place of such drama with the spectres of Heathcliff and Catherine to haunt them? Even Agnes Grey in her perfect marriage, with her perfect husband and perfect children, seems to be tempting fate to intervene. Love and marriage do not necessarily go together in these books. There are lots of double meanings and counter plots that leave the reader wondering what they have read and what will happen next.

The books are each a window on life, as seen, heard and interpreted by the Brontë sisters, and they allow the reader of any time and age, to look through that window in to the past and a world that has gone forever. And yet they deal with the universal issues of life and all the human emotions and behaviour that surround each generation. People will go on reading and interpreting these books for a very long time because they address the core of values that we all know and recognise, and they question life and death in a way that makes us want to know more about ourselves, the people around us and the world in which we live.

Bibliography

Barker, J.R.V. (2010). *The Brontës* (Paperback ed.). London: Abacus.

Brontë, A. (1982). *The Tenant of Wildfell Hall.* Harmondsworth, Middlesex, England: Penguin Books Ltd.

Brontë, A. (1988). *Agnes Grey.* (A. Goreau, Ed.) Harmondsworth: Penguin Books Ltd.

Brontë, A. (2003). *The Brontës Selected Poems.* (P. Norris, Ed.) London: The Orion Publishing Group.

Brontë, C. (1971). *Jane Eyre.* New York: W.W. Norton and Company Inc.

Brontë, C. (1980). *Jane Eyre.* (G. Maine, Ed.) London: Collins.

Brontë, C. (1982). *Shirley.* Harmondsworth: Penguin Books Ltd.

Brontë, C. (1983). *The Professor and Emma a fragment.* London, England: J.M. Dent and Sons Ltd.

Brontë, C. (1984). *Villette.* Harmondsworth, England: Penguin Books Ltd.

Brontë, C. (2003). *The Brontës: Selected Poems* (Phoenix 2003 ed.). (P. Norris, Ed.) London: The Orion Publishing Group.

Brontë, E. (1941). *The Complete Poems of Emily Jane Brontë.* (C. Hatfield, Ed.) New York: Columbia University Press.

Brontë, E. (1992). *Wuthering Heights* (Case Studies in Contemporary Criticism ed.). (L. H. Peterson, Ed.) New York, U S A: Bedford Books of St Martin's Press.

Byron, L. G. (1982). *Childe Harold's Pilgrimage in Poems of Byron, Keats and Shelley.* (E. Coleman, Ed.) London: Guild Publishing.

Daiches, D. (1965). *Wuthering Heights (Introduction).* Harmondsworth: Penguin Books Ltd.

Davies, S. (1998). *Emily Brontë* (Writers and their Work ed.). Plymouth, England: Norhcote House Publishers.

Davies, S. (2002). *The Cambridge Companion to The Brontës.* (H. Glen, Ed.) Cambridge: The Cambridge University Press.

Eliot, G. (1952). *Adam Bede.* London, England: The Zodiac Press.

Eliot, G. (1977). *The Mill on The Floss.* London: J.Dent and Sons Ltd.

Freud, S. (1917-1919). *The Complete Psychological Works of Sigmund Freud* (1955 ed., Vol. XV11 An Infantile Neurosis). (J. Strachey, Ed.) The Hogarth Press and The Institute of Psychoanalysis.

Holland, N. (2016). *In Search of Anne Brontë.* Stroud, Gloucestershire: The History Press.

Lane, M. (1980). *The Drug-Like Brontë Dream*. London, England: John Murray Ltd.

Millett, K. (1970). *Sexual Politics*. Rupert Hart-Davis.

Palmer, G. (2002). *The Brontës Day by Day*. Keighley: The Brontë Society.

Selected Letters of Charlotte Brontë. (2007). Oxford, England: Oxford University Press.

Spencer, C. K. (2000). *Reading The Brontës: An Introduction to their Novels and Poetry*. Leeds: The Brontë Society and The University of Leeds.

Thackeray, W. M. (1974). *The Brontës: The Critical Heritage*. (M. Allott, Ed.) London, England: Routledge and Kegan Paul.